WRITING AT THE END OF THE WORLD

For Frank(?),

who is helping

to make

the world a better

place.

PITTSBURGH SERIES IN COMPOSITION, LITERACY, AND CULTURE
DAVID BARTHOLOMAE AND JEAN FERGUSON CARR, EDITORS

RICHARD E. MILLER

WRITING AT THE END OF THE WORLD

UNIVERSITY OF PITTSBURGH PRESS

Published by the University of Pittsburgh Press, Pittsburgh, PA 15260
Copyright © 2005, University of Pittsburgh Press
All rights reserved
Manufactured in the United States of America
Printed on acid-free paper
10 9 8 7 6 5 4 3 2 1

Library of Congress Cataloging-in-Publication Data

Miller, Richard E. (Richard Earl), 1961-
  Writing at the end of the world / Richard E. Miller.
      p. cm. — (Pittsburgh series in composition, literacy, and culture)
  Includes bibliographical references and index.
  ISBN 0-8229-5886-4 (pbk. : alk. paper)
  1. English language—Rhetoric—Study and teaching—United States. 2. Report writing—
Study and teaching (Higher)—United States. 3. United States—Civilization—21st century.
4. Education, Humanistic—United States. I. Title. II. Series.
  PE1405.U6M535 2005
    808'.402'071073—dc22   2005013313

It is the end of the world.

And the work that lies ahead will involve,
as it always has and always will,
from moment to moment,
the building of new worlds.

Worlds end.
And worlds begin.

CONTENTS

Once a year, the former residents of the evacuation area surrounding Chernobyl are given permission to return to their homes so that they may visit with one another and tend to the graves of their ancestors. In order to document the slow decay of the deserted, radioactive towns in the evacuation area, David McMillan, a photographer and professor at the University of Ottawa, now joins those who make this annual trip. For anyone who has wondered what happened after that day in April 1986 when the nuclear power plant in Chernobyl began to melt down, McMillan's photographs track the passage of time in a landscape abruptly emptied of human life. In "Classroom, Village of Shipelicki, Chernobyl Exclusion Zone, 1995," McMillan shows us an abandoned classroom. Paint peels from the walls; crumbled plaster covers the floor; dust has quietly settled on every surface. A map of a world that no longer exists hangs on the far wall; the torso of an anatomical model rests against a radiator long gone cold. In 2135, when the evacuation area is once more habitable, all those who lived through the disaster and all their children will be dead. It's hard to resist the mesmerizing power of such apocalyptic visions, which both create and confirm a sense that despair is the only rational response to the world we have before us.

In a secular society, education is the most powerful resource citizens have to ensure a brighter future for themselves. But what is one to do when the future includes a radioactive wasteland in the northern Ukraine? The smoldering ruins of the World Trade Center? Looted museums in a bombed-out Baghdad? No meaningful discussion of the future of the humanities can proceed without confronting such examples of human depravity and indifference. And yet, the examples themselves threaten to end the discussion before it begins. Who, surveying the ruins at Chernobyl, would be persuaded either by Matthew Arnold's argument that we are ennobled by studying the best that has been thought and said in our time or by those who maintain that work in the humanities provides the foundation for a critical engagement with the world?

There is another way to phrase this question, though. In a secular society, how does one generate the sense that life is meaningful? In this form, the question has both a personal and an institutional dimension. The chapters that follow take up this question by exploring personal experience as the preeminent site where institutions and individuals intersect and meaning gets made. This isn't, however, a book about me and my individual search for meaning. Rather, it's a book for anyone working in the humanities who has wondered: Why go on teaching when everything seems to be falling apart? Why read when the world is overrun with books? Why write when there's no hope of ever gaining an audience? Posing such questions aloud is not a sign of despair; it's a way to start a conversation about how and why reading, writing, and teaching the literate arts can be made to continue to matter in the twenty-first century. Schools currently provide extensive training in the fact that worlds end; what is missing is training in how to bring better worlds into being. This book is meant to advance that project.

When I started graduate school in the mid-1980s, I had the good fortune to begin my studies in a seminar on "Literature of the End of the World," which was taught by Bob Crossley at the University of Massachusetts–Boston. Some twenty years later, Bob's mentorship and the lessons of that course remain with me, encouraging me to look beyond the latest incarnation of the apocalypse to the creative work of rebuilding and reimagining that is ever present in the world.

I couldn't have completed this book without the support of my colleague, friend, and collaborator, Kurt Spellmeyer, who has helped me to rethink what the humanities might become and how they might remain important in the twenty-first century. Along the way, Carolyn Williams, Michael McKeon, and Marian Ian read and responded to sections of the manuscript; Dean Barry Qualls offered unstinting support. Rutgers University granted me a well-timed leave, which made it possible to complete this project. Ann Jurecic was an ideal reader, respondent, and friend throughout. And for my life support network: Donna Dunbar-Odom, Barbara McCarthy, Tom Laughlin, Howard Tinberg, John Keith, Mark Estes, and my siblings, my thanks for carrying me across yet another finishing line. Finally, Elinor S. Miller read the manuscript as it neared completion; even though she is gone now, her unshakable support continues to keep me going.

My thanks to Leslie Morris of the Houghton Library and Chris Haley of the Maryland State Archives for permission to quote from their collections. An abbreviated version of "The Nervous System" appeared in *College English* 58 (Mar. 1996): 265–86 (copyright 1996 by the National Council of Teachers of English, reprinted with permission). An abbreviated version of "The Arts of Complicity: False Consciousness and the Culture of Schooling," appeared in *College English* 61 (Sept. 1998): 10–28 (copyright 1998 by the National Council of Teachers of

English, reprinted with permission). My thanks to the past editor of *College English*, Louise Z. Smith, for her support of this earlier work and to the National Council of Teachers of English for granting me permission to reprint this work here.

I presented earlier versions of this work at the University of New Hampshire, the University of Washington, the University of Michigan, Michigan Technological University, the University of Arizona, the University of Louisville, the University of Pittsburgh, and at meetings of the annual Conference on College Composition and Communication. My thanks to the many thoughtful respondents and correspondents at these venues who, over the years that this project has been gestating, have offered me helpful feedback and intellectual support.

My thanks to David Bartholomae for creating a space where the future of composition studies can be reimagined, to Kendra Boileau Stokes for shepherding the manuscript through the publication process, and to my anonymous outside readers. My thanks as well to Rachel McLaughlin, John Koblin, and Rick Lee, who provided research assistance of the highest quality during the final stages of production. And my special thanks to Jules and Jane Plangere, whose generosity and vision have helped to transform the future of writing instruction at Rutgers.

Barbara Cooper, Cara, and Rachel make the case, everyday, that optimism and perseverance are worth the effort.

There are no more words, just now, but that's okay.

There will be, soon enough.

WRITING AT THE END OF THE WORLD

THE DARK NIGHT OF THE SOUL

Though they may already have faded from memory, driven off by more recent and yet more spectacular horrors, for a few short weeks in 1999, the events at Columbine High School mesmerized the nation. There was the live footage of students fleeing in terror across the green, the boy with the bleeding head being dropped from the window, the SWAT teams moving in. There was the discovery of what lay beyond the eye of the camera: fifteen dead, a cache of weapons, a large homemade bomb made with two propane tanks and a gasoline canister, the eventual disclosure of an even more sinister fantasy that involved hijacking a plane and crashing it in New York City.[1] There was the ongoing effort to present fuller and fuller portraits of Eric Harris and Dylan Klebold, the two young men who masterminded the slaughter: they were outsiders, video-game enthusiasts, members of the Trench Coat Mafia, neo-Nazis, two boys who couldn't tell their alcohol-fueled dreams from reality, a leader and a follower, a smart kid and a loser, specimens of a middle-class value system in crisis, proof of the need for stricter gun-control laws. And finally, there were the funerals, the white caskets covered in writing from those left behind, the doves released into the air, and all those inspirational speeches about healing and hope.

Any major social cataclysm produces in its wake two responses. First, there is the search for causes: Why did this happen? Who is to blame? And second, there is an appeal to some greater authority to assist in preventing such upheavals in the future. Following Columbine, fingers were pointed at everyone and everything: inattentive parents, indifferent guidance counselors, insensitive jocks, the entertainment industry, powerful gun lobbyists, the media, the Internet, the military-industrial complex, a president who couldn't keep his pants on.[2] And then, as one would expect, there were calls both for increased external controls—new laws, regulations, supervisory agencies—and for increased internal controls—educational interventions, moral training, prayer. Surely, more laws, more education, and more religious instruction would bring these violent students back into line.

Despite heightened sensitivity and increased security, however, the schoolyard massacre has proven to be a remarkably durable and recurring social cataclysm. In February 1997, a sixteen-year-old in Bethel, Alaska, entered his high school and murdered the principal and another student. In October 1997, another sixteen-year-old, this one living in Pearl, Mississippi, killed his mother, then went to school and killed two more students. In December 1997, a fourteen-year-old took aim at a prayer circle in West Paducah, Kentucky, killing three. In March 1998, two boys, eleven and thirteen, pulled a fire alarm and gunned down students exiting Westside Middle School in Jonesboro, Arkansas, leaving five dead. And the list goes on with additional shootings over the past five years at high schools in Fayetteville, Tennessee; Springfield, Oregon; Richmond, Virginia; Conyers, Georgia; Deming, New Mexico; and Cold Spring, Minnesota. In March 2001, a skinny kid, whom classmates called "Anorexic Andy," walked into his high school in Santee, California, to reenact his version of Columbine. He killed two and wounded thirteen before being subdued. And in April 2002, Robert Steinhaeuser returned to Johann Gutenberg High School in Erfurt, Germany, to avenge his expulsion for forging a doctor's note: he killed two students and thirteen teachers before turning his gun on himself.

It's reassuring to think that either the work of the legal system or the educational system can reduce or eliminate altogether the threat of the unpredictable and the unforeseen. This is why we have childproof medicine bottles, penalties for not buckling up, informational literature on family planning for students in junior high school: these are all examples of reasonable responses to known problems. But the schoolyard massacre seems a problem of a different order. What legal or educational response could be equal to the challenge of controlling the behavior of so many students from such varied backgrounds? Just how much surveillance would be required to bring the marginalized fraction of the student population back into the fold? How invasive would a curricular intervention have to be to succeed in instilling a set of preferable values in those who currently feel so deeply alienated while at school? While the answers to these questions are unknown, what we do know is this: the day after Columbine High School reopened, after all the public and private soul-searching in the community about the killings, after all the media coverage and analysis, after an enormous pep rally replete with bouncing cheerleaders, enthusiastic athletes, and all the mandatory school spirit one could ever hope for, swastikas were found scratched in a stall in one of the high school's newly painted bathrooms.

Eric Harris certainly didn't accept the idea that anyone was to blame for his actions or that anything could have been done to stop him or Dylan Klebold in going forward with their plan. Anticipating speculation of just this kind, Harris wrote in his diary:

> i want to leave a lasting impression on the world. and god damnit do not blame anyone else besides me and V for this. dont blame my family, they had no clue and there is nothing they could have done. they brought me up just fucking fine, dont blame toy stores or any other stores for selling us ammo, bomb materials or anything like that because its not their fault. i dont want no fucking laws on buying fucking PVC pipes. we are kind of a select case here so dont think this will happen again. dont blame the school. dont fucking put cops all over the place just because we went on a killing spree doesnt mean everyone else will and hardly ever do people bring bombs or guns to school anyway. the admin. is doing a fine job as it is. i dont know who will be left after we kill but dammit don't change any policies just because of us. it would be stupid and if there is any way in this fucked up universe we can come back as ghosts we will haunt the life out of anyone who blames anyone besides me and V.[3]

If one accepts Harris's assertions, then the events at Columbine are largely without motive or meaning: the killing spree was a misguided grab for immortality by two young men at loose ends. If one rejects Harris's assertions, though, and persists in the pursuit for causes, one is left with the inescapable fact that the hierarchical, exclusionary environment of mandatory schooling fosters feelings of rage and helplessness that cannot be contained. The law drives everyone into the schoolhouse; the educational system then sifts and sorts its way through the masses, raising expectations and crushing dreams as it goes. Eventually, something has to give.[4]

What is to be done? What is to be done? Only those utterly indifferent to the suffering of others can forestall asking this question for long. And, after any tragedy that involves the death of young people, it doesn't take long for some-one to make the case that the problem lies with advanced technology and all the fantasy factories that it has spawned, which together have blurred the line between fact and fiction. After the Columbine shootings, Pat Schroeder, the former congresswoman from Colorado who now runs the Association of American Publishers, was among those who argued that we've reached the point where suburban kids are becoming mass murderers because we've cre-ated domestic spaces that isolate individuals in a technological sea of entertain-ment—the TV, the VCR, the computer, the entertainment center, the Internet, a different toy for everyone. "*This* is the beautiful family of America living the American dream," Schroeder observed wryly. "But we need some ways to relate to each other as human beings. We need to work on getting connected." Con-vinced that the virtual connections available in cyberspace tend to be divisive, Schroeder has committed herself to protecting the practice of reading books. Schroeder believes that book clubs and coffee bars provide a kind of embodied community unavailable on the Internet. These places where people go to dis-cuss the printed word are, she says, "among the few civil institutions left. [They are] places to go see other people" (qtd. in Gross).

I share Schroeder's desire for a future where physical communion with oth-ers is still an option. You might say, in fact, that Schroeder and I come from the same secular faith tradition, that we share the same belief in reading's poten-tially redemptive power. And yet, there are dark days when I doubt the activities of reading and writing have much of a future. Indeed, after Columbine, it seems almost ludicrous to suggest that the social, psychological, and biochemical problems that contributed to this massacre might have been peacefully resolved if only Harris and Klebold had spent more time talking about what they were reading. Does reading really possess such curative powers? Does writing? Does group discussion?

Reading, writing, talking, meditating, speculating, arguing: these are the only resources available to those of us who teach the humanities and they are, obviously, resources that can be bent to serve any purpose. Harris and Klebold, in fact, wrote and produced for all different sorts of media; they read a range of material that supported their beliefs and that taught them how to put together their incendiary devices; they hung out with like-minded individuals and discussed their ideas. They relied on writing to post their scathing observations about their peers on Harris's Web site; they composed poems in their creative writing class that their teacher described as "dark and sad"; they created a video for a class project in which they acted out their fantasy of moving through the school gunning down their tormentors (Pooley 30–32). Harris even had the affectation of an English teacher, declaring on his Web site that one of the many habits he found unforgivable in his peers was the tendency to pronounce the "t" in "often": "Learn to speak correctly, you morons," he commands (Barron). They read, they wrote, they talked. And at the end of the process, they tried to kill everyone they could.

For some, it will hardly come as a surprise to learn that reading and writing have no magically transformative powers. But for those of us who have been raised into the teaching and publishing professions, it can be quite a shock to confront the possibility that reading and writing and talking exercise almost *none* of the powers we regularly attribute to them in our favorite stories. The dark night of the soul for literacy workers comes with the realization that training students to read, write, and talk in more critical and self-reflective ways cannot protect them from the violent changes our culture is undergoing. Helen Keller learning to see the world through a language traced into the palm of her hand; Malcolm X in prison memorizing the dictionary word by word; Paulo Freire moving among the illiterate masses in Brazil: we tell ourselves and our students over and over again about the power of reading and writing while the gap between rich and poor grows greater, the Twin Towers come crashing down, and somewhere some other group of angry young men is at work silently stockpiling provisions for the next apocalypse.

If you're in the business of teaching others how to read and write with care, there's no escaping the sense that your labor is increasingly irrelevant. Indeed, one way to understand the dark, despairing character of so much of the critical and literary theory that has come to dominate the humanities over the past two decades is to see this writing as the defensive response of those who have recognized but cannot yet admit that the rise of technology and the emergence of the globalized economy have diminished the academy's cultural significance. And so, to fight off the sense that words exercise less and less power in world affairs, one can declare that discourse plays a fundamental role in the constitution of reality. Rather than concede that reading as an activity has come to consume less and less time in the average person's life, one can insist that the canon wars are the ground upon which the nation's political future is being determined; rather than accept the fact that technological advances have taken control of publishing out of the hands of the few and transformed everyone with access to the Internet into a potential author and critic, one can decry the movement of our culture's critical center from the university to the sound stage of the Oprah Winfrey Show. What is unthinkable in such pronouncements about the centrality of academic work is the possibility that the vast majority of the reading and writing that teachers and their students do about literature and culture more generally might not be all that important. It could all just be a rather labored way of passing the time.

I have these doubts, you see, doubts silently shared by many who spend their days teaching others the literate arts. Aside from gathering and organizing information, aside from generating critiques and analyses that forever fall on deaf ears, what might the literate arts be said to be good for? How—and in what limited ways—might reading and writing be made to matter in the new world that is evolving before our eyes? Is there any way to justify or explain a life spent working with—and teaching others to work with—texts? These are the questions that animate the meditations that follow. Those who have never felt the inner urgency of such questions need read no further.

THE PRINCE OF DARKNESS

> In a million millennia, the sun will be bigger. It will feel nearer. In a million millennia, if you are still reading me, you can check these words against personal experience, because the polar ice caps have melted and Norway enjoys the climate of North Africa.
>
> Later still, the oceans will be boiling. The human story, or at any rate, the terrestrial story, will be coming to an end. I don't honestly expect you to be reading me then.
>
> —Martin Amis, *The Information*

In *The Information,* Martin Amis's bleak and scorching send-up of the literary professions, the following beliefs are gleefully debunked: that reading makes you a better person; that writers of merit are driven to write by virtue of their deep insights into the human spirit; that a world filled with artistic creations is superior to one filled with the castoffs of consumer culture; that writing provides access to immortality. To stage his skewering of these cultural commonplaces, Amis pits two writers against each other: Richard Tull, the author of artistic, experimental (that is to say, unreadable) novels; and Gwyn Barry, who is vapid and soulless, but whose eventless, multicultural, utopian novel, *Amelior,* has become an international phenomenon. To the degree that *The In-*

formation has a plot, it revolves around Tull's repeated efforts to punish Barry for having met with popular literary success. To Tull's way of thinking, Barry's greatest literary achievement is a work of no consequence: as he describes it, *Amelior* "was about a group of fair-minded young people who, in an unnamed country, strove to establish a rural community. And they succeeded. And then it ended. Not worth writing in the first place, the finished book was, in Richard's view, a ridiculous failure" (28). And yet, in the world Amis has created for his readers, pretentious, sentimental slop of this kind has adulation heaped upon it, while work like the kind Richard Tull produces—work that strains mightily to achieve a high seriousness, work that is replete with veiled literary references, work that endlessly announces its indebtedness to the earlier classics—actually physically harms the few who can bear to read it, causing migraines, seeing disorders, and even forced hospitalizations.

Tull, who is unable to find a publisher and whose previous novels are out of print, can only view his friend's success as a cruel joke the universe is playing on him, one he's determined to counteract. But, as Tull eventually discovers, there's no fighting the ways of the universe. In the grand scheme of things, he is insignificant, and what lies in store for him is what lies in store for us all—a story of increasing humiliation. In fact, *The History of Increasing Humiliation* is one of the many books for which Tull has received an advance but has yet to write, one which is to contain his theory about "the decline in the status and virtue of literary protagonists" (92). As Tull sees it, there's a direct connection between the decline in the status of heroes in the novel and the growth in our understanding of the dimensions of the universe: with each advance in astronomical studies, "we get smaller" (93). We can see the effects of this in our literary creations, Tull argues: "First gods, then demigods, then kings, then great warriors, great lovers, then burghers and merchants and vicars and doctors and lawyers. Then social realism: you. Then irony: me. Then maniacs and murderers, tramps, mobs, rabble, flotsam, vermin" (92). And indeed, Amis uses Tull as a vehicle to prove this theory, assaulting the pieties of those who would privilege the acts of reading and writing by showing artists to be indistinguishable from criminals. By this, Amis does not mean that all criminals are like Hannibal Lecter, allknowing virtuosos who transgress and transcend social bonds at will. Rather, as Amis puts it, "the criminal *is* like an artist (though not for the reasons usually given, which merely depend on immaturity and the condition of self-employment): the criminal resembles the artist in his pretension, his incompetence, and his self-pity" (76). One could hardly say that the status of the criminal has been elevated through such a comparison.

When Tull's initial efforts to harm his rival fail, he turns to Steve Cousins, a financially secure, semi-retired criminal, who now entertains himself by pursuing "recreational" adventures in his profession: his specialty, as he defines it, is "fuck[ing] people up" for sport (116). And, for reasons that are never quite clear, "Scozzy," as his mates call him, is determined to hurt a writer, preferably Gwyn Barry. Scozzy may be motivated by his own hatred of *Amelior,* which he refers to as a "total crock" and "complete crap" (114); he may be driven by the autodidact's sense of inferiority (113); he may be acting out the aggressions of an abandoned child (Amis repeatedly links Scozzy to the wild boy of Aveyron). But to seek motivation for Scozzy's actions is, within Amis's cosmology, to misunderstand the criminal's place in the universe and our own as well. Asking why a Steve Cousins or an Eric Harris or a Dylan Klebold is violent is itself a meaningless act, not because the motivation is too deeply buried or obscurely articulated to ever be known, but because we no longer live in a world where human action can be explained. We have plenty of information; it just doesn't amount to anything. This is the logic of the history of increasing humiliation working itself out over time.

At one point in the novel, Tull's wife, Gina, is reading the newspaper in horror, trying to make sense of the actions of a child-murderer. "Words," says Gina, "—words fail me. *Why?* Won't someone tell me?" (123). Amis then interrupts this scene to introduce his own commentary on how we are to make sense of these senseless acts, the ones which rob us of speech, the ones which drive us to ask why. "A contemporary investigator will tell you that he hardly ever thinks about motive. It's no help. He's sorry, but it's no help. Fuck the why, he'll say. Look at the how, which will give you the who. But fuck the why" (124). There is no ultimate explanation for these acts of brutality, which is something the little boy, who apologized to the man who was about to murder him, could not understand: "the little boy was searching for motivation in the contemporary playground. Don't look. You won't find it, because it's gone. I'm sorry. I'm sorry" (124).[5]

As it goes with the world, so it goes with the novel: to seek out what motivates Tull to try to destroy Gwyn Barry, to try to understand why Scozzy would want to hurt Barry, to see some reason in Gina's betrayal of Tull—these are all fruitless acts in Amis's cosmos, where only the naive believe that violence is the result of some ultimately discernable act of volition. Tull understands that he lives in a world defined by random acts of violence and he is afraid, not for his own safety, but for his son's: "violence would come, if it came, from the individual, from left field, denuded of motive. The urban pastoral was all left field.

There was no right field. And violence wouldn't come for Richard. It would come for Marco" (99). And, indeed, this very scenario is acted out in the conclusion to *The Information,* with Scozzy, bent on revenge for having been publicly insulted by Tull, heading to Tull's neighborhood determined to kidnap Marco. Unaware of the danger his son is in, drunkenly planning one final plot to bring Barry down, Tull stumbles into his apartment only to discover Barry in the act of sodomizing his wife. Meanwhile, outside in the park, Barry's bodyguards happen to intercept Scozzy before he is able to harm Marco. Broken and defeated, Tull belatedly realizes that he owes his son's life to the man he viewed as being in every way his inferior. As the novel ends, with Barry proudly sauntering off victorious, Tull climbs the stairs back to his apartment "working on a way of forgiving Gina. A form of words. Because if he forgave her, she could never leave him now. Who was he? Who had he been throughout? Who would he always be?" (373). Tull, "a failed book reviewer who comes on like Dr. Johnson" (286), has been shown to be a fool who can't even read the intentions and the capabilities of those closest to him. Barry, the avowed fraud and hypocrite, gets everything—fame, fortune, even "the Profundity Requital," which guarantees him lifetime support so he can devote himself to thinking about the social good.

Although Amis explicitly outlaws such a question, one can't help but wonder why a writer would produce such a scathing portrait of the literary world and its denizens. If this is Amis's assessment both of his peers and of the reading public, then why go on writing? Is he, like Gwyn Barry, just along for the ride, cynically "doing what every man would do if he thought he could get away with it" (286)?[6] *The Information* might best be read as a meditation on the fact that sooner or later all writers encounter something that robs them of their sleep, something that deprives them of feeling that what they do matters. As the novel opens, Richard Tull is crying in his sleep, crying because the night had brought "all its unwelcome information" (4). And when he wakes, he considers calling Gwyn Barry, for whom "there would be no information, or the information, such as it was, would all be good" (5). Tull and Barry are both entering their forties and the information that awaits them on this threshold communicates different messages: Gina has given Tull an additional year to complete his latest and perhaps final novel, *Untitled,* after which time—the novel's failure being a foregone conclusion—Tull will have to commit himself to more gainful employment. Barry, on the other hand, has written two best-sellers; his marriage has been featured on the BBC; he's got an international promotional tour lined up; he's been nominated for the Profundity Requital. Tull is having "a crisis of the middle years," a crisis Amis himself has been through. Citing what are presumably notes from his own writing journal, Amis observes, "intimations of monstrousness are common, are perhaps universal, in early middle age" (44). One form this takes is a preoccupation with the question, "how can I ever play the omniscient, the all-knowing, when I don't know *anything*?" (43).

So the information that comes with age, the information that comes at night, brings news of futility, ignorance, insignificance, humiliation: "When we die, our bodies will eventually go back where they came from: to a dying star, our own, five billion years from now, some time around the year 5,000,001,995" (45). With the aging of the body and the foreclosing of future possibilities, all the inbound information serves to turn one's attention to mortality: "the information is telling me to stop saying *hi* and to start saying *bye*" (89). Throughout the novel, Amis concedes that he is not in control of what is happening, that events are unfolding and characters are developing without reference to any greater design on his part. "I don't come at these people," Amis explains in the middle of the novel, "They come at me. They come at me like information formed in the night. I don't make them. They're already there" (190–91). Whether Amis is genuinely haunted by these characters or is only mocking the terror that lesser writers experience when they lose control of their material is a matter of importance only to those who wish to argue over Amis's own literary achievements. For the purposes of this discussion, though, the salient point is to note the ways in which Amis's novel brings together the aging body, the activity of writing, and the inbound information to explore—and I would say produce—feelings of hopelessness. We live in the Information Age and all the information is telling us that whatever we have done, whatever we are doing, and whatever we plan to do will never have any lasting significance.

FOLLOWING THE WORD

> You know, Eric, you can read about this stuff, but you can't understand it until you live it.
> —Chris McCandless in Jon Krakauer's *Into the Wild*

Chris McCandless's misadventures in the Alaskan wilderness are now well known, thanks to Jon Krakauer's best-selling account of the young man's disappearance and death in *Into the Wild*. These are the facts: after graduating from Emory in 1990, McCandless donated the remains of his college trust fund to Oxfam, burned what money remained, along with his identification papers, and disappeared. Two years later, in the fall of 1992, his emaciated body was found, along with his favorite books and his journal, in a school bus deep in the Alaskan wilds. Something about McCandless's quest and his ultimate fate captured the imagination of readers across the country. For some, the story is a tragedy, one that concerns a deadly conflict between youthful idealism and a brutal, unforgiving reality. For those reading this version of McCandless's life, the loss of a young man who wanted to commune with the natural world and the disappearance of a world untouched by the mercenary desires of human society are developments to be mourned. For others, though, McCandless's story is just another example of the foolishness of those who believe more in the power of books than in the power of the natural world. For these readers, McCandless is a stock figure, a suburban rube, a dreamer who neither understood nor respected the very forces he sought to embrace. For these readers, McCandless got what he deserved.

I am interested in McCandless not because of the debate his death has sparked, but because he provides us with an opportunity to consider a reader who differs from Amis's characters in one critical regard: regardless of whether or not Amis himself actually believes that knowledge of the size of the cosmos robs the activities of reading and writing of any lasting meaning, McCandless stands as evidence that there continue to be real readers who invest the activities of reading and writing with great significance. In this respect, McCandless is just the kind of reader that Amis's character Richard Tull (and almost every English teacher) is looking for: a reader who savors the words that others have produced, who seeks guidance from the printed page, who dreams of inhabiting the landscapes that his or her most-admired authors describe in such loving detail. While one could argue that some similar utopian longing is there to be found boiling beneath Amis's bleak account of these information-saturated times, it is much more immediately clear that McCandless actually believed that it was possible to escape the bonds of the corporatized world and reach a space of greater calm. He knew this because his books told him so.

What makes *Into the Wild* remarkable is Krakauer's ability to get some purchase on McCandless's actual reading practice, which, in turn, enables him to get inside McCandless's head and speculate with considerable authority about what ultimately led the young man to abandon the comforts of home and purposefully seek out mortal danger. Krakauer is able to do this, in part, because he has access to the books that McCandless read, with all their underlinings and marginalia, as well as to his journals and the postcards and letters McCandless sent to friends during his journey. Working with these materials and his interviews with McCandless's family and friends, Krakauer develops a sense of McCandless's inner life and eventually comes to some understanding of why the young man was so susceptible to being seduced by the writings of London, Thoreau, Muir, and Tolstoy. Who McCandless is and what becomes of him are, it turns out, intimately connected to the young man's approach to reading— both what he chose to read and how he chose to read it.

After graduating from college, McCandless hopped in his car and headed west, embarking on a journey that, since Kerouac, has become a cliché for the dispossessed male. McCandless told no one where he was going or what his plans were. When his car broke down, he abandoned it and began hitchhiking. He renamed himself "Alexander Supertramp." He kept a journal and took photographs to record his adventure. He traveled to California, canoed down into Mexico, made his way toward Alaska. Along the way, he met people who looked out for him and he, more often than not, would return their kindness by encouraging them to read the books that had so moved him. To one, McCandless wrote: "Wayne, you really should read *War and Peace.* I meant it when I said you had one of the highest characters of any man I'd met. That is a very powerful and highly symbolic book. It has things in it that I think you will understand. Things that escape most people" (Krakauer 33). He took a job working at a flea market selling used paperbacks and lost himself in the pleasure of organizing merchandise and assisting in the very kind of commercial transactions he elsewhere despised. His boss reported: "Alex was big on the classics: Dickens, H. G. Wells, Mark Twain, Jack London. London was his favorite. He'd try to convince every snowbird who walked by that they should read *Call of the Wild*" (43–44). In the abandoned bus where McCandless's body was eventually found, there were books by Tolstoy and Thoreau with highlighted passages celebrating chastity and moral purity (65–66). On some plywood he had written what Krakauer calls McCandless's "declaration of independence":

> AND NOW AFTER TWO RAMBLING YEARS COMES THE
> FINAL AND GREATEST ADVENTURE. THE CLIMACTIC
> BATTLE TO KILL THE FALSE BEING WITHIN AND VICTO-
> RIOUSLY CONCLUDE THE SPIRITUAL PILGRIMAGE. . . .
> NO LONGER TO BE POISONED BY CIVILIZATION HE
> FLEES, AND WALKS ALONE UPON THE LAND TO BECOME
> *LOST IN THE WILD* (163; capitals and italics in original).

Like most readers, McCandless surrounded himself with books that reinforced his own beliefs—in this case, texts that confirmed his sense that he was living honorably by attempting to follow his beliefs *to the letter*. Alternately the evangelist and the pilgrim, McCandless moved through the world trying to convert others to his point of view and turning away from anyone who sought to make more intimate contact with him personally. As Alex, he was a hobo, a vagabond, the self-defined "super" tramp, someone who had neither the need nor the desire for human relationships: his books and his solo adventures satisfied his yearnings for connection. Or, as Krakauer puts it in his summary judgment of McCandless's motivations: "Unlike Muir and Thoreau, McCandless went into the wilderness not primarily to ponder nature or the world at large but, rather, to explore the inner country of his own soul" (183).

As much as Krakauer admires McCandless for having embarked upon such a spiritual journey, he is careful to point out that McCandless was ultimately undone by the great trust he placed in the written word. The harshest judgment Krakauer offers in his account emerges in his discussion of McCandless's way of reading Jack London's stories about life in Alaska: "He was so enthralled by these tales . . . that he seemed to forget they were works of fiction, constructions of the imagination that had more to do with London's romantic sensibilities than with the actualities of life in the subarctic wilderness. McCandless conveniently overlooked the fact that London himself had spent just a single winter in the North and that he'd died by his own hand on his California estate at the age of forty, a fatuous drunk, obese and pathetic, maintaining a sedentary existence that bore scant resemblance to the ideals he espoused in print" (44). What most interests me about Krakauer's critique of London is its vehemence: Krakauer's rage here is for an author whose life and words don't align. Because McCandless wanted to believe in the world London invented, because McCandless wanted to be enchanted, he failed to ask the question that Krakauer believes must be of concern to all readers: namely, what is the relationship between what the author says and the way the author lives? London used his writing as a place to store his fantasies about struggling to survive, about lonely battles against the elements, about the animal within, fantasies that have trapped and—Krakauer's language suggests—even killed some of those naive enough to believe them.

While Krakauer faults McCandless for being fooled by London's prose, he goes to great lengths to defend McCandless against charges of recklessness or incompetence. It is true, Krakauer concedes, that McCandless could have taken any number of actions to avoid dying in the woods. The young man could have taken a map with him; he could have done a better job exploring the banks of the suddenly uncrossable river that prevented him from returning by the route he came in on; he could even have started a forest fire to alert the authorities to his plight. But for those who see McCandless's death by starvation as irrefutable proof of his failure as an outdoorsman, Krakauer has another explanation: McCandless died in the woods not because he couldn't find enough food to survive, but because he ate seeds that no one knew to be poisonous. Relying on *Tanaina Plantlore* to guide his gatherings in the wild, McCandless trusted its author completely. As he grew weaker and as game grew scarcer, McCandless began to eat the roots of a species of wild potato that the book identified as nontoxic. The book said nothing about the seeds of the wild potato and it is Krakauer's hypothesis that, as he grew more desperate, McCandless took the book's silence on the seeds as permission to ingest them. If Krakauer is right, one could say that McCandless was killed off by a reading practice that placed too much faith in books, a practice that forgets that the world in all its infinite complexity and particularity will always exceed the explanatory grasp of any single text and, indeed, of all texts taken in their totality.

Whenever I've taught this book—and I've used it with first-year students, undergraduate literature majors, and advanced graduate students—the issue of trust inevitably arises as a problem. Why accept Krakauer's account when he is so obviously invested in defending McCandless from his critics? The fact that Krakauer is so openly identified with the subject of his research is a sign, I would say, that he is producing a kind of writing that can and should still matter. Because Krakauer has inhabited the same clichés that captured McCandless, because he understands their pull from the inside, he is able to offer an account of the young man's motivations that is simultaneously sympathetic *and* critical. By working on the materials of McCandless's life, Krakauer learns how to do what McCandless was unable or unwilling to do: he comes to understand and respect the thoughts of those who were appalled by his behavior. He is doing the work of making peace with his past. Thus, although Krakauer claims he is just trying to make sense of "why some people seem to despise [McCandless] so intensely for having died" in the Alaskan wilds, the truth is that Krakauer is equally interested in using McCandless as a vehicle for making sense of his own turbulent, and occasionally self-destructive, youth. As it turns out, McCandless and Krakauer had much in common. They read and were moved by many of the same authors; they fell in love, like many lonely, alienated, introspective young men before them, with a stark, unforgiving beauty that they could only find in books and in the natural world; and, finally, when the time was right, they both ran away from a world that did not live up to their expectations.

From a certain vantage point, McCandless's Alaskan odyssey and Krakauer's harrowing attempt to climb the Devils Thumb are clichés of modernity:

they are the stories of young men, fed up with society, determined to get away from it all. (One version of this cliché involves heading off into the wild; a more recent version, as we've seen, involves entering the schoolyard armed to the teeth.) Now that he has safely made the passage into middle age, Krakauer can see that there's nothing particularly original about embarking on such a journey and he is reluctant to require that such adventures be treated either with reverence or with scorn. On his own journey, Krakauer discovered just how fleeting the profound and transformative experience of scaling a mountain peak can be. Less than a month after realizing his dream, he found himself back in Colorado, pounding nails into frames for townhouses. Over the years that followed, Krakauer came to a different realization: "I was a raw youth who mistook passion for insight and acted according to an obscure, gap-ridden logic. I thought climbing the Devils Thumb would fix all that was wrong with my life. In the end, of course, it changed almost nothing" (155).

Since Krakauer and McCandless moved through the same experiential world for a time, Krakauer seems to know, intuitively, where to look to find a final explanation for McCandless's aberrant behavior. Why would a young man with so much going for him throw it all away? Unlike Amis, Krakauer cannot accept a world without motive, so he continues to probe until he discovers what he believes to be the series of events that alienated McCandless from his family and friends. The ultimate cause of McCandless's disaffection, it would appear, was that his father had conducted an extended affair when McCandless was a small child. Years later, unbeknownst to his parents, McCandless found out about his father's double life and confided in his sister that this discovery made his "entire childhood seem like a fiction" (121–23). To some, it will seem that in uncovering this information, Krakauer has simply succeeded in moving McCandless from one familiar narrative to another, finding at the heart of his desire to escape nothing more than another primordial example of the Oedipal struggle. However accurate such an assessment might be, I would argue that the true significance of Krakauer's discovery lies elsewhere. Having learned this dark family secret, Krakauer is able to provide us with a glimpse of how McCandless responded when confronted with a reality quite unlike the one contained in the books he had chosen to surround himself with. With his childhood transformed into a fiction, McCandless understood himself to have received a warrant to embark on a new life. He believed he was alone. He believed he owed no one anything. He believed he was free.

ON MEDITATIVE WRITING AND ITS CONSEQUENCES

> Several years have now passed since I first realized how numerous were
> the false opinions that in my youth I had taken to be true, and thus how
> doubtful were all those that I had subsequently built upon them. And
> thus I realized that once in my life I had to raze everything to the
> ground and begin again from the original foundations, if I wanted to
> establish anything firm and lasting in the sciences.
>
> —René Descartes, *Meditations on First Philosophy*

All these unhappy men, the betrayed and the betrayers, the real and the fictional. Is there any hope for them? Or for the wasted worlds they've left in their
wake? Thinking about these lives, so deeply entangled with violence, neglect,
and lies; watching the news, which is forever reporting that another angry man
has entered some building or schoolyard, guns blazing; feeling the weight of
these stories, and knowing their inevitable movement towards death, destruction, and humiliation: such thoughts only serve to plunge one deeper into the
darkness. Amis's fiction clearly offers no escape from such ruminations. And
Krakauer's real-life account confirms the fact that relying on reading as a mode
of escape has its own unique set of dangers. Against the backdrop of Columbine (or Kosovo or Rwanda or September 11 or Afghanistan or Iraq—the news
never fails to offer up another example), there is little these authors can do. The
senseless loss of life always trumps the efforts of the meaning makers. Why
bother with reading and writing when the world is so obviously going to hell?

One could say that the course of Western philosophy was forever altered by
an encounter with a differently phrased version of this question. When Descartes reached that point in his life when he felt that nothing he had been told
in the past could be trusted, he, too, sealed himself off from the rest of society
and contemplated the dark possibility that he might be doomed to live out the
rest of his days in a dream world. This, at any rate, is the opening conceit of his
Meditations on First Philosophy. To rid himself of all the false opinions that he
had been fed in his youth, Descartes tells us that he waited until he had
both the maturity and the free time necessary to devote to the harrowing task
of self-purification. In his mid-forties, he sits by the fire, in his dressing gown,
all alone. He is transported by the idea that he can attack his past and demolish
it. He, too, wants to be free. And so Descartes settles down to the task of dis-
mantling and reassembling his cosmology, a process that takes him six days to
complete.[7]

On the first day of his meditations, everything collapses under the force of

Descartes' determined skepticism. There is nothing Descartes has ever thought or felt that cannot also be doubted. Since everything that comes to him through his senses is misleading, he finds it impossible to distinguish dream states from states of consciousness. He even imagines the possibility that there might well be "an evil genius, supremely powerful and clever" who whiles away his time deceiving him at every turn (62). While the first act of the God of Genesis is to separate light from darkness, Descartes' accomplishment, on his first day, is to plunge his readers into the pitch of night. In the inverted world he has created with his skepticism, one dreams in the light and fears waking to toil "among the inextricable shadows of the difficulties" that have been produced by the workings of his mind (63).

On the second day, Descartes sets out to inhabit the world of doubt he has created: "I suppose that everything I see is false. I believe that none of what my deceitful memory represents ever existed" (63). Shorn of his past, of his body with all its misleading signals and vague impressions, Descartes discovers his true essence: he is first and foremost a "thing that thinks" (*une chose qui pense*) (65). And as a "thing that thinks," he determines that the senses are not to be trusted: in the midst of this meditation, Descartes looks out the window and believes he sees men walking by on the street. "[Y]et," Descartes asks, "but what do I see aside from hats and coats, which could conceal automata?" (68). To get to the essence of any thing, be it a man or a piece of wax, we must strip "it of its clothing" and "look at [it] in its nakedness" (68): we must remove all outward appearances and get to that which does not change.

On the third day, having shut his eyes, stopped up his ears, withdrawn all his senses, and abandoned his past, Descartes surveys the world of his creation and determines that he is alone. The only way out of this bleak environment that is haunted by malicious demons and the illusory reports of the senses is to posit the existence of a firm foundation, which, for reasons we'll discuss shortly, Descartes designates "God." Descartes' "proof" or "discovery" of God's existence is well known: God is the perfection that Descartes can conceive of but does not actually possess in his thoughts. Since Descartes' thoughts cannot be the cause of this state of perfection (because "what is more perfect [that is, what contains in itself more reality] cannot come into being from what is less perfect"), this perfection must exist outside of him (73). From this, "it necessarily follows that I am not alone in the world, but that something else, which is the cause of this idea, also exists" (74).

Alone with his God in the fourth meditation, Descartes turns his thoughts to an issue that has been at the center of our current discussion: how to distinguish between truth and falsity. For Descartes, the crucial task before him is to explain how God, who is perfect, could have created a thinking thing so defective that it struggles to distinguish fact from fiction, truth from lies. Setting to the side the question of *why* his creator elected to design him in this way, Descartes posits that his own errors result from the fact that he has been endowed by his creator with a will that has a much wider scope than his intellect. On the fifth and sixth days of his meditations, in a repetition that bespeaks a certain anxiety, Descartes once again proves the existence of God and then, after some deft negotiations, is returned to his body and the sensuous world. Before resting, Descartes looks back on where his thinking has taken him and concludes that "the hyperbolic doubts of the last few days ought to be rejected as ludicrous" (103). By doubting everything, he has found the firm ground that is necessary for going on: there is a God; everything that happens is not a lie; the mind can provide us with direct access to the truth. Descartes, it would appear, is home free.

Why should the thoughts this lonely man had more than 350 years ago warrant our attention now? Descartes contributed to the larger effort to liberate reason from the prison of religious dogma and he did this, in part, by driving a wedge between the mind, which traffics in clear and distinct ideas, and the body, which transmits and receives the innately imperfect data of the senses. Fearful of how his thoughts might be received at the time, Descartes had his meditations published first in Latin in Paris and only later allowed them to be translated into French and reprinted in Holland where he was staying. He also placed at the front of his meditations an open letter "to the Most Wise and Distinguished Men, the Dean and Doctors of the Faculty of Sacred Theology of Paris," explaining his reasons for seeking to make public the transcripts, as it were, of his own encounter with the darkness. For those readers prone to skipping such front matter and jumping straight to the body of the text, it will probably come as something of a surprise to learn that Descartes' meditations, which seem like such an earnest attempt to find some solid bedrock upon which to build a life free of falsehoods, are actually a ruse. As Descartes makes clear in his letter to the faculty, he never really had any doubts at all about God or the eternal life of the soul: he's simply trying to put together an argument that will persuade the "unbelievers" (*infidèles*) of what he and his fellow believers "believe by faith" (47). So, the darkness, the radical doubt, the mind floating free of the body are all just props to add to the drama of the fiction he's created —ways of getting those outside the circle of believers to share in his illusion.

That's one way to read Descartes' opening remarks to the Faculty of Sacred Theology. There is, however, yet another possibility. (There always is.) Maybe the letter to the deans and doctors is the sham, just Descartes whispering sweet nothings to those in power in hopes of securing a protected space where he can carry out his scientific research without threat of being harassed. And, given that Descartes is so good at creating the illusion of compliance, what can the illustrious deans and faculty do? He's poured it on so thick—he's just doing what any fellow believer would do, contributing to the cause, etc.—that they just have to get out of the way. If the God that emerges from Descartes' meditations is one more likely to be found residing in the theorems of analytical geometry than in the sanctuaries of the Vatican, what's the harm? That's how advertising works: it's just food for the infidels. It poses no threat to the believers, for what true believer would doubt the existence of God or that the soul separates from the body at death?

There's no resolving the question of whether or not Descartes was being completely sincere when he wrote to the deans and doctors of the Faculty of Sacred Theology in Paris seeking their protection. All we can know is that he had good reason to fear their powers and the institution they represented. For our purposes, what matters most is pausing to take note of the intellectual regime that has risen in the wake of Descartes' effort to break free of dogmatic belief by locating the self at the nexus of reason and the will. To resolve his crisis in certainty and construct a working space that is not contaminated by the lies of the past, Descartes established an internal hierarchy that gives primacy to the mind and its universal truths—truths that, like the properties of a triangle, are clear, distinct, and without a history. The body and its voyage through time are without interest: nothing is to be gained by exploring what happens to the body as it moves through the social institutions that govern life. These are just accidents of time and place. The mind is where the action is.

Whether Descartes himself learned anything as a result of writing down these meditations isn't clear. We know only that Descartes' meditations were designed to provide their author with a method for protecting himself from being deceived by the world and its denizens. Encased in this regulatory mechanism, Descartes is, I believe, more alone at the end of his meditations than when he started. For now that he has rid himself of his fictions and screwed himself into the real, he has no need to consider these fundamental matters any further: "I will say in addition that these arguments are such that I believe there is no way open to the human mind whereby better ones could ever be found" (48). True to this claim, Descartes spends much of the rest of his life defending the veracity of his proofs and the cogency of his line of reasoning. He wanders off into the dreamy world of argumentation.

JOINING THE LIARS' CLUB: WRITING AND THE GENERATION OF HOPE

> I never knew despair could lie.
>
> —Mary Karr, *The Liars' Club*

It's safe to say that the spirit of our time differs markedly from the spirit of Descartes' time. While he wrote to banish the particular and to revel in the universal, now that we inhabit the age of the memoir, we find ourselves surrounded by those who write to distinguish themselves from the crowd by capturing the deep particularity and pathos of their own past experiences. Frank McCourt describes the grueling poverty of the Irish immigrant; former Princeton professor Michael Ryan records having sex with his dog; Kathryn Harrison, sex with her father; David Denby, sex with himself (while reading the Great Books no less); James McBride, what it's like to grow up black while having a white mother; Susanna Kaysen, what it's like to be institutionalized. The list goes on and on, because every shoe salesman and waitress, every schoolteacher and cop, every politician and pundit has a story to tell and wants to share it now via the Internet, on some television talk show, or on the printed page. The chosen media doesn't seem to matter. The stories will out.

While there has been much fretting in the critical community about this "turn to the personal" and all that it may be said to signify, the memoirs just keep coming, flooding over the outstretched arms of all those who would like to contain the spread of this genre. That the memoirs, in general, return to scenes of violence and violation is worth pondering, for here one finds evidence of one way in which writing continues to matter at the current moment: the memoir allows one to plunge into the darkness of the past; it provides the means both for evoking and for making sense of that past; and it can be made to generate a sense of possibility, a sense that a better, brighter future is out there to be secured. When judged by these criteria, Mary Karr's *The Liars' Club* stands out as one of the most remarkable representatives of the genre.

The Liars' Club opens with fragments of a recovered memory, "a single instant surrounded by dark": Karr, at seven years old, being inspected by her family doctor; the Sheriff and his deputies moving through her house; the backyard on fire; her mother being taken away; the concerted effort to find a place for the children to stay (3). One of the central projects of *The Liars' Club* is to make sense of these fragments, to relocate them in a more coherent, more comprehensive account of Karr's past. What happened that night? Why did no one ever speak of it again? To answer these questions, Karr has to wade through the faulty, inexact evidence that her family—which is its own liars' club—makes available to her and then find a way to tell not only her story, but also the stories of Pete Karr, her father, Charlie Marie Moore Karr, her mother, and Lecia, her sister.

By the middle of Karr's memoir, she has succeeded in finding out what led to the appearance of the police and the firemen in her house. She eventually remembers being with her sister, hiding in the dark, their mother in the bedroom doorway holding a knife and then, moments later, her mother in the hallway calling the police, saying, "Get over here. I just killed them both. Both of them. I've stabbed them both to death" (157). But to get to this moment, Karr must first detail: life among the working poor in Leechfield, Texas; the odd union of her father, an oil worker, and her mother, a highly educated woman with artistic aspirations; her parents' spiral into alcoholism, the violent fights, the long separations; the slow, agonizingly painful death of the grandmother; her own rape by a neighborhood boy. She is participating in a form of revelation, a ritual of purging and purification. She is telling the family secrets, pulling the ghosts out of the closets, waking the dead, and she does so with no overt sign of shame.

At one point, in retaliation for a beating she received in a fight with the boys who lived next door, Karr credits herself with going on "a rampage that prefigured what Charles Whitman—the guy who shot and killed thirteen people from the tower at the University of Texas—would do a few years later" (161). She got a BB gun, climbed a tree, and waited for her victims to walk out into a nearby field. And when the enemy clan appeared, Karr opened fire, hitting one of the children in the neck before the family fled out of range. When one of the boys hid behind his father, Karr reports that her response was as follows: "*You pussy,* I thought, as if Rickey's not wanting to get shot were a defining mark against his manhood" (162). For this activity, Karr received a whipping. She notes, as well, that her "morning as sniper won [her] a grudging respect. Kids stopped mouthing off about Mother" (162). Violence silenced her tormenters and it kept the enemies at bay. Within the psychic economy of the world Karr inhabited at the time, this doubtless seemed the only rational response available to her.

Eventually, Karr recovers the psychically charged world surrounding her memory of that dark night. Trapped in a life she never wanted serving as a "hausfrau" to an oilman in a "crackerbox house," surrounded by people she despised, Charlie Marie Karr tried to set her world on fire. She burned down her studio. She made a bonfire of her paintings, the children's toys, their books, their furniture, their clothes, their shoes.

As Mary and her sister mutely look on, they are transformed by the experience: they are ready to be led into the fire themselves. "We are in the grip of some big machine grinding us along. The force of it simplifies everything. A weird calm has settled over me from the inside out. What is about to happen to us has stood in line to happen. All the roads out of that instant have been closed, one by one" (152).

They are doomed.

No neighbor intervenes to stop what is happening. No one calls the police. The children don't run away to save themselves. The father doesn't appear to rescue them. The mother is not restrained by some maternal instinct. On the familial level, this is the apocalypse: this is a time without hope. And yet, for reasons that are never explained and perhaps never can be, Charlie Marie doesn't actually go through with murdering her children. She only thinks she has. The disaster passes. The mother is institutionalized. Mary takes her BB gun into the tree. And eventually Charlie Marie comes back home.

From a certain vantage point, this would appear to be the logical place for Karr to end her meditation. She's cast light into her memory of that dark night in the bedroom and now knows what happened. Why keep *The Liars' Club* going for another two hundred pages? What else is there to know? The story continues, I would argue, for two interrelated reasons. First, Karr only knows the *how* and the *what* regarding that night; she does not know *why* her mother went over the edge. Second, Karr's writing has not yet delivered her from those memories because she knows only the facts, not the truth of what happened. At the age of seven, thinking magically, she understood only that her mother had tried to kill her for failing to clean up her room. By the middle of the book, she recognizes the inadequacy of such an explanation. Without the *why* she has nothing, just information coming in the dead of night.

Pursuing the question of motivation takes Karr into still darker waters. After her mother's psychotic episode, her parents move to Colorado and eventually divorce. Her mother remarries and sinks deeper into a drunken stupor. Karr walks in on her mother having sex with another man; Karr is raped again; Charlie Marie tries to kill her new husband, buys a bar, stays up late reading French philosophy and "talking in a misty-eyed way about suicide" (230). Eventually, Charlie Marie puts the girls on a plane back to their father, but it's the wrong plane and they end up flying to Mexico. The calamities continue without ever exposing the cause of all this senseless, self-destructive behavior. Why is it that no one seeks help? What is it that fuels Charlie Marie's all-encompassing sense of despair? Why is it that Pete Karr seeks refuge with the other members of "the Liars' Club," a group of men who drink together and tell tall tales that keep their pasts shrouded in darkness?

When Karr finally finds the key that unlocks the mystery of her family's past, it is long after she has grown up and moved away. Her parents have reunited. She has watched her father's steady decline after a stroke, sat by his side during his final days, listened to him ramble on about his life in the war, a time he never before mentioned. She discovers that he was wounded twice, one time stuck with "a bayonet through his forearm, leaving a scar [she'd] seen a thousand times and never once asked about" (307), the other time left for dead under the rubble of a bridge he'd helped to explode. This last news sends Karr up to the family attic in search of military papers that might be used to get her father additional medical assistance. While moving amongst the family's remains, she discovers four jewelry boxes, each containing a wedding ring. She has, quite unexpectedly, found her mother's hidden past and she then finds the strength to use this material evidence to compel her mother to speak. As Karr confronts her ever-reticent mother, she observes: "Few born liars ever intentionally embark in truth's direction, even those who believe that such a journey might axiomatically set them free" (311).

Karr uncovers the systemic violence that defined her mother's past—the sudden, inexplicable disappearance of her first husband and her first two children, the years she spent trying to find her first family, the reunion where she was convinced to leave the children with their father and return to her studio apartment in Texas—and as she does so the fragmented pieces of her own life begin to fall into place. In the end, the mystery is not so mysterious: "Those were my mother's demons, then, two small children, whom she longed for and felt ashamed for having lost." The explanation for Charlie Marie's years of silence about her past is both simple and profound. She tells her daughter that she kept these events a secret because she was afraid that, if Mary knew, she "wouldn't like [her] anymore" (318).

It would be easy to ridicule such an explanation. After all, Charlie Marie has done much in her life that her daughter did know about that would have justified rejection. She neglected her children, placed them in harm's way, tried to kill herself, tried to kill them. Karr herself finds her mother's reasoning to be "pathetic" (318). However one judges Charlie Marie's excuse, though, the fact that she cannot produce a satisfying or reasonable account for her silence is compelling evidence of just how much power stories *can* exercise over the lives of individuals. By clinging to her silence, by keeping her story trapped inside, she invested her untold story with such a monstrous power that she came to believe that speaking it aloud would make her essentially unlikable. Left alone with this story, Charlie Marie transformed a series of events where she was outmatched, unprepared, and cruelly victimized into irrefutable proof of her own unworthiness as a mother. Without some other connection to the world, without some other voice to counter her interpretations, Charlie Marie was left to suffer her own perpetually punishing judgments. Within this psychic economy, the only possible way for Charlie Marie to remain likable was to keep her story a secret. To remain likable, she had to lie.

The revelation of Charlie Marie's story did not produce the anticipated effect, though.

As Karr puts it: "what Mother told absolved us both, in a way. All the black crimes we believed ourselves guilty of were myths, stories we'd cobbled together out of fear. We expected no good news interspersed with the bad. Only the dark aspect of any story sank in. I never knew despair could lie." As the book ends, Karr escapes the darkness that has defined her past and contemplates "the cool tunnel of white light the spirit might fly into at death." Acknowledging that this description of what it's like to die may simply be an account of "death's neurological fireworks, the brain's last light show," Karr insists that this is a lie she can live with. She is content to at least entertain the possibility of a future communion with her loved ones, a time when "all your beloveds hover before you, their lit arms held out in welcome" (320).

In Karr's hands, the memoir thus becomes a vehicle for arriving at an understanding that produces forgiveness. Writing, as she uses it, is a hermeneutic practice that involves witnessing the mundane horrors of the past in order to make peace with that past. And, as the preceding account makes clear, it also becomes, however briefly, a means for gaining access to the light of the universal. While the other writers and events I've discussed here have turned our attention to death and decay, Karr offers an encounter with the prospect of one's mortality that leads neither to despair nor cynicism nor violence nor suicide nor escape. Even if it's a lie, the lie Karr tells herself at the end of *The Liars' Club* is a lie that keeps her inside the realm of social relations, helping her make what she can of what life has put before her.

AN EXPERIMENT IN INSTITUTIONAL AUTOBIOGRAPHY

It might seem that, by organizing these readings in this way, I've been building up to a spirited defense of the social and therapeutic value of writing one's memoirs. After all, this kind of writing worked for Karr, why shouldn't it work for us all? But the genre of the memoir is no more likely to compel a writer to make peace with the past or to find some sense of connection with others than is poetry, fiction, the meditative essay, the policy statement, the well-honed critique, the bulleted memo, the forced confession, the suicide note. When Martin

Amis composed his memoirs, for instance, the genre didn't force him to shift his world view: he ends *Experience* with atrocity, Auschwitz, ruminations on the murder of one of his cousins, and "the usual articles of faith for a man of fifty . . . : that the parents are going, the children are staying, and I am somewhere in between" (371). When Eric Harris began his diary with the statement, "I hate the fucking world," he wasn't laying the groundwork for a transformative inner voyage; he was girding himself for battle.

If we accept Amis's bleak view of the future of publishing—and I think we should—then the challenge, for all whose lives are inextricably bound to the literate arts, is to make a compelling case for why writing might be said to matter in the twenty-first century. Amis taking the long view, Alex Supertramp running into the wild, Descartes alone with his thoughts: it is clear that these men knew that writing could be used to articulate and extend one's sense of despair and one's sense of superiority. What isn't clear, though, is whether these men knew what Karr knows—namely, how to use writing as a practice for constructing a sense of hope and optimism atop the ruins of previous worlds. Is it possible to produce writing that generates a greater sense of connection to the world and its inhabitants? Of self-understanding? Writing that moves out from the mundane, personal tragedies that mark any individual life into the history, the culture, and the lives of the institutions that surround us all?

In working my way up to this set of questions, I have unexpectedly found myself relying on words and phrases that immediately produce religious connotations: the dark night of the soul, the generation of hope, the power of forgiveness. While I did not set out to consider religious matters, the language I've fallen into using has inevitably led me to a set of concerns that tends to be avoided by those who share my secular sensibilities. Under normal circumstances, I might find other, less volatile terms. But these aren't normal circumstances. There will never again be a book that can credibly be labeled "great," not because outstanding books are no longer being produced, but because the world is now awash with writing that no one reads, with last year's blockbusters ending up in the dump next to this year's most insightful critiques. If one is in search of fame or truth and one has placed all one's hopes on the activity of writing, this fact can be a devastating blow. But, however painful it may be to admit, it is clear that those of us who remain committed to books are part of a residual culture whose days are numbered. The fetishization of the written word is coming to an end and in its place one finds a fascination with moving what is known from here to there in the shortest amount of time and with the elusive pleasures of religious conviction. One finds as well a haunting sense of disconnection, as one tightly wound individual after another hatches a plot to make others pay for these ambient feelings of placelessness. The world as we have known it is passing away and the world that is emerging is one that appears to be fraught with danger.

What to do? These concerns about the diminishing power of reading and writing serve as the launching point for a sustained investigation into the value of humanistic inquiry at the present moment. In fashioning the oxymoronic phrase "institutional autobiography" to describe the collection of meditations that follows, I mean to highlight a brand of intellectual inquiry that is centrally concerned with what might best be termed "the felt experience of the impersonal." The course of any given individual life cuts through or around a set of institutions charged with responsibility for nurturing both a sense of self and a sense of connection between self and society—the family, the school, and, for some, the church or the house of worship. It goes without saying that the relative influence each of these institutions has on any given individual depends on a number of variables, including race, class, and gender. By linking the institutional with the autobiographic, my goal is not to draw attention away from our individual differences, but rather to show that we all internalize institutional influences in ways that are both idiosyncratic and historically situated, open-ended and overdetermined, liberating and confining. We all go to school, bringing both our minds and our embodied histories: what happens there is both utterly predictable and utterly mysterious, the circumscribed movement of a statistical norm and the free flight of aberrant data.

Historically, schooling in the United States has served as the battleground where the nation works out its evolving understanding of social justice—through, for example, busing, affirmative action, the student loan program, the multicultural curriculum. What has changed recently, though, is the power of weaponry that students bring to the schoolyard and the magnitude of the notoriety that accrues to those who show up ready for a fight. The police investigating the actions of Harris and Klebold concluded that the two young men were driven, above all, by a desire for fame: "[A]ll the rest of the justifications are just smoke. They certainly wanted the media to write stories about them every day. And they wanted cult followings. They [were] going to become superstars by getting rid of bad people" (Cullen, "Kill Mankind"). We might say that Harris and Klebold wanted what all writers are said to want, what Richard Tull and Alexander Supertramp dreamed of and what Gwyn Barry, Amis, Krakauer, Descartes, and Karr have all, to varying degrees, achieved. The costs of such fame are quite high and the benefits fleeting at best.

Can writers learn a different set of desires? Can writing itself be made to serve some other function besides aiding in the search for fame and immortality? Can secular institutions of higher education be taught to use writing to foster a kind of critical optimism that is able to transform idle feelings of hope into viable plans for sustainable action? These are the questions that animate the meditations that follow. Violence, suicide, war, and terrorism recur in these discussions, as do fraudulence, complicity, and woundedness. If there is to be lasting hope for the future of higher education, that hope can only be generated by confronting our desolate world and its urgent, threatening realities. The only way out is through.

2

THE NERVOUS SYSTEM

For his second attempt, my father selected a set of kitchen knives and, when he got to the garage, a hammer from his toolbox. Shortly after my mother found him, the emergency crew rushed him to the hospital and the neighbors and the parish priest arrived to offer what services they could. Then, amidst the frenzied activity in the intensive care unit, my father struggled to explain the presence of the hammer. At a loss for words, he could only say that he had felt at the time that it "might have been of some use." There is a dark logic to such thoughts, perhaps, one that trades in the various means and mechanisms of self-annihilation, and it is the relative inaccessibility of this logic that interests me here. If the decision to end one's life is the most important decision of one's life, then how do we gain access to the line of thinking, the chain of events, the preliminary acts and feelings that lead to such a conclusion? How are we to understand a hermeneutic system that courts its own destruction?

Though shocking, experiences like this are not entirely unfamiliar, partly because of the media's increased ability to provide us with a glimpse of such personal tragedies as they unfold: we spend days mesmerized by images of planes slamming into the towers, bodies falling, soot-covered survivors emerging from the dark; we huddle around our sets as the white Bronco makes its slow drive down the freeway; we watch the boy with the bullet in his head drop from the window in Littleton, the SWAT team standing by. That the media feast on the misfortunes of others is a point we in the academy never seem to tire of making. Indeed, I was on a panel a while back where one of my fellow presenters successfully entertained the packed room with his exposition of how the popular television show, *Rescue 911*, which was broadcast from 1989 to 1995 and dramatized real-life rescue efforts, satisfied its viewers' need to witness disasters week after week. Although there was little in the speaker's analysis that was meant to surprise, everyone—myself included—enjoyed being treated to the usual pratfalls that intertextuality provides (references to the narrator as "Captain Kirk, er, I mean William Shatner"), the inevitable revelation of a master narrative (the show was not, actually, about rescuing people in danger but about the necessary dependence of average citizens upon a massive bureaucratic system of experts for survival), and the familiar set of tropes about the media's manipulative powers and the consequent need for producing critical viewers who can see beyond the mystifying image of a bureaucratic utopia where the experts always get there . . . just in the nick of time.

It was, as I've said, an amusing performance, but the speaker got his biggest laughs by far when he commented on the fact that, after the show had been on the air a few years, it began to run regular episodes about how the show itself helped its viewers avert tragedy. There were stories about a mother who learned CPR by watching the show and who was then able to revive her own son when it was his turn to fall into the pool while playing unattended in the backyard; a schoolgirl who saved a choking classmate by employing the Heimlich maneuver which she had heard about the previous night on television; a man who fell while hiking but succeeded in fashioning a brace out of fallen branches and strips of his own clothing because . . . etc., etc., etc. The possible permutations were endless, of course, and one way to account for *Rescue 911*'s self-referencing and self-promotion was to assert, as the speaker did, that the producers had simply found a way to make the entire show one long advertisement for itself. Thus, when the survivors turned to the camera, as they inevitably did, and said, as they inevitably did, "[Fill in the blank] wouldn't be here with us today if [fill in the blank] hadn't seen that episode on *Rescue 911* about [fill in the blank]," from a certain perspective, all that was really going on was a sustained effort by the producers to convince the viewers that remaining glued to their television sets was literally a matter of life or death.[1]

The detection of this clever strategy for keeping the audience mesmerized is what enables the very kind of reversal upon which so much academic work depends, for it puts us in a position to see the survivors as, in fact, victims; mere puppets responding to the tugs and twitches of the invisible, but nefariously motivated, television producers. With the world so turned, it becomes clear that what the viewers really need is not this show at all, with its diverting pleasures, its lifesaving tips, its pathetic stories about kids without bicycle helmets going through windshields and skydivers plummeting earthward in hopelessly tangled parachutes. No, what they really need is us, the bearers and producers of cultural critique, the ones who can expose the hegemonic function of the show and reveal its drive to convince viewers that their relative sense of powerlessness is inevitable, necessary, even desirable.

On one hand, then, we have the scene in the garage with the knives and the hammer, the rescue workers on their way, the ultimately inaccessible, illegible event. On the other, the speaker at the podium, the performance of a masterful reading, the laughing crowd, the erasure of lived experience, the claim to possess truly useful knowledge. To stage the debate in this way, however, is both to establish a familiar set of oppositions and to guarantee an equally familiar outcome. That is, if I'm going to follow the generic conventions that I have been working with and that have been working with me up to this point, I must now argue for a return to "personal" or "non-academic writing" as a way to reclaim a form of expression that really matters—writing that reaches beyond the walls of our conferences, that eschews jargon to make a bigger tent, that dismantles the sense that the writer is the master of her past or of all that she surveys. To head down this road to individualism is, perhaps ironically, to travel an increasingly crowded path: it is one that has already been covered, in one way or another, by Jane Tompkins, Nancy Sommers, Linda Brodkey, Peter Elbow, Lynn Z. Bloom, and Donald McQuade, to name a few of the most prominent participants on this side of the discussion.[2] And who among us has not felt Tompkins's weary dissatisfaction with the performative aspects of teaching; Sommers's sense of the invasive threat posed by theory; Brodkey's desire to speak without citation, weaving together one's past experiences with one's current academic preoccupations?

This is important work, both in itself and for the discussions it has started. And yet, as moving as the personal narratives are that it has showcased, I must confess that my own reading in this area has not provided me with a resource for hope about the possibilities of reimagining what it means to write in the academy. Although one could say that my problem with the personal is personal, I think it would be more accurate to say that my increasing dissatisfaction with this side of the debate is the result of my own inability to get the stories of these authors to provide me with "an idea to think with"—to borrow a favorite phrase of Ann Berthoff's. Thus, whether I'm plunged into a vivid, personal account of how one has come to read the way one has or I'm regaled with a semiotic decoding of how the act of reading is represented in the paintings of Georges de La Tour, I tend to come away feeling equally disaffected: neither event helps me to think about the interplay between personal experience and academic training, which is—although both sides of the debate give this point wide berth—also part of personal experience. For these reasons, in what follows I want to explore the extent to which it is possible to escape the confines of this debate in order to see if its polarized positions can, perhaps, be reworked to produce an idea with which we can think anew about writing as a place where the personal and the academic, the private and the public, the individual and the institutional, are always inextricably interwoven.

Desire says: "I should not like to have to enter this risky world of discourse; I should not like to be involved in its peremptoriness and decisiveness; I should like it to be all around me like a calm, deep transparence, infinitely open, where others would fit in with my expectations, and from which truths would emerge one by one; I should only have to let myself be carried, within it and by it, like a happy wreck."
—Michel Foucault, "The Order of Discourse"

Within the context of this ongoing debate about the role of the personal in academic writing, I risk, in opening with a passage from Foucault's "The Order of Discourse," being perceived as already allied with one side in this debate since, far from shifting the terrain of the discussion, my choice of citation returns us once again to the work of the central figure in the debate, the writer whose name alone has become the line in the sand that separates academic writers and writers of the personal essay, theorists and practitioners, knowers and doers, company men and caring women. It is Foucault's voice that inaugurates one of the most widely read and cited essays in composition studies—David Bartholomae's "Inventing the University"—and whose presence is felt throughout Bartholomae's argument that the problem basic writers face when they sit down to write in the academy is that the very syntax of their thoughts is defined by cultural and discursive commonplaces. In a similar vein, Kurt Spellmeyer has argued that Foucault's "The Order of Discourse" illustrates "with unparalleled clarity the dilemma of many beginning writers" and that

Foucault's work is to be valued because it "reminds us that learning is the process through which we deliberately fashion our lives—and that the outcome of this fashioning, this 'assaying' of ourselves, is always an open question" (72, 89). While Bartholomae and Spellmeyer argue that the application of Foucault's ideas to the composition classroom can enable a critical reassessment of what the business of being trained into academic discourse entails, their opponents tend to describe the rejection of Foucault's ideas as a liberating experience in its own right. The turning point in Nancy Sommers's Braddock Award–winning essay, "Between the Drafts," comes when she realizes that it is only by getting out from under Foucault's influence and, by extension, the demands of academic convention more generally, that she can begin to ground her authority as a writer in her own experiences and her own stories (28). And in "Resisting the Faith," Nancy Welch's much-cited send-up of graduate training at "University B," Foucault's influence on the discipline of writing instruction is seen to be even more pernicious: as Welch describes it, when she attended University B, she was required to read Foucault as part of a training regime designed "to promote the violence, struggle, and loss assumed to be inherent in any act of writing" (396). Repulsed by this approach, Welch returned to University A, where "freewriting and stargazing" were encouraged, and where it was assumed that "we write and learn in an environment that is safe and supportive" (398).

This quick summary of Foucault's presence in the debate about the nature and purpose of academic writing suffices to illustrate how differently his work has been received in the two camps. And it is because Foucault's work has had this polarizing effect that I wish to return to the opening moment in "The Order of Discourse," where Foucault dreams his impossible dream of self-annihilation. Foucault opens this talk with the enunciation of his desire to slip into the lecture hall unnoticed, to have his voice imperceptibly join the unnamed voice of another and thus to be borne along "like a happy wreck" on a sort of discursive sea. As we have seen, this vision of a disembodied linguistic encounter, where one does not so much speak as one gets spoken by an array of discourses, has been cast as both the utopian promise and the dystopian nightmare of poststructuralism. But what has been overlooked in these discussions is Foucault's realization at the end of his talk that there was, in fact, one voice in particular that he wanted to hear speaking as he entered the lecture hall—the voice of his dead teacher Jean Hippolyte.[3] "I know now whose voice it was that I would have liked to precede me, to carry me, to invite me to speak, to lodge itself in my own discourse. I know what was so terrifying about beginning to speak, since I was doing so in this place where once I listened to him, and where he is no longer here to hear me" (76). Were Foucault to attempt to dissolve into his teacher's discourse in the way he describes, he would either have to fall into a silent reverie at the podium or begin to ventriloquize verbatim his teacher's past lessons—in which case his auditors would still be stuck with the fact that the words emerged from Foucault's body, not Hippolyte's corpse.

I'm being blunt, but the corporeality of the human body is, finally, a blunt matter. There's no doubting that the kid facedown in the swimming pool, turning blue, is a floating signifier of a kind, deployed for material gain by corporate sponsors as a bit player in a ceaseless drama about the virtues of panopticism. He is also drawing real water into his lungs and, thus, is moving toward death much more rapidly than most of us would like to ourselves. While he is not simply discourse yet, he will be if the only intervention that occurs takes place at the level of language. Similarly, the man losing consciousness in the garage is, undoubtedly, a site of discursive contestation, his plight seeming to reference a wide array of psychological and classical narratives about the confrontation between patriarchal systems and the aging body (*Oedipus the King, King Lear, Absalom, Absalom!, Things Fall Apart*) or, for those better positioned to read this particular event, the silent struggle of a creative spirit trapped by the drudgery of domesticity (*The Yellow Wallpaper, A Room of One's Own, The Awakening*). He is, also, my father, and to see him as being spoken by either of these narratives does not, at least not immediately, provide any of us (him, me, you) with any clear guidance about how such narratives might be disrupted and alternatives devised within the confines of his individual situation. And the same, blunt corporeality of the body applies to Foucault's teacher, as well. Although Foucault may dream of hearing his teacher's voice again, following Hippolyte's death, Foucault can never again be swept away by his teacher's discourse. Thus, as seductive as it may be to say that all the world is a text, the dramatic structure of "The Order of Discourse" illustrates the ultimate barrenness of the simile: no amount of "revising" or "rereading" can revive or resurrect Foucault's fallen teacher because "discourse" and "the body" are terms that apply to irreducibly different and distinct aspects of the human condition.

Seen in this light, "The Order of Discourse" is best read as Foucault's effort to understand why being asked to speak where his teacher once spoke made him feel so physically anxious, an effort that leads him to consider how institutions stimulate, regulate, and deny speech simultaneously. As productive as it has turned out to be for those who work primarily with language to accept Foucault's invitation to explore the interplay between discourse and the body, one consequence of the overwhelming success of "the Foucauldian project" has been the steady transformation of *everything* into a discursive matter. Indeed, the fact that academics trained in the literate arts have shown themselves so eager to lay claim to being experts on the discourses of popular culture, economic theory, and political practice can only be seen, within the Foucauldian paradigm, as an expression of the very "will to truth" that Foucault is at such pains to criticize. Foucault's rhetorical question about the ultimate goal of the will to truth highlights the personal and institutional investments that motivate all such claims of mastery: "what is at stake in the will to truth," Foucault asks, "in the will to utter this 'true' discourse, if not desire and power?" (56).

I should mention at this time that the man in the garage spent his entire adult life as a writer. The results of his labor included two novels (both unpublished), two chapbooks, and hundreds of short stories and poems that appeared in numerous small literary magazines. He also bore principal responsibility for the day-to-day business of raising his four children.

Increasingly, I have felt the need to escape both the seductive allure of Foucault's interest in discourse and the neutralizing force of his rhetorical question, which forever compels me to recognize that any intellectual endeavor— including, and perhaps especially, the one I'm engaged in right now—is always already contaminated with self-interest and larger disciplinary interests. Pierre Bourdieu's *Distinction: A Social Critique of the Judgement of Taste* provides a way to reroute the discussion of the relationship of the personal and the academic through the materiality of the body, offering an alternative explanation for the nervousness a writer feels at the moment of composing a piece that brings the personal and the academic together, for example, or the anxiety a speaker feels when approaching the podium. Bourdieu's book, which he terms "a sort of ethnography of France," sets out to expose the social machinery at work in the hierarchization of the various standards of taste one finds in that country (xi). Bourdieu wants, in short, to account for that very thing that common sense would have us believe there's no accounting for; he wants to show that "taste" is neither a natural attribute of the self nor a sign of one's innate superiority, but is simply the internalization of a socially constructed set of likes and dislikes.

Without doing any research at all on this subject, most people would state, as Bourdieu does, that it is "self-evident" that class of origin and level of education are the two most important factors influencing the level of taste an individual acquires (99). Bourdieu looks beyond this self-evident relationship between class, education, and taste, however, to trace out what he calls the "series of different *effects*" this relationship has at the level of the lived experience of individuals (22; emphasis in original). Thus, while it is fairly obvious that advanced education in English studies seeks to foster a taste, say, for the works of James Joyce, Bourdieu is interested in seeing what other effects flow from such a system of instruction. What kind of person is produced through this process? What other tastes does he or she develop? What kind of bodily experiences does he or she come to prefer? In order to answer these questions, Bourdieu has to put aside the vaunted musical pieces, the esteemed works of art, and the prized photographs he asked his subjects to work with at the beginning of his study and reconceive of taste not as some thing "out there" in the world of culture, but as some feeling experienced "in here" in the bodies of individual citizens.

It is at this point that Bourdieu's study becomes most provocative and most disturbing, for it is here that he maps the interrelationship between "taste" defined as the kind of culture one is drawn to and "taste" as a way of being in the world. Bourdieu moves from the realm of music (which he defines as "the 'pure' art par excellence" on the grounds that it "says nothing and has *nothing to say*") to the realm of the senses, specifically the kinds of food (or drugs or body parts or other instruments) one is willing and able to put into one's body (19; emphasis in original). Bourdieu's argument is that, regardless of the amount of cultural capital one inherits as a birthright or acquires through education, the end result is an overwhelming sense that one's tastes are natural, rather than the product of one's social class or one's schooling. And, he concludes, the "naturalness" of one's taste is experienced most immediately as the sense of revulsion one might have at the thought, say, of sitting down to a steaming plate of spaghetti smothered in a sauce of pork parts, of having a nipple pierced, of contemplating the crucifix submerged in a jar of urine, of hearing someone discuss a personal tragedy in an academic forum.

Bourdieu goes on to explain: "tastes are perhaps first and foremost distastes, disgust provoked by horror or visceral intolerance ('sick-making') of the tastes of others. 'De gustibus non est disputandum': not because 'tous les goûts sont dans la nature,' but because each taste feels itself to be natural—and so it is, being a habitus—which amounts to rejecting others as unnatural and therefore vicious. . . . The most intolerable thing for those who regard themselves as the possessors of legitimate culture is the sacrilegious reuniting of tastes which taste dictates shall be separated" (56–57). With this enhanced definition, taste is reconceived as an acquired way of feeling that is nevertheless experienced as natural and, therefore, inherently superior to other possible tastes, which are also experienced as naturally distasteful. The very act of making distinctions maps out the circulation of cultural capital at the level of lived experience. So, though the debate about personal writing would make it seem otherwise, what's at stake when one experiences discomfort while reading an academic article that includes autobiographical elements, say, is not one's innate sophistication or one's essential earthiness. Rather, Bourdieu would have us see that "[a]t stake in every struggle over art there is also the imposition of an art of living, that is, the transmutation of an arbitrary way of living into a legitimate way of life which casts every other way of living into arbitrariness" (57).

The argument that one's preference for academic or personal writing is, ultimately, an arbitrary inclination naturalized by culture isn't likely to change how one feels or to alter the debate about the place of personal experience in the academy, of course. Nonetheless, entertaining the idea that such preferences may be linked to and otherwise expressed in bodily responses can spur those of us who spend our lives working with words to begin to think again about the various ways in which writing matters. Specifically, this idea might help us to consider the force of the written word as it is revealed not only in a reader's response to well-formulated arguments others have produced, but also in the writer's experience of the act of composing itself. In other words, those of us who teach might leaven our ongoing preoccupation with training readers in the arts of textual analysis with a consideration of the kinds of writing that produce visceral reactions in actual readers and the kinds of writing that evoke in a given writer a similarly profound felt response at the moment of production. To pursue such an investigation is to escape the Aristotelian trap of proclaiming how one is supposed to feel during a tragedy and to attend, instead, to the varying responses people actually have when they observe a given tragedy, read a given book, hear a given paper. In this way, we can move our discussion of how texts might work under ideal conditions to an examination of how they actually work in a given context, excavating bodily responses for material evidence of the ways culture is present in the writer's very act of experiencing the composing process and in the reader's responses to the writer's text.

Obviously, one could commence such work by turning to the opening of this chapter. For the moment, though, I am less interested in investigating the reader's visceral response to one kind of primal scene ("Oh no, he's not really going to talk about suicide and writing is he?" "I can sense a reference to Hemingway or Plath coming any minute now," etc.) than I am in pursuing the possibility that the writer's response, during the process of composing, might become a site for exploring the relationship between modes of writing legitimated by the academy and the circulation of cultural capital in our society. Pursuing such an investigation, I believe, serves both a lexical and a pedagogical function: it allows us to widen the definition of what it means to write self-reflexively and it provides a way to index those places in the text where a true revision of not only the writer's argument but also of the writer's circumstance can occur.

In order to illustrate this, I must now turn to an experience I had many years ago in a poetry workshop where I produced a piece of writing that mattered in the sense I have in mind here. At a certain point during my efforts to finish my assignment, which was to write a poem about the first house I could recall living in and to use the phrase "I remember" as a kind of incantation, I found myself overwhelmed with grief. Although I was frequently visited by such feelings as I struggled to complete my dissertation, this particular experience was qualitatively different: the unfolding poem and its narrative energy became, to improvise on I. A. Richards's phrase, a machine to feel with. That is, writing the poem provided me with a different kind of emotional experience which, in turn, supplied me with a new set of analytical machinery to think anew about a host of problems related to "composition," which I construe to mean the art of putting oneself and one's writing together. Thus, the poem was writing that mattered in two senses: it mattered at the level of experience, in that I physically responded during the process of composing to what I was composing, and it mattered at the cognitive level, because it provided me with the material for a revision of both my professional and my personal circumstances.

AROUND THE HOUSE

I remember the way the pink neon filled the sky at sunset.
I can't see the words it wrote out into the darkness,
I'm not sure if the sign flashed or not.
The particulars aren't what's important:
the feeling produced by the buzz of the sign,
the way the pink held out against the rising stars:
these are the things that matter.

The sign promised candy, I think,
long slabs of marbleized taffy,
the labor of peeling the paper off,
the long walk back down the hill,
a hand reaching up into my father's,
my mouth full of taffy and wax.

I remember the yard as immense,
miles and miles of grass and my three-year-old butt
poised in full focus, filling the frame,
landing without hesitation
in a patch of thistles.
Afraid to cry, afraid to turn towards the house.

I remember that Dad would let the grass grow:
we would roam around like lions
pounding through the bush
pouncing suddenly into their vision.
I can hear you. I can see you.

I guess the neighbors would start to talk
or the house would disappear or
one of the kids would disappear
or I don't know what but
Dad would mow through the fields
winding trails so we could snake behind him
run through circles and curlicues
collapse in laughter.

By the side of the house
I remember Dad built a kind of amphitheater
not for people to come and sit
not for any kind of performance
but for layers and layers of tulips
that would rip up the countryside in the Spring,
their violent colors banging back and forth in the breeze.

I was probably wearing a sweater that day,
a green one with arrowheads on it,
sitting on the front stoop
with fat cheeks and a shock of blond hair
while the Spring billowed and filled my clothes.
Sitting and thinking about burning the house down.

I don't remember where I found the matches,
the long wooden ones that scratch so against the boxside.
The firm feel, the loud pop into flame.

Matchstick after matchstick.
The whole box spent as I stood against the rafters
trying to find just a splinter that would go.

I don't remember if they found
the four hundred burnt matches in the attic
or the box, which I remember watching fall
as the last match failed me,
or if they missed me while I was up there
trying to start a fire that wouldn't start.

The whole day disappeared with a breeze
that whispered across that shock of hair
and left that little kid on the porch
looking at those tulips
banging against each other.

I've just finished reading through a large stack of submissions for my department's creative writing prize. It hasn't been a pleasant experience, partly because I've been unable to escape the fact that the familiar understanding of
poetry as *the* place where the authentic self gets expressed profoundly limits
what the students feel they can and cannot do in a poem. As the poems and
short stories wander between tales of loss and alienation and evocations of
natural beauty and serenity, the authors repeatedly relent to the pressure to
record what "really" occurred. Although "creative writing" tends to attract students in search of a place where truth-telling of this kind is promoted and rewarded, and although I myself have thought about my own work along these
lines for many years, what struck me in the experience of writing "Around the
House" was the way that poetry can be called upon to imagine alternatives to
what the world offers—how it can, for instance, allow one to set fire to the past.
Under these circumstances, the very vagueness of what comes to mind during
the ransacking of memories becomes an ally: the sheer immateriality of the
conjured images invites, or one might say requires, the intervention of an organizing, revivifying principle for an act of composition to occur. In this case, that
principle is realized through narrative, which draws together a disparate set of
images (culled from memory, fantasy, the mass media, wherever) and places
them in the sequence of a story, all of which seemed, at the time, to unfold quite
naturally. In place of chaos and confusion, order and clarity: a perfect universe,

where narrative serves to structure lived experience into a coherent, stable event for others to perceive.

Thus, far from being a private record of emotion recalled in tranquility, poetry as it has been put to use here re-presents the private as already organized by publicly held narrative structures: "the boy's" "private" story becomes, in effect, a familiar tale of loss, loneliness, abandonment—becomes, that is, everyone's story, at least potentially. While it is safe to say that one of the central concerns of literary studies is the promotion of just such disembodied textual encounters, where readers suddenly discover in the words before them a description of their own experience, what interests me here is the writer's embodied encounter with the words as they were produced. What, if anything, can we learn from the fact that, in this instance, composing the line, "I can hear you. I can see you," caused tears to run down my face? That is, regardless of the poem's effects on its readers, I want to see if it is possible to use a writer's reaction to the composing process as the starting point for an investigation into the ways that institutional forces manifest themselves in the realm of personal experience.

"I can hear you. I can see you." This is the familiar script from an equally familiar game parents and children play: a dual pleasure is evoked in one's ability to draw attention to oneself both through one's absence and through the revelation of one's presence. Indeed, it could be said that the central tension in the poem is between the pleasure of this game and the boy's felt sense of being invisible, where the matches are used in an effort both to be missed and to be seen. While the inclination is, no doubt, strong at this point to use the poem as a vehicle for analyzing the author's relationship to the described figures, to follow this inclination is, I would argue, to once again safely relocate this specific poem, and the production of poetry more generally, in the realm of the private. It is, in other words, to seek to alleviate, through the invocation of a series of psychoanalytic tropes, the discomfort that is the seemingly inevitable and natural result of a social situation where the speaker begins to reveal signs of vulnerability. Once this discomfort has been dissipated by the revelation of the master narrative of psychoanalysis, the affront to one's dignity assuaged, and bodily composure regained, it then becomes possible to return to the business at hand, namely producing theoretical work that "critically intervenes," but never stands in danger of being accused of a "therapeutic" intent. The mind touched, the body left unsullied.

What I want to draw attention to, then, is the profound sense of discomfort that can be produced when, in an academic setting, the request is made that one see or hear the actions, events, or details of another's life as warranting sustained attention. (A similar sense of discomfort could be produced, of course, by requesting in a poetry workshop that the participants attend, with interest, to one's insights into the power of narrative to structure seemingly disjointed events into a coherent, manageable whole.) We begin, then, by considering these bodily responses—the sense of agitation and impatience, the jumping knee, the unfocused look from the watch to the phony chandeliers to the ground—over against the bodily response that accompanies the production of the text—the sense of relief and release, a sort of revelatory exhalation of spirit and excitation. And once we've done this, we can start to see the effects of the allocation of cultural capital in the academy played out at the level of experience. What is happening in this moment where taste and distaste collide is the performance of a cultural drama that centers on the form and function of academic work. To present a paper, to write an article, to teach a class is to assume, whether one wants to or not, a role where one instructs others in how to see and manipulate the world: how to organize an argument, how to establish a dialogue between texts, how to decode the exploitative ploys of the mass media, etc. To be present in any of these contexts and to receive, instead of a demonstration of the speaker's mastery, a request to acknowledge the speaker's presence, an invitation to focus on the minutiae of the speaker's life, a petition to witness a personal declaration of independence, is to be asked (some might say forced) to do a different kind of work as an auditor. The bodily discomfort arises, I believe, because it is unclear exactly what is being asked of those who are within reach of the speaker's words. Beyond saying, "I can hear you. I can see you," beyond authorizing the speaker's version of events, what can the listeners do? What other role can they play? We come together and express our sorrow that the world is so ruthless, that marriages can be so awful, family systems so destructive, patriarchy so relentlessly degrading. We say what we have to say and leave feeling either that nothing has happened or that a new sense of community has been established or perhaps, even, that some act of violence has occurred at the level of discourse.

After an extended class discussion following Kurt Cobain's suicide, where the predictable range of angry, heartfelt, and agonized responses to the musician's final actions were voiced, one of the students raised his hand and said, "It seems to me that all we've been doing is trying to cover the mouths of the dead with words."

Now that I have introduced "the body" into the discussion, the question remains: What can we learn from the conflict between the pleasure that comes in, as the popular phrase puts it, "breaking the silence" and the tangible sense of revulsion that frequently surfaces in response to such ruptures of the academy's discursive norms? What we can say, so far, I believe, is that this conflict is an expression of cultural expectations about what constitutes academic work and what warrants the profession's attention. The academy, in general, is not concerned with the production of writing that matters, if we mean by that phrase writing that provides a therapeutic outlet for the author. This does not mean that the academy is not interested in the production of writing that matters, but rather that it defines this phrase differently: in this context, it means writing that establishes the author's position within the field of study, that demonstrates the author's analytical and diagnostic powers, that clearly attests to the author's ability to break new ground. If writing that matters in the therapeutic sense expresses the writer's need for the world, writing that matters in the academic sense verifies the world's need for the writer.

When phrased this way, it becomes clear that the rhetorical relationship academics establish with their audiences is remarkably similar to the rhetorical relationship that the producers of *Rescue 911* adopted with their audiences: from a certain perspective, both groups can be seen as centrally concerned with laying claim to the power to disseminate "really useful knowledge." Far from dismissing the claims of either group, I would recommend that the claims of both groups be taken seriously in order to revitalize the discussion of how best to define these loose, overly familiar terms to which I have repeatedly returned. What is "really useful knowledge"? How do we get students and their teachers to produce "writing that matters"? Thus, I am not insisting ahead of time that the academy's claim to possess really useful knowledge be ridiculed any more than I am arguing that academic writing be seen as the empty, inevitable result of a process whereby the self is evacuated of its content. To go this route is to slip back into a familiar round of accusations and recriminations that serves the important ritualistic function of rehierarchizing and reauthorizing competing standards of taste and distaste, but does little to help us imagine alternative ways of defining what really useful knowledge might mean, or what other forms writing that matters might take, or, finally, what other kinds of content such writing might contain or reference. To resist the immense gravitational pull of this dichotomous, stereotyped world, where the only options available are understood to reside at the polarized extremes, it may be helpful to turn to two scenes where the expression of a desire to be seen elicits a response other than revulsion.

At the initial meeting of a graduate seminar for first-time teachers of composition that I taught a few years ago, one of the instructors asked if I was going to address the issue of "coming out" in the classroom. Specifically, as a gay teacher, he wanted to have the opportunity to discuss strategies for coming out and to have an open discussion about the benefits and dangers of pursuing such a project. I agreed that it was an important and appropriate topic for the seminar and arranged to have one of the assistant directors of our writing program, a veteran teacher who is gay, participate in the discussion. On the appointed day, which came when the assigned series of readings was on resistance in the classroom, the beginning instructor eloquently detailed the advice he had received from friends about how to negotiate coming out to his class. He then described the silence that followed his mentioning to his students, during their work on Gloria Anzaldùa's *Borderlands/La frontera,* the fact that, as a gay man, he objected to her characterization of gay men as being more in touch with their femininity than straight men. Although he felt that coming out had ended up being something of a nonevent in his class, this instructor spoke compellingly about the importance of gay people making themselves visible to the straight world, in general, and to younger gay people, in particular. Citing the high rate of suicide among gay and lesbian adolescents, the instructor went on to make the case that the lives of students could well hang in the balance while their teachers ponder over whether or not to emerge from the closet.

Acknowledging these powerful reasons for coming out and the courage it takes to do so, the assistant director nonetheless went on to explain his reasons for not doing so in his own courses. For him, the act of coming out only serves to stabilize the very category he most wants his students to problematize— namely, identity. From the assistant director's point of view, while the out instructor runs the risk of having his or her intellectual positions being read as nothing more than "the way gay people think," the instructor who has not self-identified his or her sexual status to the class is in a position to disturb dominant assumptions about "the way gay people think" and to draw attention to those moments when the students' automatic assumptions about a heterosexual world have an impact on their reading and writing. In this way, not coming out manifests itself as a local strategy within a larger pedagogical project concerned with establishing a classroom where the relationship between sexual preference and identity might be productively explored over the course of a semester.

Two curious things happened in the highly animated and engaged discussion that followed this opening exchange of views as we moved between and among a series of contrasting observations about the construction of identity, the establishment of authority in institutional settings, and the legibility and accessibility of the range of semiotic systems drawn up in the representation of one's sexuality. First, a number of the instructors took the opportunity to deploy the structure of the coming out narrative to tell their own stories: one instructor described first writing a set of hostile responses in the margins of a student essay that referred to "queers" rather than "gays and lesbians," only to have to scratch the comments out when she discovered, on the final pages of the student's essay, the student writer's own coming out story. Alongside this tale of a teacher's reading problem, another instructor added a story of her students' reading problem: once, while team teaching, she and her colleague fell in love. Although they thought their attraction to one another was obvious to the students, they discovered, to their surprise, in the evaluations for the course that the students thought the two women hated each other.

Story made way for story, with some instructors, gay and straight alike, drawing on the tropes of the coming out narrative for their own devices and others, gay and straight alike, remaining studiously silent. And then, something happened that pulled the plug on the high-pitched energy of the class: one of the instructors hijacked the narrative structure and "came out" to the class as a . . . Christian. Speaking about the separation of church and state, this instructor went on to share her fears about the consequences of making this aspect of herself known to her students (her students might complain; she might be accused of proselytizing; she might lose her job). In the moment, no one knew quite what to say, so we took a break, and came back to reflect on what had happened in the discussion and its aftereffects, including the rush some instructors made to meet the final speaker in the hall and thank her for having the courage to break the silence.

What interests me about this concatenation of events is the way it dramatizes the impossibility of maintaining the opposition between "the academic" and "the personal." As this example has shown, the question of which kind of personal experience produces revulsion and which kind garners cultural capital is always a contextual matter. Of course, what gets seen as merely personal and better left unsaid in the academy has shifted and continues to shift over time and across locations. In this instance, the birth of gay and lesbian criticism has made it possible to place issues of sexuality and marginality on course syllabi, on conference programs, and in class discussions, whereas at one time such a move would have been thought impossible. And, as these issues have moved towards the center of work in the humanities, other issues, such as spirituality and religion, have inevitably either receded to the horizon of concerns or emerged as undeveloped, newly marginalized areas to be exploited. In the ebb and flow, some academic careers are brought to shore and others are taken out to sea.

It goes without saying that what is permissible in one English graduate seminar is generalizable neither to all English departments nor to the culture at large: my point is not that the discussion of personal experience in public academic settings has been legitimized, so long as talk is restricted to the topic of sexual preference. I would argue, rather, that the chain of stories taken from my seminar shows how the solicitation of one kind of personal narrative simultaneously prohibits the production of other kinds of narratives. In this case, as in all cases, to have the "right" kind of personal experience is what matters, for this is what allows one to accrue cultural capital within a given institutional context. This explains why, in this instance, once a certain kind of personal narrative was seen to be institutionally authorized, there was the seemingly natural proliferation of a series of stories, which, however ambiguous, served to sanction the right of certain members of the seminar to speak and to withhold that right from others. Thus, in place of revulsion, attraction and reproduction: not, "when is this guy going to stop talking about his life," but "how can I find a way to show that this guy's life and my life aren't so different?" And then, just as quickly, the sense of community that is established through the telling of similar tales is disrupted when someone brings the "wrong" kind of experience to the table, setting in motion new waves of revulsion and attraction.

———

I want to consider one final example of what the stakes are in getting seen and being heard. In *The Bluest Eye,* Toni Morrison describes a world where the option of telling one's story and having it heard is not available to the novel's central character, Pecola Breedlove. Living a life of almost unspeakable horror, Pecola is beaten by her mother, taunted by fellow classmates for being ugly, stupid, and poor, and eventually raped and impregnated by her drunken, violent father. Unable to escape her situation or to understand what has been done to her, Pecola dreams of becoming beautiful, of acquiring the physical attributes that the dominant culture most values in its little girls: she is, as her savior/destroyer Soaphead Church describes her, "an ugly little girl asking for beauty. . . . A little black girl who wanted to rise up out of the pit of her blackness and see the world with blue eyes" (174). It is Soaphead who provides Pecola with the ritual she must perform in order to get her wish: Soaphead gives her a piece of meat that she, in turn, is to feed to her landlady's dog. If the dog acts strangely, she may expect her wish to be granted within two days. Pecola does as she is told, unknowingly poisoning the dog, and then watches helplessly as the following scene unfolds: "The dog gagged, his mouth chomping the air, and promptly fell down. He tried to raise himself, could not, tried again, and half-fell down the steps. Choking, stumbling, he moved like a broken toy around the yard. The girl's mouth was open, a little petal of tongue showing" (176).

In this way, through the machinations of a particularly brutal sort of logic, Pecola gets what she asked for. The novel ends with a dialogue between two voices in her head, arguing over whether or not she has the bluest eyes. As Claudia, the novel's narrator puts it, we have seen in this story that "[a] little black girl yearns for the blue eyes of a little white girl, and the horror at the heart of her yearning is exceeded only by the evil of fulfillment" (204). But, what exactly is it that Pecola yearns for? The answer is not as obvious as it may at first seem, though Claudia's explanation and the at times weighty didacticism of the novel might lead one to stop with the answer provided by the title. Soaphead Church assumes that she "wants to see the world with blue eyes," but the truth is that Pecola already sees the world with blue eyes when she appears in his doorway asking for his help: she needs him precisely because she already sees herself as ugly by all the standards of beauty that are metonymically invoked in the symbol of "blue eyes." The horror of Pecola's desire is not that she wants to see the world the way white people do, but that she wants to be seen by the world that is ruled by this standard of beauty. She thinks that having blue eyes will allow her to surface in other people's vision, that possession of these eyes will shatter her loneliness and isolation by providing her with the physical material necessary to be a member of the human community. In short, she doesn't want to change how she sees the world: she wants to change her body so that the world will begin to see her. And the only way for Pecola to realize her desire, given the blunt, inertial resistance of the body to a transformation of this magnitude, is to go mad.

Having set out to focus on the interplay between the personal and the academic, the body and the mind, the private and the public, I have ended up working through a variety of ways of defining the project of rhetoric. I began with the most familiar definition, that of rhetoric as persuasion, as the process of convincing others of their need for us. I then looked at rhetoric as production and reproduction, as a discursive process of creating a space, a frame, a narrative structure where others can begin to have our experiences, to see the world the way we do. I have concluded with a view of rhetoric as transformative, as an activity whereby we remake ourselves in the image of those in power. I have also tried to imply throughout that the constitution of the "we" in the previous sentences varies according to context and that both those in power and those on the margins draw on all three definitions of rhetoric in their mutually antagonistic efforts to secure access to the ephemeral, but nonetheless real, effects of possessing cultural capital.

Although being fluent in these various modes of rhetorical work is important, fluency alone does not ensure that any of these rhetorical approaches will include the dialogic aspect, which must be present if the process of composing is ever to serve the function of generating hope. Thus, I would like to suggest that we expand our notion of the rhetorical project to include the ongoing work of learning how to make oneself heard in a variety of contexts. In making this suggestion, I mean, for the moment, to uncouple the pieces of the game I've referred to throughout this meditation, to separate "I can see you" from "I can hear you." Pecola perhaps best illustrates the limits of concentrating exclusively on the importance of being seen, which, within the context of our current discussion, can be extended to mean establishing one's presence in the field, making oneself a visible member of the profession, bolstering one's vita, publishing just to publish. All of these activities are vital: all of them have their pleasures; all are unmistakably important to maintaining one's employment; and all provide opportunities for reallocating the distribution of cultural capital. But, granting this, what would happen if we also thought about our work as learning how to speak and write so others could hear us? How might we do this? And how might we learn to teach others how to do this?

In "Nihilism in Black America," Cornel West says that "cultures are, in part, what human beings create (out of antecedent fragments of other cultures) in order to convince themselves not to commit suicide"(24). This is a remarkable postulate, one that implies that the threat of self-annihilation is ever-present and that the work of culture is to sustain an ongoing battle against this threat. Although I am uncomfortable with the "politics of conversion" that West goes on to advocate as the way to address the nihilistic tendencies he sees as posing a specific threat to the black community, I know now that this discomfort itself needs to be explored as a site where my own cultural assumptions express themselves as a naturally experienced sense of distaste. We work in different locations, which is one reason why we know different things. It is by virtue of his position as a renowned scholar and theologian that West can say: "Nihilism is not overcome by arguments or analyses; it is tamed by love and care"; and it is, no doubt, by virtue of his experiences helping to combat this nihilism that West knows it to be "a disease of the soul" (29). But it is by virtue of my own position as a writing instructor that I know that "love and care" alone can't be counted on to provide a pedagogical practice that leads students, regardless of their race, to embrace what West and I agree is the antidote to nihilism—namely, the sense that "there is hope for the future and a meaning to struggle" (29). Pursuing this goal only becomes imaginable to me when I conceive of the work in the classroom as an ongoing project in which I am learning how to hear what my students are saying. Learning to do this helps me, in turn, to find a way to speak that they can hear. It also makes it possible for my students to learn how to hear what I, as a representative of the academy, am saying and how to speak, read, and write in ways that I can hear. This is the only approach I know of for making the classroom a possible resource for hope and it is the only mechanism I've found for transforming recitations and revelations of personal experience into moments for reflection and revision about the complex, conflicted, and contradictory ways that culture makes its presence known in the day-to-day workings of one's life.

To use the classroom in this way is to attend quite closely to the inevitable conflicts that occur between the expectations created by the student's lived experience of the world and the academy's efforts to master that world. This doesn't mean that the teacher is restricted to soliciting either recordings of personal experience or rehearsals of the assigned material. On the contrary, it means that students are persistently required to play the personal against the theoretical, the fictional against the real, and facts against interpretations, not to establish the primacy of any one of the terms in these binary oppositions, but rather to forestall for as long as possible slipping into the simple and satisfying binarism that allows anyone the comfort of relaxing into a settled position. What the students are required to do, instead, is to perform the same activities as they read and write in the academy that everyone must perform every day of their lives out in the world—that is, they must test out their theories about what it means to live a good life against their own lived experiences and their own internalized set of standards. The inevitable gnarl of contradictions that results when such a project is embarked upon—when the personal and the academic are set loose and allowed to interrogate one another with no predetermined outcome—is evidence, I would argue, that a different kind of "writing that matters" is getting produced, a kind of writing that seeks, as Foucault himself sought in revising his project on the history of sexuality, *The Use of Pleasure,* "to learn to what extent the effort to think one's own history can free thought from what it silently thinks, and so enable it to think differently" (9).

———————————

The importance of revision, of learning to speak in ways that others can hear, has never impressed itself with the force that it has on me now. Following my father's second attempt, I have had to ask myself whether or not my professional training in the literate arts has provided me with anything that I would call, in the context of this discussion, "really useful knowledge." As Adrienne Rich has said in "When We Dead Awaken: Writing as Re-Vision," (an essay I've had in the back of my mind throughout this meditation), "For a poem to coalesce, for a character or an action to take shape, there has to be an imaginative transformation of reality which is in no way passive. . . . Moreover, if the imagination is to transcend and transform experience it has to question, to challenge, to conceive of alternatives, perhaps to the very life you are living at that moment"(43). With Cornel West's postulate about the purpose of culture in mind, we might well say that the means to combat nihilism and to hope for change is contained in this ability to imagine a transformed reality. For it is this ability (as both Rich's own biography and West's discussion of the achievements of black Americans amply illustrate) that provides us all with the potential to construct alternatives to the lives we have been living.

Sitting in my father's room on the psychiatric ward, holding his shaking hands, paring his fingernails so he won't cut himself, I see just how difficult such an imaginative transformation of reality is. He is afraid, he tells me, of everything: of being locked away for good this time, of his decaying body, of what his doctor is going to think, of things innumerable and unnameable. It is as if he were physically trapped inside his own fears. As I listen to him struggle to find some way to relax, I sense that he is making his way back from the madness, battling a set of internal and external systems that had once again made the decision to live untenable. I think he understands now that just medicating the body is insufficient; he will also need to learn how to tell the stories he has never told in order to escape the terrible power they have over him.

Sustaining a self and sustaining a culture are ceaseless activities. Both projects are always under construction and always under repair, although this endless work may escape our notice until a moment of crisis makes the grinding of the machinery suddenly audible to us. To engage actively in the process of constructing a self is to replace a sense of destiny with the vision of an uncertain future. Similarly, to think of culture as not only present in a series of intellectual debates carried out in the academy but also as the varying registers of taste and distaste physically experienced in the body is to take down the cordon separating the public and the private and to recognize that all intellectual projects are always, inevitably, also autobiographies. Thus, whether one is constructing a self or studying a culture, one must confront the sheer necessity for acquiring a kind of multivocal fluency, an ability to hear things previously shut out or ignored, to attend to matters that might otherwise be overlooked or dismissed as irrelevant, to accept, in effect, the fact that learning to speak in such a way that one gets heard is a lifelong project that involves, perhaps paradoxically, first learning how to listen better to others.

With the judicious substitution of a word here, a phrase there, it would be obvious that the lessons outlined above could be said to be basic to any writing classroom that conceives of revision not as the act of tidying up past transgressions, but as the ongoing process of entertaining alternatives. For it is through such revision that change becomes imaginable, escape from the lonely, isolated world of the merely personal becomes possible, and the redemptive power of the kind of critical optimism I've pointed to here becomes tangible. And the writing that results from such a revisionary practice can, I believe, generate material for constructing a more humane and hospitable life-world by providing the very thing the academy is most in need of at this time: a technology for producing and sustaining the hope that tomorrow will be better than today and that it is worth the effort to see to it that such hopes aren't unfounded.

3

SMART BOMB

smart (smärt) *adj.* **1. a.** Characterized by sharp, quick thought; intelligent; bright. **b.** Amusingly clever; witty. **c.** Impertinent.

—*American Heritage Dictionary*

What does it mean to be smart? Is this something acquired at conception or something learned over time? Is it possible to teach oneself or to teach others to be smart? There is, it is safe to say, no more highly valued commodity in the academic marketplace today than "smartness": in conference corridors, behind closed office doors, and in faculty meetings governing hiring and promotion, the activity of assessing the smartness of others is ceaseless. In the classroom, teachers seek out "the smart ones," joyously celebrate having "a smart class," gush over their "A" students. Now, at my university, thanks to an administrative initiative that links technology and pedagogy, one can even speak of "smart classrooms"—learning spaces where students and teachers alike can, with the stroke of a few keys, gain instant access to all the World Wide Web has to offer. I've long been puzzled by the high premium we place on the vaguely defined notion of smartness, but those "smart classrooms," which come with thirty-two-inch monitors, DVD players, ethernet cards, and ribbon-cutting ceremonies, puzzle me the most. If those classrooms are "smart," what about the other ones? Are they the "dumb classrooms"—the ones reserved for those students and teachers destined to be left behind by the technological revolution? Can you have "smart classrooms" without also having "smart teachers"?

It's no accident I find myself rehearsing a version of what I call "the schoolhouse melodrama," where those who have dedicated their lives to teaching struggle to make sense of a world created by administrators only interested in the latest educational gimmick. In this genre, it's always the teacher against some faceless system—be it bureaucrats demanding accountability, consumer culture generating mindless customers, or even the deeply embedded indifference of the students themselves—and it's always the teacher's job to strike out against these crushingly oppressive systems, to unmask the forces of corruption, and to create a better, smarter world. For teachers, the appeal of retelling this story is obvious and all but irresistible, as the following two articles on the current state of education illustrate.[1]

In "Education by the Numbers," Daniel Ferri, a sixth-grade teacher in Lombard, Illinois, recounts how he responded when his students, squirming under an endless regime of government-mandated tests, demanded an explanation for why their education had been reduced to endless days of filling in bubbles. The best Ferri could do was say:

> Look, neither of us has a choice about this: I have to give you this test, you have to take it, and some poor soul in North Carolina has to read and grade 500 of them a day. The graders don't care about what you write; they only care about the rules. If you don't follow the rules, they lower your score. The scores are printed in the newspaper. If they're bad, people will think our school is bad and they won't want to move here, which will make the real estate people mad, and they will yell at the school board, who will yell at the superintendent, who will yell at the principal, who will yell at me. This is not about writing, this is about not getting yelled at. (21)

In the world Ferri inhabits, the great chain of being has been transformed into the great chain of humiliation, and education has devolved into nothing more than compliance and constraint. In this dying world, all the teacher can do is transmit ever-bleaker reports from the front lines as the indomitable forces of the mindless bureaucrats overwhelm the meager defenses of those truly committed to "critical thinking."

In "On the Uses of the Liberal Arts," Marc Edmundson devotes his energies to decrying the university's transformation into a combination resort area and shopping mall, where students are more interested in the athletic facilities than the thoughts of their distinguished professors. As Edmundson tells it, the situation isn't improved by having these product-driven consumers drag themselves to class, since they arrive eager not for the grueling work that goes into becoming scholars, but for "info-tainment"—a kind of teaching that is enjoyable and mildly informative at the same time. In this stupefied state, Edmundson's students don't announce that "they've been changed by the course" he has taught, but rather that they've found "the Oedipus complex and the death drive . . . interesting" (40).[2]

For those who make a living working with words, such stories are not without their uses: they demonstrate our critical powers; they cast our work in a heroic light; they make our difficult working conditions more bearable. Nevertheless, I think the time has come for us to put these exhausted tales of moral victories and institutional stupidities to bed and to begin, instead, to imagine alternate ways of accounting for the lives we live in school—ways that might allow us to revalue the work we do. It is in the interest of launching such a project that I pose the following set of admittedly impertinent questions: If Mr. Ferri and Professor Edmundson are so smart, why can't they free themselves from the traps they've described in such detail? Or, to state this as a more general problem, if those of us who stand in front of language-arts classrooms across the country really are the purveyors of critical thinking and the masters of rhetorical persuasion, as we so often claim, then why is it that our critiques and our carefully crafted arguments rarely produce any measurable results? If being smart is so valuable, why are the typical products of smartness—namely, critiques of the status quo—so easily absorbed by the targeted institutions, which continue to generate tests and seemingly indifferent students with relative ease?

These are, as I've said, impertinent questions. In posing them here, I do not mean to denigrate the work that we do as teachers or to wish away the problems that Ferri and Edmundson have identified. Rather, I wish to grant from the outset that we live and teach in an environment saturated with alien bureaucratic demands and consumerist desires, so that we can move on to the more difficult and more imaginative work of thinking about how best to reenchant the business of teaching. To that end, I will focus on what I see as the greatest impediment to institutional change—not the stupidity of the system, but rather the mystifying appeal of "smartness," which produces in its wake an undervaluing of bureaucratic detail, an attraction to "critical interventions," an unwillingness to disappear into the anonymous work of generating sustainable reform, and a sense that the written word is imbued with magically transformative powers.

smart—*intr. v.* **1. a.** To cause a sharp usually superficial, stinging pain, as an acrid liquid or a slap.

—*American Heritage Dictionary*

THE BOMB

Smartness acquired a new referent on January 18, 1991. On that day, millions of viewers the world over watched as General Norman Schwarzkopf and General Charles Horner narrated the opening air assaults of Operation Desert Storm. That the Persian Gulf War was the first made-for-TV war is now a critical commonplace: as the initial major news briefing made clear, the public's access to this war would be restricted to a series of carefully choreographed successes. And, as those who watched this telecast at the time will recall, it was this news conference that provided the public with the first visual evidence of the overwhelming technological superiority of our weaponry. It was here that we were allowed to witness our laser-guided missiles flying through the night, zeroing in on the enemy targets, cleanly and accurately delivering their deadly force while our pilots escaped to freedom unscathed.

As the war continued, we were treated to endless variations of this scenario: those luminous crosshairs superimposed on some dark, shadowy target, and then the satisfying explosion as the bracketed building, tank, bridge, or rocket launcher was destroyed, with the gasps and laughter of the reporters in the background. Or, in the variations involving the Patriot missiles, we would look up into the wide open, seemingly empty sky, see the trail of smoke, and hear the dull thud signifying that the Scud missiles had been intercepted and neutralized well out of harm's way. This was the new generation of smart bombs, which, unlike their dumber siblings, swiftly and accurately delivered the kind of lethal force that practically guaranteed, from the outset, a quick and tidy conclusion to Operation Desert Storm.

There can be no doubt that this made for compelling theater. As Alex Thomson reports in *Smokescreen,* his book on censorship and the Gulf War, the videos that captured the smart bombs in action were "Central Command's most powerful tactical media weapon. The technology was undeniably impressive and conveyed the profound feeling of invincible power deployed and somehow being deployed in a clean way" (102). To my mind, the most lasting image of the war came from the briefing led by Schwarzkopf and Horner, in which Horner walked his audience through the first series of smart bomb videos. When Horner arrived at the last clip, he drew the enthralled reporters' attention to the grainy image of a building flickering on the monitor before them: "And this," he said, "is my counterpart's headquarters in Baghdad," to which his audience responded with a hearty laugh.[3] Then the exciting denouement: "This is the headquarters of the airforce. Keep your eyes on all sides of the building as the airplane overflies the building and drops the bomb down through the centre of the building" (qtd. in Thomson 103–4).

Another successful strategic strike. This time, the office of General Horner's double in the Iraqi military was identified and eliminated. And to a certain way of thinking something significant had happened: a central building in the military's bureaucratic infrastructure had been destroyed, as had the other paper-pushing strategists who, presumably, inhabited the building. In this way, we were treated, once again, to a lesson about the virtues of informed aggression— given the requisite military intelligence and the necessary military force, one could move rapidly to eliminate an inferior military system. Change could happen and it could happen quickly. In just one thousand hours, the Iraqi soldiers could be driven from Kuwait, Saddam Hussein's tyranny could be brought to the brink of collapse, and the flow of oil to the Western world could be restored.

Within a few years, there was reason enough to wonder about the lasting effects of this massive critical intervention and now, a little more than a decade later, with the occupation of Iraq entering its second year and resistance continuing long after the capture of Hussein and many of his top officers, even those who declared victory in the first war have been forced to concede just how little was accomplished by the spectacle of liberating Kuwait back in 1992. Of course, in the euphoria that followed the conclusion of the first Gulf War, the idea that Hussein would survive such a humiliating defeat seemed unthinkable. Surely, given how smart our smart bombs were, given our superior intelligence, all our military needed to do was punch in the right coordinates and Hussein would be history.

It turns out, though, that the success of the bombing campaign had been overstated. A few months after the first war ended, senior military officials disclosed that only 7 percent of the bombs dropped on Iraq were "smart" and that no fewer than 70 percent of the 88,500 tons of bombs dropped on Iraq *missed* their targets (Thomson 104). The Patriot missile defense system's performance was even worse. In a letter dated September 8, 1992, Professors Theodore Postol and George Lewis of MIT reported to the Congressional Committee on Government Relations that, after reviewing 140 videotapes of the Patriot system's actions during the war, they had concluded that there was "no convincing evidence in the video that any Scud warhead was destroyed by a Patriot" (Postol). Representatives for Raytheon, the maker of the Patriot system, vigorously and successfully contested Postol's and Lewis's interpretation of the data, ensuring that funding for the ongoing development of this defense system would continue to flow. It would be many years before Defense Secretary William S. Cohen would admit publicly, without qualification, that "the Patriot didn't work" in the Gulf War (qtd. in Farrell).

For those who aren't already inclined to disregard the official version of historical events, statements like these by people directly involved in the war unsettle those tidy images of smart bombs whistling toward their appointed destinations, of precise strikes with low "collateral damage," of deserving bureaucrats sitting in their offices being blown to bits. While it is tempting to think that noting these disjunctions between image and event is an act freighted with political significance, the painful truth is that critical work of just this kind was produced *during* the war without any noticeable effect on its intended audiences. Robert Fisk, for example, writing for the British newspaper the *Independent,* warned in February 1991: "the unquestioning nature of our coverage of this war is one of its most dangerous facets. Many of the American television pool dispatches sound as if they have been produced by the military which, in a way, they have"(19). And revered figure Walter Cronkite complained in the pages of *Newsweek* later that same month that "the greatest mistake of our military so far is its attempt to control coverage by assigning a few pool reporters and photographers to be taken to locations determined by the military with supervising officers monitoring all their conversations with the troops in the field"(43). Many others joined in mounting this critique at the time, but all their passionate words made absolutely no difference: before it was possible to build and consolidate a sense of outrage over the public's restricted access to the events in the Gulf and the extermination of tens of thousands of Iraqi civilians, the first Gulf War was over.[4]

---

smart—*intr. v.* 2. To suffer acutely, as from mental distress, wounded feelings, or remorse.

American Heritage Dictionary

THE BOMBER

That we live in an age enamored with the notion that violence constitutes a viable politics is obvious. The terrorist bombings of the American embassies in Kenya and Tanzania in 1998; President Clinton's "retaliatory and preemptive"[5] assault on what appears to have been a legitimate pharmaceutical plant in the Sudan;[6] the attacks of September 11 and the vengeful acts that have followed: all of these events attest to the fact that the world is overrun with those who feel the only solution available to them involves grievously harming others—particularly others chosen at random. For some reason, the belief persists that revolutionary change is sparked by such quick, incisive blows—that one smart shot will set off a chain of events, which will, in turn, bring the offending forces crashing to the ground. There's James Earl Ray standing in the parking lot as the sun sets in Memphis; Lee Harvey Oswald climbing the stairs of the book depository in Dallas; Charles Manson directing his followers to crawl through the windows of the Tate and LaBianca mansions. Somewhere, there's always someone ready to light the match that will release some world-cleansing apocalyptic blaze.

In our time, perhaps no figure more fully embodies the murderous, careless rage of the impotent than Theodore Kaczynski, the Unabomber. From May 26, 1978, when Kaczynski placed his first bomb in the parking lot of the engineering department at Northwestern University, until April 3, 1996, when he was captured in his now famous one-room log cabin in Lincoln, Montana, Kaczynski successfully carried out more than two dozen attacks on wholly unsuspecting individuals, killing three and seriously injuring five more. Early on in his campaign, he left his bombs in campus parking lots and meeting rooms, and then switched to targeting the airline industry, thus earning the Unabomber nickname and the attention of law-enforcement figures around the country. And after seventeen years of eluding the FBI and all others, he was clearly unafraid of the forces of intelligence arrayed against him. Indeed, convinced of his superior intellect, Kaczynski wrote to the *New York Times* on April 24, 1995, ostensibly as the leader of the terrorist group "FC," to demand publication of the group's manifesto. If this demand was not met, the group could be counted on to continue its war against human targets indefinitely since, Kaczynski crowed, "it doesn't appear that the FBI is going to catch us anytime soon. The FBI is a joke" (Douglas and Olshaker 184). As it turned out, though, insisting on getting into print was the Unabomber's fatal error: Kaczynski's brother read the published manifesto, recognized the arguments and the turns of phrase, pointed the authorities in the direction of that small cabin in Montana filled with books and bombs. It was a stupid mistake and, for that reason alone, one worthy of a teacher's attention.

By all accounts, Kaczynski is a bright man. When he was six years old, he took an IQ test and is reported to have scored 167, a result that placed this working-class boy living on the South Side of Chicago safely among the geniuses (Chase 49). He distinguished himself early on academically: he graduated from high school at the age of sixteen, received his degree from Harvard at twenty, did his doctoral work in mathematics at the University of Michigan, and then, at the age of twenty-five, became an assistant professor in the mathematics department at Berkeley. In another context, Kaczynski would be a shining example of the American Dream Realized, but for the fact that he walked away from a promising academic career and disappeared into the wild, driven by his desire to live out the fantasies he had been nourishing since his first years at Harvard—"fantasies of living a primitive life and . . . [of] himself as 'an agitator, rousing mobs to frenzies of revolutionary violence'" (S. Johnson 9; pt. 1).[7]

Beneath the resume of Kaczynski's academic success, though, there is another, more mundane record of the emotional consequences of his having been marked for intellectual distinction. From the beginning, Kaczynski was uncomfortable with other children, so much so that his mother considered enrolling him in a study conducted by Bruno Bettelheim regarding autistic children, before deciding to rely on "advice published by Dr. Spock in attempting to rear her son" (S. Johnson 4; pt. 1). By the age of eight, Kaczynski was no longer accepted by the children in the neighborhood or at school. Save for a brief moment in junior high school, a profound loneliness enveloped Kaczynski. He skipped fifth grade; he skipped eleventh grade; he walked through a world where, as he experienced it, he was "the subject of considerable verbal abuse and teasing" (5; pt. 1). He failed to establish meaningful relationships with others.

When he got to Harvard, this sixteen-year-old boy encountered what Alston Chase describes as a general education curriculum that celebrated the accomplishments of science and denigrated the moral and ethical issues raised by progress, thereby promoting a sense that life is without meaning and "that there was no hope" (50). Kaczynski experienced the excess of scientific enthusiasm quite directly as a result of his having been one of twenty-five students selected from his entering class to participate in Professor Henry Murray's study of personality development among gifted college men. Following the instructions given to all who participated in this study, Kaczynski wrote an essay on his personal philosophy of life, handed it in, and then returned, at the appointed time, to debate his ideas with "a young lawyer," while his responses were monitored.

Kaczynski entered a dark room with a two-way mirror, electrodes were attached to his body, a bright light was directed at his face. Someone he could not see began barking questions at him. Contrary to what Kaczynski and the other participants had been told, the goal of the study was to measure how the personality changes under stress. A sixteen-year-old boy. His life's philosophy.

Answer the question.

Participants wept, became enraged, felt defeated, limped back to their dorms to be with peers who knew nothing about Murray's project. And then they returned and took more tests. Over his four years at Harvard, Kaczynski spent nearly two hundred hours providing the researchers with the data required to develop his psychological portrait. He composed an autobiography in which he was directed to answer specific questions on "a range of subjects from thumb sucking and toilet training to masturbation and erotic fantasies"; he provided a fantasy inventory, an inventory of self-description, a range of experience inventory, a food-preference inventory. He submitted himself to an odor-association test, a word-association test, a Rosenzweig picture-frustration test (Chase 56). He put his trust in his teachers.

And then, suddenly, while in graduate school, he experienced "several weeks of intense and persistent sexual excitement involving fantasies of being a female." He sought help initiating the process of sex-reassignment, but panicked while waiting in the psychiatrist's office. When he did get in to see the doctor, he spoke only of being depressed and then left "feeling rage, shame, and humiliation over this attempt to seek evaluation" (S. Johnson 6; pt. 1). This was one test he didn't want to sit for. In 1967, after he completed his degree at the University of Michigan, he was hired by the Berkeley mathematics department, where student-published evaluations labeled him "a poor teacher who was intellectually arrogant, a generally poor communicator who showed little interest in his students" (Douglas and Olshaker 89). After two years of such work, he abruptly resigned, refusing to be persuaded by the department chair that he had "a brilliant career as an academic mathematician ahead of him" (90). Buffeted along by a host of motivations, including this fear of how others would judge his mental health and his growing hatred of technology,[8] Kaczynski moved into the wild, eventually buying a small piece of land outside Lincoln, Montana, in 1971, where he built the one-room cabin that would come to house his strange, delusional plans for changing the world. He felt "compelled to live a life of extreme isolation and to focus his energy against the aspects of society that are attempting to control the masses," including "advertising, genetic engineering, computer technology, business, certain aspects of education, chemical companies, etc." (S. Johnson 2; pt. 2). He began writing. He broke his life up into six periods and composed extended, detailed accounts of every wrong that had ever been done to him. He penned an article about the destructive powers of technology. He amassed evidence to show posterity that he wasn't a "sickie" (11; pt. 1). And, in April 1978, after seven years of subsisting in the wilderness, he traveled back to his hometown to find an audience for his ideas, an outlet for his feelings.

He approached math professor Donald Saari of Northwestern University to seek help getting his article published. When none of the readers at Northwestern or at the University of Illinois would support publication, Kaczynski became enraged and vowed to "get even" (Douglas and Olshaker 99). On May 26, 1978, he left a package addressed to a professor at Rensselaer Polytechnic in the parking lot reserved for the University of Illinois's engineering department. When the package was found, it was returned to the address of the presumed sender, a professor at Northwestern University's Technological Institute. Not recognizing the package, this professor immediately turned it over to the authorities, one of whom was slightly injured upon opening the package. The following year, Kaczynski left a rigged cigar box in a study carrel on the second floor of Northwestern's Technological Institute which, when opened, caused minor injuries to a graduate student. In November of 1979, setting his sights higher, Kaczynski put a bomb in the mail that was then placed aboard an American Airlines flight out of Chicago. This bomb malfunctioned, causing a fire in the cargo hold, which led to an emergency landing. In June 1980, Kaczynski struck again, this time successfully. He mailed a package bomb to the home of the president of United Airlines, who was injured on his hands, face, and thighs when he opened the box.

To those untrained in reading the criminal mind, this series of acts is bound to appear both random and pointless. What did he stand to gain by blowing up members of the university or the airline industry? Since none of the victims had ever had any encounter of any kind with Kaczynski, the logic behind his choice of targets seems elusive and the desired outcome obscure. But, for John Douglas, a profiler for the FBI called in on the case early in 1980, there was enough evidence to piece together a portrait of the individual responsible for these four events: "[D]espite the early crudeness of the bombs, I felt we were dealing with someone with a strong connection to the academic world, either to Northwestern or the University of Illinois at Chicago, or both. Maybe he was an instructor who'd been turned down for tenure. Maybe he was an 'ABD' . . . a frustrated, long-suffering grad student who just couldn't get it together to finish. Maybe he had some other type of grudge. But I was relatively certain this wasn't a blue-collar type. This guy was well educated and intellectual, with a strong grounding in the sciences" (Douglas and Olshaker 39).

Setting to the side Douglas's reasonable assumption that the bomber's grudge could only be the result of having *failed* in the academy, one finds a remarkably accurate portrait of the Unabomber's academic background. One might be tempted, in fact, to say that Douglas has shown his smarts by making so much from so little.

At the time, though, few in the FBI were impressed by Douglas's profile. Indeed, according to Douglas, one reason the FBI had such difficulty tracking the Unabomber was because of an ongoing "tussle between the operational people and the behavioral people" in the bureau about how to go about the business of solving crimes. From the operational perspective, those who produce profiles have left the realm of science and have entered the more fluid domains of art, experience, and interpretation. From the behavioral perspective, profilers make the best of a bad situation: they run their minds across the data, cross-check their insights with what they know about human behavioral characteristics, and then invent, create, or fabricate a portrait of the perpetrator's psychological predispositions for an audience of disbelievers. By Douglas's account, the Unabomber might have been captured more than a decade earlier if the FBI and the other governmental organizations with investigative responsibilities had coordinated their actions, trained agents to "apply creative proactive techniques," and supplemented their methods of detection with the insights offered by those skilled in the arts of profiling (155). Douglas ends his book by imagining the kind of fantastic dream of bureaucratic cooperation that drives most any reform project. In this case, Douglas points to "the unfortunate outcomes at Ruby Ridge and Waco" and expresses his support for combining the FBI and the ATF in order to create a single body with a "unified leadership, unified goals, and unified operational policy." Working out the details of such a project must, Douglas concedes, be left "to the politicians to work out" (154).

So on one hand, we have the highly constrained life of the investigator, who toils away in the interstices of a large, inefficient, ponderous, internally divided bureaucratic body; on the other, we have the seemingly unconstrained life of the Unabomber, riding his bike along the backroads of Montana, paying for everything in cash, using a sponge to dampen his stamps, flying beneath the radar of what some would have us call "our panoptic society." Because Douglas's version of the investigation is embedded in a larger institutional framework, it assumes, almost of necessity, the same shape and texture as "the schoolhouse melodrama," in which a marginal and marginalized way of knowing struggles for legitimacy in a world controlled by the blind. There's no escaping this story or the familiar feeling of Douglas's own thinly veiled rage because, as the Unabomber puts it: "Bureaucracies HAVE TO be run according to rigid rules. To allow any substantial personal discretion to lower-level bureaucrats would disrupt the system and lead to charges of unfairness due to differences in the way individual bureaucrats exercised their discretion. . . . GENERALLY SPEAKING the regulation of our lives by large organizations is necessary for the functioning of industrial-technological society. The result is a sense of powerlessness on the part of the average person" (qtd. in Douglas and Olshaker 228; par. 114; emphasis in original).[9]

Who, in their darkest hours, hasn't entertained ideas about the value of obliterating such a world and starting over? Surely a differently organized world, one where reasoned arguments prevailed over petty turf wars, would be in every way superior to the murky world where Douglas and the rest of us are destined to spend the rest of our days.

In his manifesto, the Unabomber provides his theory about the root cause of the felt sense of powerlessness he believes characterizes life in the modern era generally. As the Unabomber defines it, "human beings have a need (probably based in biology) for something that we will call the 'power process,' which has four elements—goal, effort, attainment of goal, and autonomy" (201; par. 33). Humans need to have goals they can strive for and attain autonomously. It is through this process, the Unabomber asserts, that "self-esteem, self-confidence and a sense of power are acquired." And when humans are denied access to this process and the felt sense of autonomy that attends it, the results are "boredom, demoralization, low self-esteem, inferiority feelings, defeatism, depression, anxiety, guilt, frustration, hostility, spouse or child abuse, insatiable hedonism, abnormal sexual behavior, sleep disorders, eating disorders, etc." (205; par. 44).

From a certain perspective, one could say that the Unabomber has merely described, in other terms, the world that Mr. Ferri and Professor Edmundson gesture toward when they write of being trapped by testing mechanisms and the soulless byproducts of consumer culture. The important difference, though, is that the Unabomber actually believes his words have the power to set in motion the revolution that will bring all of technological society crashing to the ground. As he sees it, the only option available to those who are troubled by our society's reliance on technology and dehumanizing bureaucratic systems is "a radical and fundamental change in the nature of society" (240; par. 140), a "revolutionary movement" that will offer "to solve all problems at one stroke and create a whole new world" (240; par. 141). The Unabomber's hope is that his words will set off this anarchic, apocalyptic, redemptive revolution, bringing together all the dispossessed in a coordinated effort to dismantle the technological advances that have increasingly deprived life of its meaning and its pleasures. What arises to replace the current system is of no particular concern to the Unabomber: "we have no illusions about the feasibility of creating a new, ideal form of society. Our goal is only to destroy the existing form of society" (258; par. 182).

The Unabomber's reluctance to trouble himself with the details of imagining the world that might be built upon the ruins of technological society could be seen as evidence either of his faith that such work would eventually be carried out by others more experienced in the arts of crafting a state or of his belief that, after the revolution, such work would never be necessary. I would argue, though, that the Unabomber's silence on this matter suggests that the primary function of his manifesto is simply to provide a retroactive political rationale for his deeper commitment to causing pain indiscriminately. After all, if the Unabomber had truly wanted to create the kind of havoc dreamed of in his manifesto, why didn't he pursue figures who are central to the spread of technology—Bill Gates comes to mind—rather than the insignificant, low-level functionaries he successfully targeted: graduate students in engineering, the owner of a computer store, a host of security personnel, the odd academic specializing in computer science or genetic research? Or why didn't he devote his considerable mental powers to releasing a series of stunningly toxic computer viruses on the world at large, viruses that would destroy the machines without necessarily causing human harm?[10]

We will never have definitive answers to such questions. At best, we have the Unabomber's explanation, included in his letter to the *New York Times* seeking publication of his manifesto, for the sixteen-year silence of "FC": "We were very young then and our thinking was crude. Over the years we have given as much attention to the development of our ideas as to the development of bombs, and we now have something serious to say. And we feel that just now the time is ripe for the presentation of anti-industrial ideas" (qtd in Douglas and Olshaker 186). To put this another way, one could say that it wasn't until early in 1995 that the Unabomber was able to complete his work on a theory that retroactively gave shape and meaning to his random acts of violence. But even if we take seriously the Unabomber's claim that he worked as hard on his ideas as he did on developing increasingly sophisticated timing and detonation devices for delivering "his message," we are stuck with the fact that he didn't reserve time for choosing high-profile targets. The Unabomber had no difficulty justifying this allocation of his mental resources: "the single overriding goal must be the elimination of modern technology, and . . . no other goal can be allowed to compete with this one" (266; par. 206)—especially not a socially engineered concern for the indiscriminate suffering caused by the revolutionist's actions.

It's hard to imagine just who the Unabomber thought would travel with him as he made his way from articulating a vague, nagging dissatisfaction with modern life to promoting a cause with no vision of a better life and no coherent rationale for justifying who the revolution was targeting or why. The writer bent over his typewriter, pounding away in his one-room garret, dreams that his words possess some mystical power to transform the masses and that his readers will study his text with care, unlock its secrets, and come together to join him on the field of battle against the forces of evil. The writer dreams this dream, refusing to concede the obvious—that all words written for others eventually become dead letters, their powers muted, their messages scattered to the wind. To date, the manifesto's call to action has received no reply.

Given the faith that the Unabomber placed in the power of the written word, it's worth considering what kind of a reader he was during the time he was actively waging his war against technological society.[11] On June 18, 1993, apparently driven by his concern over the news coverage of the bombing of the World Trade Center and the debacle in Waco, the Unabomber sought to put himself back on the terrorist map by sending off two bombs on the same day. The first one seriously injured Dr. Charles Epstein, a geneticist at the University of California, San Francisco; the second caused equally grievous injuries to Dr. David Gelernter, a computer scientist at Yale University. While the Unabomber's decision to target a geneticist makes a certain immediate sense, given the Unabomber's concern over scientific efforts to manipulate the future form of the human race, why choose Gelernter who, by his own account, is "one of the very few persons in the field who doesn't *like* computers" (*Drawing* 28)? Gelernter's doubts about the advance of technology were no secret: his book *Mirror Worlds*, which was published two years before he was attacked, concludes with a dialogue between two professors—one a techno-enthusiast who believes that "the real live warm joyful *emotional* cutting edge of human experience today *is* science and *is* technology," and the other a techno-skeptic who fears that the revolution in interactive software will forever "stratify society based strictly on a person's fondness for playing games with machines" (224, 218).

When it came to light that the Unabomber had blown up a potential ally, Kaczynski broke with his past protocol and contacted his victim directly in July 1995. He was motivated to write neither by remorse nor embarrassment over his possibly faulty reading of Gelernter's text,[12] but rather by a need to comment on the intelligence of his victim: "People with advanced degrees aren't as smart as they think they are. If you'd had any brains you would have realized that there are a lot of people out there who resent bitterly the way techno-nerds like you are changing the world and you wouldn't have been dumb enough to open an unexpected package from an unknown source." The Unabomber then went on to contest Gelernter's argument in *Mirror Worlds* that the ongoing development of computer technology is inevitable. Such developments, the Unabomber asserted, "are inevitable only because techno-nerds like you make them inevitable. If there were no computer scientists there would be no progress in computer science" (qtd. in Douglas and Olshaker 181). And so, in this way, the Unabomber justified to himself and to his victim the necessity of refusing to discriminate among members of a given category: to be a computer scientist of whatever stripe is to invite annihilation.[13]

The transcripts from Kaczynski's preliminary hearings give us another glimpse of his indifferent reading practice. Here we learn that, three days after the Unabomber posted his packages to Professors Epstein and Gelernter, the journal *Earth First!* published an issue that eventually found its way into Kaczynski's cabin in Montana. Included in this issue was an article claiming that the advertising firm "Burston-Marsteller" (really Burson-Marsteller)[14] was responsible for burnishing the image of the Exxon Corporation after the Valdez spill. For whatever reason, this piece of information stuck with the Unabomber and, when he attacked again on December 10, 1994, he targeted Thomas Mosser, a former executive for Burson-Marsteller, who was killed instantly upon opening a package with a return address for a professor at San Francisco State University. In his letter to the *New York Times* on April 24, 1995, the Unabomber repeated the information contained in the *Earth First!* article to justify his choice of target: "We blew up Thomas Mosser last December because he was a Burston-Marsteller [*sic*] executive. Among other misdeeds, Burston-Marsteller helped Exxon clean up its public image after the Exxon Valdez incident. But we attack Burston-Marsteller less for its specific misdeeds than on general principles. Burston-Marsteller is about the biggest organization in the public relations field. This means that its business is the development of techniques for manipulating people's attitudes. It was for this more than for its actions in specific cases that we sent a bomb to an executive of this company" (qtd. in Douglas and Olshaker 182).

When it subsequently came to light that Burson-Marsteller did not have the Exxon Valdez account and that Mosser was no longer employed by the ad agency at the time he received the bomb, the Unabomber was again wholly unperturbed by the consequences of his incomplete research. In his cabin, detectives found a letter to *Earth First!* in which the Unabomber declared: "to us [the mistake about Burson-Marsteller] makes little difference" (*United States v. Theodore Kaczynski*). One advertising executive is just like any other advertising executive—the people in those offices who do that kind of work are all interchangeable and equally culpable.

The letter explaining the rationale for murdering Thomas Mosser was sent out on the same day that the Unabomber mailed what was to be his last bomb. In this instance, the victim, Gilbert Murray, president of the California Forestry Association, was killed upon opening a package addressed to his predecessor. The success of this attack and the previous one lent considerable force to the Unabomber's request that his manifesto be published. Frustrated with the ways his message was being distorted in the media, the Unabomber wanted to reassure the public that his organization had nothing against "universities and scholars as such. . . . We would not want anyone to think that we have any desire to hurt professors who study archaeology, history, literature or *harmless stuff like that*. The people we are out to get are the scientists and engineers, especially in critical fields like computers and genetics" (qtd. in Douglas and Olshaker 183; emphasis added). Asserting that the goal of FC was "less to punish [those who promote technological progress] than to propagate ideas," and declaring that "we are getting tired of making bombs," the Unabomber offered to strike a bargain: if the *New York Times, Time,* or *Newsweek* would publish his manifesto and allow him the opportunity, over the next three years, to respond to criticisms of his piece, FC would "permanently desist from terrorist activities" (184–85). To assist the editors while they deliberated over the ethics of relenting to the demands of a terrorist, the Unabomber mailed another letter asserting his plans to plant a bomb aboard an LAX flight sometime that week. Havoc ensued and, as debate over the issue swirled, on June 28, 1995, a copy of the Unabomber's manuscript arrived at the offices of the *New York Times* and the *Washington Post*. The presses had three months to decide whether or not they would accede to the Unabomber's demands.[15]

This restriction struck John Douglas as particularly odd: "The time frame of the ultimatum roughly equated with the academic summer vacation. Could it be that our guy was some prominent professor who would be overseas or somehow otherwise engaged until the next school year began?" (75). Or was this a ploy to steal the headlines back from the Oklahoma City bombing, which had occurred on April 19, 1995? There was no way of knowing what motivated the Unabomber's time constraints or whether he could be trusted to keep up his end of the bargain if the newspapers agreed to publish his work. What we do know is that when the *New York Times* and the *Washington Post* jointly published the Unabomber's manifesto on September 19, 1995, they simultaneously gave into his demands and released the textual evidence that ultimately led to his capture. In the end, it was the Unabomber's belief in the power of the word to wreak the kind of revolutionary havoc his explosive devices could only gesture toward that brought him down, for there can be little doubt that, had Kaczynski kept his writing to himself, he would still be free today, mailing his packages and devastating the lives of the unsuspecting.

The manifesto itself hardly merits attention. Retrospectively providing a justifying argument for his actions, the Unabomber would have his readers believe that, all along, he has been responding to the devastating effects of technology on the environment, the destruction of the family, and the emptiness of modern life. It is hard to imagine a reader who wouldn't agree with his general characterization of life in contemporary society as one where "the modern individual . . . is threatened by many things against which he is helpless: nuclear accidents, carcinogens in food, environmental pollution, war, increasing taxes, invasion of his privacy by large organizations, nationwide social or economic phenomena that may dispute his way of life" (213; par. 68). But it is also hard to imagine the document Kaczynski has produced stirring the masses to join his cause: it is only in the fantasy-ridden world dominated by rhetoricians and advertisers that one believes words have such magical powers of persuasion. It may have pleased Kaczynski to write his philosophy of life, but his belief that doing so might have some larger impact on the world outside his cabin was as delusional as his belief that putting bombs in the mail might bring technology to its knees. However fond we are of asserting that the pen is mightier than the sword, the truth is, as the Unabomber's manifesto inadvertently makes clear, words don't explode. Mute and all but irrelevant on the page, words rarely exercise the transformative power we so often seek to grant them. Just as even the most well-placed bomb has little to no chance of altering the social order, the well-placed essay or article, book or manifesto has little hope of significantly changing the lifeways of individuals acting alone or collectively.

Once Kaczynski was captured, his greatest fear was realized—not that he would die, but rather that, despite the evidence of his high test scores, his success in school, his degrees, his voluminous journals, and his carefully crafted manifesto, he would be judged not to be of sound mind. And, indeed, without his knowledge or his consent, his own lawyers set about building a defense based upon a plea of insanity. When Kaczynski learned what his lawyers were up to, he vigorously fought this strategy for saving his life: he wanted the chance to present the reasons for his actions and to make it clear, as William Finnegan has put it, that he "was not only refusing to recant his ideas but also refusing to recant his acts. He had done what he had done for the reasons he had given. And he was apparently prepared to explain those reasons to the jury and the world" (55). When Kaczynski's efforts to retain other legal counsel were blocked by the judge in his case, he exercised his right to insist upon representing himself, which forced the judge to delay the trial so that a psychological exam could be performed to determine his competency.

That night, January 7, 1998, Kaczynski returned to his cell, placed his underwear around his neck, fashioned it into a tourniquet, and attempted to strangle himself to death. As he drifted toward unconsciousness, he considered the possibility that he might not succeed, that he might end up "brain damaged" [his words], that he might have to live out the rest of his days deprived of his mental powers. And so he stopped (S. Johnson 15; pt. 1).[16]

Although declared competent in the psychological report, Kaczynski was nevertheless denied his rights to self-defense and to the council of his own choosing. Faced with the prospect of a defense that argued his insanity and the certainty that he would not be allowed to speak in his own defense, Kaczynski pled guilty and was sentenced to life without parole. He was shipped to the federal penitentiary in Florence, Colorado, where he crossed paths with Timothy McVeigh, who was awaiting execution for the Oklahoma City bombings, and Ramzi Yousef, who is serving out a 240-year sentence for masterminding the first World Trade Center bombing. Kaczynski immediately set to work on a book-length manuscript entitled *Truth Versus Lies* and found a publisher who promoted the book as describing "in penetrating prose [Kaczynski's] undergraduate years at Harvard, his budding activism, and the Cain and Abel nature of his relationship with the brother who eventually turned him in." And then, at the last minute, the book was pulled as it went to press because, according to the publisher, "Kaczynski was uncooperative and expressed himself in ways that made it impossible for the book to be published by Context, or anybody else" (Weeks). Silent on the subject of the bombings, *Truth Versus Lies* remains in search of a publisher.

Through super human computers and mind control there simply will be no place for a rebellious person to hide and *my kind of people* will vanish forever from the earth.

—From the journals of Theodore Kaczynski (emphasis added)

THE BOOK

But, surely, books and manifestos, scholarly articles and vicious screeds can rip through society and change the world—can't they? Examples of the power of the written word abound: Luther pounding his ninety-five theses to the cathedral door at Wittenberg; Marx and Engels penning *The Communist Manifesto;* Hitler in his cell, scratching away at *Mein Kampf;* Chairman Mao's *Little Red Book* next to every beating heart. Leaders write and the masses follow, revolutionizing the world of social relations as they go (or so those of us wedded to a life with books like to tell ourselves). While it may have been true at one time that the written word exercised such extraordinary powers over the literate and the illiterate alike, never again will there be another written text that plays such a transformative role in a nation's history because no single text will ever again be able to occupy center stage. This does not mean that books will no longer be marketed as bringing the good news in one form or another to humankind—as being earth-shattering bombshells, as delivering stunning critiques, as inaugurating paradigm shifts, as altering consciousness, as riding on the cutting edge of a new way of thinking. These claims will continue to be made because what is true about advertising in all other consumer realms will continue to apply to the textual world as well: namely, that underneath all the self-serving chatter about the product's transformative powers rests a humbler reality, one where the object being celebrated exercises, at best, a modest, transitory claim on one's attention.

To illustrate this point, I'd like to turn to one of the most incendiary books published in the last thirty years, a book which, as it happens, is centrally concerned with the consequences of being smart—Richard J. Herrnstein and Charles Murray's *The Bell Curve: Intelligence and Class Structure in American Life.* Since *The Bell Curve* came out in hardback in the fall of 1994, Herrnstein and Murray's revival of the argument that race and IQ are correlated has been the subject of nearly continuous debate. It was immediately reviewed in nearly every major journal, weekly magazine, and newspaper in the country, where it was proclaimed in one corner to be the work of "brave scholars" who "dare to re-examine the evidence that different ethnic groups score differently in IQ tests" (Hawkes) and denounced in another as "a scabrous piece of racial pornography masquerading as serious scholarship" (Herbert). The *New Republic* devoted its October 1994 issue to showcasing brilliant rebuttals and cautious endorsements from leading scholars and critics working in the fields of geology, law, political science, history, literary criticism, and education. These responses were subsequently expanded and collected together in a book entitled *The Bell Curve Wars: Race, Intelligence, and the Future of America* (Fraser) and were soon joined by no less than four additional book-length critiques of Herrnstein and Murray's work: *The Bell Curve Debate: History, Documents, Opinions* (Jacoby and Glauberman); *Inequality by Design: Cracking the Bell Curve Myth* (Fischer et al.); *Measured Lies: The Bell Curve Examined* (Kincheloe, Steinberg, and Gresson); and *Intelligence, Genes, and Success: Scientists Respond to The Bell Curve* (Devlin, Fienberg, Resnick, and Roeder). And there's more: since 1999, no less than 135 articles have been published that focus on *The Bell Curve*. This is, it's safe to say, a book about which most everyone has an opinion.

Why produce a book that sets out to recuperate a form of intelligence testing that the coauthors themselves acknowledge "has been variously dismissed as an artifact of racism, political reaction, statistical bungling, and scholarly fraud?" As the authors see it, the truth is that "intelligence is a reasonably well-understood construct, measured with accuracy and fairness by any number of standardized mental tests" and it is their job to show how the public came to discredit legitimate psychometric efforts to measure innate human intelligence (Herrnstein and Murray 1). Because the behaviorists have been so successful in persuading the public and the policy makers to believe that human potential is "almost perfectly malleable" and that it can be improved and increased through "the right public policies—redistribution of wealth, better education, better housing and medical care" (8–9), research on the genetic foundations of human intelligence has been forced underground where, in the academy's "cloistered environment," as they term it, Herrnstein, Murray, and their fellow "classicists" have carried on the effort "to identify the components of intelligence much as physicists seek to identify the structure of the atom" (14). Outside the public's view, the classicists remain convinced of the existence and the measurability of g, a unitary mental factor that the statistician Charles Spearman hypothesized represented "general intelligence"(3). It is *The Bell Curve*'s thesis that the nation's declining productivity and the general reduction in the quality of civic life are both a direct result of the government's refusal to contend with the social, political, and economic implications that follow once one has conceded that g exists and is measurable. As Herrnstein and Murray put it, "by accepted standards of what constitutes scientific evidence and scientific proof, the classical tradition has in our view given the world a treasure of information that has been largely ignored in trying to understand contemporary policy issues" (19).

One reason this information has been largely ignored, Herrnstein and Murray believe, is that those in a position to bring about lasting, meaningful social reform come from "the cognitive elite," a group that consistently and mistakenly assumes that their own experiences are generalizable to the populace at large. To illustrate how this dynamic works, Herrnstein and Murray instruct each reader to think of his or her closest friends and colleagues. Then they make a prediction about what kind of readers would pick up a book about intelligence testing in the first place: "For most readers of this book, a large majority [of their friends and colleagues] will be college graduates" (47). Now, if social relations were truly fluid and random, they calculate, the odds against having half of one's twelve closest friends be college graduates is six in a thousand, with those odds growing to more than one in a million against having a similar number of close friends with advanced degrees. Later in the book, Herrnstein and Murray speculate about how their readers' friends and colleagues might be mapped on to a bell curve for IQ distribution: "In all likelihood, almost all of your friends and professional associates belong in that top Class I slice [people with IQs higher than 125]. Your friends and associates whom you consider to be unusually slow are probably somewhere in Class II [people with IQs between 110 and 125]. Those whom you consider to be unusually bright are probably somewhere in the upper fraction of the 99th centile, a very thin slice of the overall distribution" (121). Surrounded by fellow members of "the cognitive elite," the average reader of *The Bell Curve* simply does not see the world as it actually is for those of lesser intelligence.

Concessions of this kind are, of course, little more than rhetorical moves meant to ease the fears of their readers. They say: we know the topic is volatile, but you're not to worry, because you're one of the smart ones. They say: your good judgment has been skewed by the uniqueness of your experience. They say: we think you can handle the bomb we're about to drop.

———————————————

The bomb, of course, concerns the relative intelligence of whites as measured against blacks and other ethnic minorities. Herrnstein and Murray put off wandering into this murky, forbidden territory as long as possible: they even go so far as to advise those precocious readers who jumped to the middle of their book to get to the discussion of race and intelligence to "turn back to the Introduction and begin the long trek" (315). Readers who follow the prescribed path will get the argument as Herrnstein and Murray want it to unfold. They will see that Herrnstein and Murray quite self-consciously initially neutralize race as a category in their discussion about the important social consequences of having a low IQ by showing in the second part of their four-part book that, when the white population is considered in isolation, there is a strong correlation between having a low IQ and having a life characterized by poverty, incarceration, illegitimacy, broken families, and a host of other social ills. That is, before they rank the races according to average intelligence, Herrnstein and Murray first show that "cognitive ability affects social behavior without regard to race" (125). Having established that people at the lower end of the bell curve are more likely to live horrible, unproductive lives, Herrnstein and Murray are free to tackle the most fraught issue of all. Before doing so, though, they offer a warning to their readers: "The facts about these topics are not only controversial but exceedingly complex. For our part, we will undertake to confront all the tough questions squarely. We ask that you read carefully" (267). And with this caution, the bay doors open.

The problem is this: whatever one calls it—IQ, "native intelligence," g, or smarts—the cold, hard truth, as Herrnstein and Murray see it, is that general cognitive ability is not equitably distributed amongst the races, with approximately one standard deviation separating the scores of whites and blacks on reliable IQ tests. "Translated into centiles, this means that the average white person tests higher than about 84 percent of the population of blacks and that the average black person tests higher than about 16 percent of the population of whites" (269). In light of what Herrnstein and Murray have argued earlier in *The Bell Curve,* the significance of this "fact" is clear: taken as a whole, African Americans are a drag both on the economy and on the social well-being of the nation. In an effort to defuse the possible implications of these findings, Herrnstein and Murray maintain that news about the differential allocation of cognitive ability across the races should have no practical impact on how individuals in our society treat one another. To prove this point, they make yet another appeal to their readers' sense of reasonableness and civility: "If tomorrow you knew beyond a shadow of a doubt that all the cognitive differences between races were 100 percent genetic in origin, nothing of any significance *should* change. The knowledge would give you no reason to treat individuals differently than if ethnic differences were 100 percent environmental. By the same token, knowing that the differences are 100 percent environmental in origin would not suggest a single program or policy that is not already being tried" (314–15; emphasis added). The only force that stops the revolutionary dawning of this new era of social harmony is governmental efforts to intervene in the natural order of things. As Herrnstein and Murray would have it, almost nothing that has been done to improve the IQs of underperforming individuals has made a measurable, sustained difference in the lives of the target population—not Head Start, not desegregated schooling, not affirmative action. Indeed, Herrnstein and Murray contend that all such programs, working in concert with the democratizing effect of mass education, have served to siphon off the most promising members of every class and race, collecting the best human genetic material in the restricted realm of the cognitive elite, while leaving the least desirable genetic material behind to dwell in misery. If this unnatural state of affairs is allowed to continue, Herrnstein and Murray envision a nightmarish future where the government, run by this increasingly out-of-touch cognitive elite, "will continue to try to engineer behavior through new programs and regulations," ultimately generating a "*custodial state*, . . . a high-tech and more lavish version of the Indian reservation for some substantial minority of the nation's population, while the rest of America tries to go about its business" (525–26; emphasis in original).

The only way to escape this apocalyptic world and make the United States "a place for everyone," Herrnstein and Murray believe, is to dismantle the bureaucratic structures currently dominated by people with high IQs who "think that complicated, sophisticated operationalizations of fairness, justice, and right and wrong are ethically superior to *simple, black-and-white versions*" (541; emphasis added). Preferring a system where it is clear that black is bad and white is good, Herrnstein and Murray call for the elimination of governmental rules and regulations that unnecessarily complicate the moral and commercial worlds of the average person, because these very rules and regulations, purportedly meant to ensure fairness, actually "effectively block off avenues for people who are not cognitively equipped to struggle through the bureaucracy" (542). Thus, to protect the cognitively disenfranchised, everything must be made simpler and more accessible to the average person. As Herrnstein and Murray put it, since "the cognitive elite has come to power, it has trailed in its wake a detritus of complexities . . . that together have reshaped society so that the average person has a much tougher time running his own life. Our policy recommendation is to stop it and strip away the nonsense" (542). Herrnstein and Murray then close their eyes and end their book by asking their readers to join them in dreaming of a better world: "Imagine living in a society where the rules about crime are simple and the consequences are equally simple. . . . The meaning of criminal offenses used to be clear and objective, and so were the consequences. It is worth trying to make them so again" (543–44). Ah, the simpler world, the one without bureaucrats and cumbersome rules, the one where the difference between right and wrong is as clear as the difference between night and day, the prelapsarian world where everything stays in its rightful, preordained place. And with this exhausted, cliché-ridden, ridiculous last gasp, *The Bell Curve* comes crashing to an end.

———————————

But haven't we been here before? The evil bureaucratic system, the corruption of the schoolhouse by outside forces, the enfeebled teacher-scholars wailing against the injustices of the world—when considered generically, *The Bell Curve* makes a number of rhetorical moves that aren't all that different from the ones found in the versions of the schoolhouse melodrama discussed at the opening of this chapter or, for that matter, from the ones the Unabomber makes in his manifesto. There's a malevolent force out there tampering with the natural order of things and this force must be neutralized. The bureaucrats or, if you prefer, "the cognitive elite," have rigged the game so that the little guy—the enterprising one who just wants to run his small business without all the governmental red tape hamstringing him at every turn—doesn't have a chance. The little guy's only hope is that the system devised by the intellectual fat cats to maintain their positions of privilege can be destroyed. On the glorious day that this comes to pass, we will all be able to return to a simpler, purer time—one characterized by social harmony, mutual respect, self-sufficiency, and freedom from the intrusion of either the government or the market into one's daily life.

Could *The Bell Curve* really exercise the dangerous powers it dreams of having? Could it change people's minds about the connection between race and intelligence? Could it influence public policy? Could it foment a revolution that would quash all entitlement programs? Could it lead to the termination of all the egalitarian goals of mass education in a democracy? It is certainly the case that many of Herrnstein and Murray's critics have attributed such fantastic powers to the book. Joe Kincheloe and Shirley Steinberg suggest, for instance: "If Herrnstein and Murray are able to convince their fellow citizens that they are correct and that IQ fairly and accurately portrays the worth of individuals, African Americans, Latinos, and poor Whites face a psychic, economic, and political disaster. . . . [T]he viewpoints promoted in the book, if taken seriously, will explode the dreams of millions of oppressed people in America" (12). Henry Giroux and Susan Searle declare: "the popularity of *The Bell Curve* signals the rewriting of history by omitting the legacy of slavery and racism in the United States" (79). Catherine Lugg argues: "the authors have effectively marketed their policy proposals for eliminating affirmative action, cloaking their rhetoric in notions of merit and white supremacy" (368).

It is the abiding assumption of the critical community that books have such powers and that there are masses of readers out there who are in danger of being seduced by all the statistical mumbo-jumbo, mystified by the veneer of scientific objectivity, and duped by the savvy marketing of this intentionally controversial commodity. But let's suspend for a moment our belief in this threatening reader so ready to embrace the unthinkable. As a thought experiment, try to imagine the reader most likely to pick up *The Bell Curve* at the local bookstore or library. Recall that the book weighs in at a hefty 845 pages and that nearly 300 of those pages contain densely worded appendixes, long blocks of statistical data, footnotes, and bibliographic information. Recall, as well, that the body of the text is repeatedly interrupted with graphs and charts of every kind. In what sense does a book of this kind pose a threat? And to whom does it pose that threat? It can't be the case that it poses a threat to those who are convinced, either by academic training, upbringing, or faith, that environment plays the most important role in determining one's success later in life: if such readers ever bothered to familiarize themselves with Herrnstein and Murray's book, they would do so only to learn more about the opposition. And the book obviously also does not pose a threat to those readers who already agree with the positions staked out by Herrnstein and Murray: if anything, the book gives these readers more ammunition to make their case. Since ammunition of this kind simply bounces off the chests of those readers who reject out of hand the notion that genetics is destiny, it must follow that the book and its avid supporters assume frightening proportions because of its purported ability to persuade those who have long harbored secret, inchoate doubts about the effectiveness of the welfare state and about the equality of the races but who have yet to find a place to focus their anger.

While I have my doubts that there are, in fact, many people who have not already made up their minds about the relationship between race and intelligence, I find it nearly impossible to picture some genuinely undecided reader methodically working his or her way through *The Bell Curve,* analyzing its charts and statistics, nibbling on a pencil, weighing "the evidence." Herrnstein and Murray harbored similar doubts and thus designed *The Bell Curve* so that it could be read at a number of predetermined levels. "At the simplest level," they write, *The Bell Curve* "is only about thirty pages long," with the little blurbs heading each chapter giving the reader "the main findings and conclusions minus any evidence for them, written in an informal style free of technical terms" (xix). At the next level, things get a bit more difficult: the main text is "accessible to anyone who enjoys reading, for example, the science section of the news magazines." For such readers, "no special knowledge is assumed: *everything you need to know to follow all of the discussion is contained within the book*" (xix; emphasis added). And the levels continue, adding further qualifications, extra data, scholarly references, appendixes. Perhaps the reader who is put in danger by this book is the one who works with the thirty-page version of *The Bell Curve*, the part that's all assertion and no evidence. Perhaps the nation is filled with such readers who, up to the point that they came into contact with *The Bell Curve*, were undecided or agnostic on the issue of racial differences and then, after a quick spin through Herrnstein and Murray's tome, found themselves wholly convinced of the need to dismantle the welfare state. Even Michael Willis, the director in charge of marketing *The Bell Curve*, doubted the existence of such readers: as he put it in an article on unread bestsellers, "We thought it was very much the case that both professionals and the general public bought [*The Bell Curve*] to have it and didn't read it. We got the sense even from reviews that people basically read the first chapter and the last" (Goldstein).

It seems an easy enough matter to dispel such skepticism about *The Bell Curve*'s transformative powers: all one need do is produce evidence that the book has swept through the realms of the undecided, convincing all in its wake that intelligence is destiny. While evidence of real, rather than putative, acts of reception is notoriously difficult to come by, in this case, one would think that such evidence would be everywhere ready to hand—that the journals and airwaves would be littered with testaments from readers who were converted by Herrnstein and Murray's "irrefutable" data. In the interests of unearthing evidence of such readers, I made an initial venture into an area where the literate responses of those who work outside the mainstream community of liberal and conservative critics and scholars are recorded—the customer review pages of amazon.com. What I found there genuinely surprised me: a decade after its publication, long out of print, *The Bell Curve* continues to attract customer reviews, having racked up, by the day I checked in the summer of 2004, a total of 142 reviews—an extraordinarily high number for an "academic" book.[17]

Closer inspection of the reviews, however, revealed that only a handful of respondents represent the book as having produced a change of mind on the subject. For the vast majority of the respondents—by my count, 134 out of 142 (94 percent)—writing about *The Bell Curve* serves as the pretext for fronting an agenda already held. Thus, for every reader who declares the book "utterly courageous science and writing in an Age of Unreason," there is another who sees it as "Mein K[a]mpf hidden behind pseudoscience" or "completely ridiculous and racist."[18] There's even a reader who recommends the book and gives it five stars, "but not for the reason you might suspect"—not because the reader approves of what Herrnstein and Murray have to say, but because it is important "to know thy enemy." In the cacophony of this response, slavishly devoted gurglings like this—"Personally, I don't know which I admire most, the intelligence, the scholastic abilities, or the courage of the authors"—find themselves right next to calm observations like this—"The explanations offered by the authors of *The Bell Curve* do not acknowledge entire fields of study which have long ago established the critical role of society in the development of human behavior. It is important to seek out explanations that do not rely on single and simplistic variables to establish causal relationships. This is especially true when discussing the complexities of social structure." Readers trade blows, regularly complain that the book has been misrepresented in the press and in previous customer reviews composed by "idiots," insist that the book should be placed on a pedestal or set on fire.

Amongst the shouting and the deafness, there are, indeed, four readers who represent themselves as coming to *The Bell Curve* with an open mind and then having been persuaded by the book's thesis. A reader from St. Paul says she put off reading the book because of the reviews she had read, fearing that its argument was "too racially antagonistic," but she concluded, after finishing the text, that "it is actually very well written and has a clear purpose." A reader from Boston is less reserved in marking how much the book altered his thinking: admitting to an initial bias against *The Bell Curve*'s thesis, this reader ended up being "amazed by the incredibly new thinking contained in it. It was a whole new way of looking at the societal problems that face the United States. It drew connections that I did not think existed, or possibly could exist. It relied on a wealth of evidence to support its claims, and used sufficient evidence and sound reasoning to refute every 'but what about . . .' question/objection." A registered Democrat from Boulder confesses that she "was forced to agree with the conclusions made in *The Bell Curve*" even though she "did not like the book's thesis." Finally, a reader from Ontario admits that he "started reading [*The Bell Curve*] with a heavy dose of skepticism, but . . . found its arguments, its conclusions and the researches they are based on flawless and utterly believable."

As it turns out, though, there are also four readers who represent themselves in their customer reviews as having come to the book with an open mind and then having exactly the opposite reaction to *The Bell Curve*. A reader from Alaska writes, "When I first read *The Bell Curve* I admit it presented cogent arguments. Now I question its putting so much weight on intelligence as a determining factor for success. The statistical information in the book leaves gaps that need to be filled in." This reader concludes his review by recommending just the kind of work that Herrnstein and Murray most disapprove of: "*Emotional*

Intelligence or *The Millionaire Mind*. These two books do more to prove that intelligence is only one factor—and not necessarily the most important one — that leads to success in later life." A reader from Stamford, Connecticut, reports that he read *The Bell Curve* "shortly after it was first published six or seven years ago and came away with the sense that while the authors' arguments sounded plausible, they really were saying nothing that many of us thought [*sic*] we knew already, particularly as it concerns the hereditary nature of intelligence." For this reader, the problem with the seemingly plausible arguments provided in *The Bell Curve* is that they are grounded in social science rather than in research in the hard sciences "conducted by geneticists, evolutionary biologists, even quantum physicists." For this reader, conducting research in this way "is akin to writing a book about fractal geometry while citing the works of Shakespeare as one's sources." Another reader from Houston, Texas, a self-confessed fan of Charles Murray, feels, after reading *The Bell Curve* that he must take his "hero to task" for his "bizarre assertion that a study of possible racial differences in IQ serves us well in devising viable social policies." This reader says that Murray, who is "normally a superb thinker deserving of much respect" has, in this instance, "made a fool of himself. He has latched onto a band wagon inevitably doomed to crash and burn." A reader from Sacramento, California, conducted an independent study at Cal State Fullerton on *The Bell Curve,* and was astonished both by the anger the book generated and by the tendency of his professors to condemn a book they admitted having never actually read. After calmly recasting the book's thesis in his own words, this reader observes:

> The whole idea of valuing people on the basis of intelligence and Darwin's debunked theory of evolution with its corollary of the survival of the fittest and the filter or strainer of natural selection is flawed. Instead . . . we hold these truths to be self-evident, that all men are created equal, that they are endowed by their Creator with certain unalienable rights. . . . Jesus is greater and kinder and more inclusive than Natural Selection, an unscientific theory that has always promoted racism and discrimination. . . . Dr. Martin Luther King, Jr. didn't quote Darwin but he did quote the Declaration and the Bible, Jesus Christ. You decide which system is more beneficial to mankind . . . hard unforgiving debunked Darwinism or merciful, kind, loving Christianity. (ellipses in original)

This, surely, is not a response anyone could have anticipated. How does one connect the dots that run between the reading of this book and the preaching of this critique grounded in a vision of the sacred?

Far from establishing *The Bell Curve* as capable of robbing its readers of their critical powers, these responses all depict readers at work deploying what they've read to support their belief systems. And in those few cases where readers represent themselves as having had their opinions changed by the book, it turns out that there's no predicting where that change will lead—to a belief in the value of intelligence testing and the need for the abolition of all the bureaucratic "nonsense" that supports egalitarianism or to the sense that the book's seemingly reasonable argument actually violates one's most cherished political and religious commitments. Thus, one could say that, to the degree that *The Bell Curve* exercises any power over its readers, it does so not through rational argument but rather by providing the information and the occasion for bolstering a set of beliefs, a faith structure, or even a rage already firmly in place before the book arrived on the scene. When any number of the amazon.com reviewers speak of Herrnstein and Murray's "courage," the individual reviewers inadvertently suggest not that the book has changed the reader's mind, but that it has allowed the reader to bring his or her inchoate beliefs out into the open—that the book, in effect, confirms something the reader has suspected all along, but didn't quite know how to put into words. And if books in general work in this way, it doesn't mean that they can't be dangerous, but rather that they can't be dangerous in the ways most of us have typically imagined—that they can never, on their own, exercise a profound influence over the mass of society or shape how society as a whole thinks about any given idea.

Even if the allegiance of the average reader isn't really at stake in this game, it doesn't necessarily follow that *The Bell Curve* has had no influence over those readers from "the cognitive elite" who actually have the power to shape public policy. Indeed, many critics of *The Bell Curve* have linked its publication with, among other things, the ascendancy of Newt Gingrich and the establishment of a Republican majority in the House of Representatives, the passage of Proposition 209, which effectively dismantled affirmative action in California, and signs of growing racial intolerance in the nation. In such arguments, *The Bell Curve* is seen as part of a downward trend, a strong indication that the tenuous advances made in race relations in the second half of the twentieth century are being undone. And, sure enough, shortly after *The Bell Curve* was published, *USA Today* listed Murray as one of "the most influential minds" in "the Republican brain trust" responsible for shaping GOP strategy. While this way of accounting for the direction of Republican policy in the mid-1990s will appeal to those who wish to believe that books continue to play a major role in political affairs, to accept such a simplistic account of history is, as Randall Kennedy has warned, to miss the actual significance of how Herrnstein and Murray's work has been received. For, unlike the debates about racial inferiority that preceded the publication of *The Bell Curve,* in this instance, Kennedy insists:

> It must be appreciated that Murray-Herrnstein have been met by a quick, vigorous, sustained, and knowledgeable rebuttal. . . . The reaction against *The Bell Curve,* moreover, has not been animated only by liberals or leftists; a significant number of centrists and conservatives have joined in the repudiation as well. While clearly powerful, the cultural-political-social network which loudly and unequivocally champions *The Bell Curve* ethos is by no means ascendant. That is due, in large degree, to effective efforts undertaken by a wide range of people to uproot the racist beliefs, intuitions, and practices that are buried so deeply throughout this culture. (186)

And then there's the fact that, just two months after Murray was declared part of the Republican brain trust, leaders of the Republican party were lining up to declare publicly that they wanted nothing to do with *The Bell Curve:* Phil Gramm, eyeing a possible presidential campaign, said he hadn't read the book and didn't "know anything about it," as did Dick Armey; Henry Hyde, chair of the House Judiciary Committee, confessed, "It's one of the jillions of things I haven't gotten to"; Jack Kemp stated flatly that it was "pseudo-scientific" and "unambiguously wrong"; and Gingrich announced through his spokesman that he'd read enough of the book to know one thing—"It's completely wrong" (Tilove).

If this evidence suggests the relative irrelevance of *The Bell Curve* as a force for social change, one could still insist that another book was primarily responsible for setting in motion the effort to put an end to the welfare state: not the largely unread and ineffectual *The Bell Curve,* but Newt Gingrich's *Contract with America.* It is certainly the case that Newt's foot soldiers in the House of Representatives cited the Contract at every turn, declaring that they were going to shrink the federal government and shift power back to the states; abolish the commerce and education departments, introduce amendments to the Constitution on flag burning, school prayer, and term limits; and, once Clinton's affair with Monica Lewinsky came to light, see the president impeached and morality restored to the White House. Confident that such momentous changes were at hand, buoyed by his convictions, Gingrich warned those who dared get in his way, "On those things that are at the core of our Contract, those things which

are at the core of our philosophy, and on those things where we believe we represent the vast majority of Americans, there will be *no* compromise" (Gingrich
186; emphasis added).

What exactly did the Contract with America change? Just three years after
making this outlandish and politically untenable declaration of a refusal to
compromise, Gingrich was at work on another book, significantly entitled *Lessons Learned the Hard Way: A Personal Report*. Using his writing to try to understand why the Contract with America had failed to bring about the changes he
had hoped for, Gingrich did not conclude that the problems he had encountered were the inevitable result of his having presented revolutionary change as
possible or desirable, or of his principled stand against compromise, or of his
mistakenly thinking that a book could ever exercise such power; rather, the vil-
lain in his narrative, as one should be able to predict at this point, is . . . a top-
heavy, bureaucratically administered government that resists the call for fundamental change. And then, in a stunning reversal, shortly after *Lessons Learned
the Hard Way* was published, Gingrich, unable to contain a rebellion in his own
party, was forced to resign, undone by the zealotry of his own followers, by his
involvement in a series of ethical scandals, and by an election year in which
fully a third of his revolutionary foot soldiers were turned out of office
(Milbank).

This is not to say that the effort to advance an agenda that Gingrich, Herrnstein, and Murray would approve of came to a sudden, abrupt end, of course.
Efforts to curtail affirmative action are vigorous and ongoing, as evidenced
most recently in the Bush administration's support for the white defendants in
Grutter v. Bollinger, the 2003 Supreme Court case involving the use of race as
one criteria among many at the University of Michigan's Law School. Even as
such attacks persist, it is important to listen to the fears expressed by those who
had hoped that the Supreme Court would put an end to affirmative action in
higher education. Prior to the Supreme Court's decision in favor of the University of Michigan, Roger Clegg, general counsel for the Center for Equal Opportunity, announced that he wanted the Bush administration to take the
strongest, most uncompromising position possible against the use of race as a
criteria used in the admissions process; otherwise, he said, whatever the courts
decided would "change almost nothing. If the door to discrimination is left ajar,
colleges and universities will drive a truck through like they have in all the years
since Bakke" (Lewis). What Clegg fears is what Gingrich, Herrnstein, Murray,
and Kaczynski all fear: the protean character of bureaucratic systems and the
ability of those who work inside these systems to circumvent, ignore, and un-
evenly enforce whatever rules are handed down from on high.

DIVING FOR COVER

While few of us would have difficulty explaining our general distaste for bureaucracies and the tests they administer, Mike Rose would seem to have more
reasons than most for holding both the school system and the testing industry
in contempt. Rose's award-winning book, *Lives on the Boundary,* opens with an
account of how the course of his own life was forever altered by a bureaucratic
filing error made when his parents placed him in a Catholic secondary school.
Despite the fact that Rose was an avid reader and had been a student in good
standing at his previous school, in his new environment, he found himself on
the "Voc. Ed." track and there he remained taking business math, typing, and
English-level D until one of his teachers checked the school records and discovered the placement office had somehow confused his test results "with those of
another student named Rose" (24). "The telling thing," Rose observes, "is how
chancy both my placement into and exit from Voc. Ed. was, neither I nor my
parents had anything to do with it. I lived in one world during spring semester,
and when I came back to school in the fall, I was living in another" (30). In less
capable hands, this material would have been deployed as one more opportunity to take a turn through the schoolhouse melodrama, where the reader
would be treated, once again, to a tale about the stupidity of administrators, the
failure of test-designers, and the indifference of school counselors. The value
of *Lives on the Boundary,* though, resides in Rose's refusal to wallow in the
dichotomy that drives the schoolhouse melodrama, where the noble individual
is pitted against the mindless institution, and his determination to devote his
energies to thinking in concrete ways about how to improve the instruction
provided to those the educational system would otherwise be content to leave
behind.

Rose continues this project of constructive engagement in *Possible Lives,* in
which he reports not only on the failures and lost opportunities he has seen in
his visits to classrooms across the country, but also on "what schooling for all in
a democratic society can be and how we can meaningfully talk about it" (413).
Rose comes to view successful classrooms as those that give students "the *experience* of democracy" and he comes to see that such classrooms have three attributes in common. First, students have a sense of mental and physical safety
—"safety to take risks, to push beyond what you can comfortably do at present"
(413). Second, there is a multilayered respect, which involves both "fair treat-
ment, decency, an absence of intimidation and, beyond the realm of individual
civility, a respect for the history, the language and culture of the peoples represented in the classroom" and an intellectual respect for the students that is re-

flected in a challenging curriculum. And, finally, the teacher's authority comes not from "age or role" (or test scores, one assumes), but rather from "knowledge, care, the construction of safe and respectful space, solidarity with students' background." In classrooms that had these attributes, Rose found that, no matter what form the teacher's pedagogical practice took, the teacher's authority was always distributed in such a way that the "students contributed to the flow of events, shaped the direction of discussion, became authorities on their own experience and on the work they were doing" (414). The teachers became, in a sense, environmentalists, by recognizing that whether one learns and what one learns are both profoundly influenced by the surroundings within which one is meant to learn.

One could say that the classrooms Rose has described enact, on a daily basis, the slow, cumbersome, unending process of laying the foundations for a democratic society. Of course, Rose's refusal to commit to a more "radical" project than asking that students be provided with safe learning spaces is bound to disconcert those who feel that the whole stupid system needs to be torn down. Equally disturbing, no doubt, is Rose's contention that there is "no single profile of the Good Teacher, . . . no final list of good practices, no curricular framework or set of instructional guidelines" that emerge from his study of actual teachers working with actual students (*Possible Lives* 9). At best, Rose asserts: "teaching well means knowing one's students well and being able to read them quickly and, in turn, making decisions to slow down or speed up, to stay with a point or return to it later, to underscore certain connections, to use or forgo a particular illustration. This decision-making operates as much by feel as by reason: it involves hunch, intuition, a best, quick guess" (419). What does it mean to be "smart" in an environment that requires operating "as much by feel as by reason"? How is one to get one's bearings in a world of such shifting, unpredictable responses? In accepting this essentially ungovernable state of affairs and committing himself to the language of possibility, hasn't Rose abandoned the fundamental responsibility of all members of the critical community— namely to judge the world and find it lacking?

As alluring as it is to dream that the intellectual can play a guiding role in the lives of others by revealing bureaucratic incoherence and inefficiency, the truth is that the world of social relations is no more responsive to the quick, penetrating "critical intervention" than a stone is to the pounding of the rain. The missiles go in and a building falls in Baghdad; a lonely, tormented man puts a bomb in the mail; a poisonous book briefly finds an avid audience of supporters and critics in the United States: these events all seemed critical at the time, having caused immediate and grievous harm to many people but, just as quickly, life and the cascading flow of information has resumed. Beneath this world of raging manifestos and symbolic victories resides a humbler reality, one where change occurs, if it occurs at all, as a result of quiet, patient, all but anonymous efforts like the ones Rose describes, where teachers, working away in imperfect systems, help their students to learn about language and its limits, the social world and its possibilities. In this fallen world, there are no stories of decisive victories; there is only movement toward and away from an ever-receding goal and the ceaseless—some might say mindless—work of building on the ruins of the past.

FALLING BODIES
CLEANING UP AFTER THE APOCALYPSE

Everyone has a story now.

Nine-eleven wasn't the first time Time stopped. Time stops all the time. In the past, we'd sit, hands clasped, watching the flickering newsreels. Assassinations, surprise attacks, mushroom clouds, concentration camps. Paying homage to other people's stories. But now, after all the waiting, the racing from one place to the next, the putting of this thing here and that thing there, it seems Time has finally stopped for us and our own lives have been marked as important.

We can all say we were alive when. We were there when. We were together when.

And we can all tell these stories that begin:

I was waking up. I was reading the paper. I was on my way to work. I was at my desk, talking on the phone. I was doing this or that and then someone came in and said.

Look, even our president was passing the time in a typical way. There he is, sitting in a classroom, listening to some students read, smiling benignly. And then someone comes in and says.

One reason we tell each other these stories, staging and restaging the moment when our expectations were violated is because the telling weaves us back into the familiar. Yes, this happened and it was unimaginably horrible, we tell each other, but we are together now. Those who speak and those who listen. Whatever else has happened, this much hasn't changed.

Immediately, even as the attack was unfolding, some experienced a felt need to preserve a record of the stories set in motion by the central event of the day. If you so choose, you can, for instance, visit Web sites with screen shots taken that day of news telecasts from around the world, the compilation of some peculiar global response to tragedy: Quick, photograph your television set! This is what the smoking towers looked like in Sweden, Germany, Slovakia, Israel, Brazil.

There are memorial pages with funereal music, the names of the dead and missing scrolling by.

There is the official September 11 Digital Archive, jointly hosted and maintained by CUNY's American Social History Project and George Mason University's Center for History and New Media. Here you can read firsthand accounts from people who were there, were near there, just missed being there, wished they had been there, felt like they were there, had premonitions that it wouldn't have been a good idea to be there. You can click through images of the towers before, during, and after. You can read reports about everything from the backlash against minorities that followed the attacks to a running assessment of the quality of the air in and around Ground Zero. You can spend days, weeks, months, wandering the archives, reliving that day.

Although there are those who would prefer that the attack and its aftermath be seen as an unprecedented violation and as the occasion for unparalleled heroism, the cumulative effect of casting about in all these documents is to be placed in the presence of a different kind of story, one that is about the wide-ranging mundaneness of catastrophic events. Whose job is it to clean up after the apocalypse? After all the judgment calls have been made, what does life begin to look like on the other side of the unthinkable?

Of that day and its aftermath, there are two images that remain fresh in my mind, one seen, one left behind by a story I was told. First, there are the falling bodies tracking against the white blur of the towers. And then there's the guy sifting through the layers of dust and broken glass that cover his apartment. The guy who, toiling away on his balcony, pushing stuff here and there, finds three fingers.

———————————

About a month after the attacks, the *Chronicle of Higher Education* invited a group of educators and publishers to describe how they were making sense of September 11. Not too surprisingly, a number of people involved in the colloquy were wondering whether being an especially gifted reader was of much use at times of crisis. Two of the participants were particularly interested to know about the books other people had turned to after the attacks. While such questions are bound to strike those who don't spend their lives working with words as odd ones to ask, the very fact that these questions were posed is a valuable index of the secularity of the teaching and publishing professions, for where else but in a secular world would one not know, *in advance,* where people would seek refuge in troubled times?

In "The Way We Read Now," William Germano, vice president of Routledge, describes wanting to read in the days after the towers fell, but being unable to find the escape he was looking for in fiction. Ultimately settling on a worn Latin grammar because this "offered immersion in another world," Germano then polled friends and colleagues to find out what they were reading and ends up with a hodgepodge: newspapers, a Buddhist self-help book, *As You Like It,* a natural study of the chickadee, French theory, the Bible. In "The Solace of Literature," Carolyn Foster Segal recounts how, in the immediate aftermath of the attacks, she found she had nothing convincing to say about the lasting value of the humanities, either to herself or to her students. When she asked one of her students whether or not literature could provide solace at such times, the student responded with an answer her teacher found disappointing: "Maybe not reading, but perhaps writing could . . ."

Segal ends her piece rummaging through the bookcase in her mind, rearranging the coming semester's syllabus. She knows she'll never teach Don DeLillo's *White Noise* again because his description of "the airborne toxic event" just isn't funny anymore. She may come back to *Underworld*, "which tempers irony with sympathy," but not right away. She plans on replacing Emerson, "who did not want to acknowledge that there was evil in the world," with Walt Whitman, "who believed that poetry could actually heal a nation," and Lincoln, who "honored the dead and created contexts to comfort and inspire the living." Unable to find the pattern or the unambiguous sign they're seeking, both Germano and Segal conclude their essays with the hope that the act of reading literature will regain for them the salvific powers it has exercised in the past.

Carrying this project of exploring the literate response to tragedy just a bit further, we discover a number of other readers reporting that, on or shortly after September 11, they turned away from their television sets and went to their bookshelves in search of the very book Segal has decided to pull from her syllabus: Don DeLillo's *Underworld*.[1] At first blush, this seems a peculiar response, given the fact that the questions driving DeLillo's wayward exploration of waste management at the end of the twentieth century offer neither solace nor comfort. Where, DeLillo asks, does our garbage go? Not just our refuse and our toxic waste, but our memories and all that we collect and preserve to remind us of cherished times gone by? Where does it all go?

The readers who reached in their shelves for *Underworld* weren't seeking to reconnect with DeLillo's questions, though, nor were they trying to wrap themselves in his vision. They just wanted to look once more at the cover of his book, to see André Kertész's grainy picture of the Twin Towers, shrouded in a hazy mist, looming over the belfry of a church, a bird soaring in flight. They just wanted to look away from Ground Zero, hold the book in their hands, and bring the towers back into view.[2]

Whatever relief this provided was only momentary, of course. The towers are gone and what they left behind when they fell is one of the greatest environmental disasters in our nation's history. Few of us would ever willingly choose to contemplate the contents of Ground Zero. Where's the drama, the heroism in sifting through the wreckage? Where's the nobility in the ghoulish work of cleaning up after the tragedy is over and the camera crews have all gone home? Aren't these matters best left to others?

But picking through the trash is precisely what the most important characters in *Underworld* do, and it is the activity, DeLillo believes, that best captures the state of civilization at the end of the twentieth century. This is a realization that Brian Glassic, one of the central characters in *Underworld,* comes to after watching bulldozers move garbage around the Fresh Kills landfill on Staten Island. Where others would look away, Glassic, a waste management engineer, found himself admiring:

> All this ingenuity and labor, this delicate effort to fit maximum waste into diminishing space. The towers of the World Trade Center were visible in the distance and he sensed a poetic balance between that idea and this one. . . . He looked at all that soaring garbage and knew for the first time what his job was all about. Not engineering or transportation or source reduction. He dealt in human behavior, people's habits and impulses, their uncontrollable needs and innocent wishes, maybe their passions, certainly their excesses and indulgences but their kindness too, their generosity, and the question was how to keep this mass metabolism from overwhelming us. (184)

What would happen if we followed DeLillo's lead here and shifted our attention from contemplating civilization's major cultural achievements to tracking the flow of civilization's refuse? Would there be any benefit, say, in retelling the story of September 11 from the point of view of waste management, now that both the "poetic balance" and the distance between the World Trade Center and the Fresh Kills landfill has been eliminated? Consider this a thought experiment, one designed to serve as a limit case in discussions about the value of the humanities at times of crisis. Should a novel be taken this seriously or is lending so much credence to the insights of a fictional character a special kind of madness?

Before embarking on this quixotic journey, we need first to better understand DeLillo's reasons for making waste management the Prime Mover of civilization—an understanding we can only acquire by retracing his steps as he moves through his *Underworld*. The novel's prologue, which bears the recycled title, "The Triumph of Death," provides an extended and loving evocation of the final playoff game between the Brooklyn Dodgers and the New York Giants on October 3, 1951. Throughout this historic contest between the two hometown rivals, the fans throw whatever they can onto the field, the tone and meaning of their actions changing as the game moves into the final innings: "If the early paper waves were slightly hostile and mocking, and the middle waves a form of fan commonality, then this last demonstration has a softness, a selfness. . . . [I]t is happy garbage now, the fans' intimate wish to be connected to the event, unendably, in the form of pocket litter, personal waste, a thing that carries a shadow identity . . . " (44–45). The game ends with Bobby Thomson's improbable three-run homer with two outs in the ninth, handing the victory to the Giants and capping what remains, more than fifty years later, one of the most dramatic comebacks in sports history. Fans pour onto the field as Thomson rounds the bases; there's a mad scramble for the home run ball in the stands; and more celebratory trash rains down.

J. Edgar Hoover, who knows just how much can be learned by going through other people's garbage, is in attendance at the game, but his thoughts are elsewhere. Because he has just been informed that Russia has conducted its second secret testing of an atomic bomb, he cannot share in either the euphoria or the despair unleashed by Thomson's home run. As he watches the trash fall from above, thinking about what the official response to this test will be, a reproduction of Brueghel's *The Triumph of Death* lands at his feet. He picks it up, studies it, and puts in his coat pocket for future contemplation. It is a picture that excites Hoover: "It causes a bristling of his body hair. Skeletons with wispy dicks. The dead beating kettledrums. The sackcloth dead slitting a pilgrim's throat. . . . The old dead fucking the new. The dead raising coffins from the earth. The hillside dead tolling the old rugged bells that clang for the sins of the world" (50–51). As Hoover leaves the stadium, he stops to take in the scene one final time: "He turns toward the field on an impulse and sees another body dropping from the outfield wall, a streaky length of limbs and hair and flapping sleeves. There is something apparitional in the moment and it chills and excites him and sends his hands into his pocket to touch the bleak pages hidden there" (55). The following day, the story of Thomson's blast, which is termed "the shot heard 'round the world," shares the front page of the *New York Times* with the news of the atomic explosion in Russia.

The steep challenge that DeLillo has given himself in *Underworld* is to bring these widely divergent histories into relationship. He is concerned, on one hand, with imagining the itinerary of Thomson's home run ball as it passes through the hands of a string of lost and lonely men foolish enough to invest such things with value. And, on the other hand, he wants to follow the creation, movement, and storage of a kind of trash whose dangers transcend time and pose an ever increasing threat to human civilization as we know it: radioactive waste. In the pages that follow "The Triumph of Death," DeLillo constructs the elaborate narrative infrastructure required to cover the seemingly vast distance that stretches out between these two kinds of trash—the distance that separates the entertaining pleasures of baseball and the serious business of atomic warfare, the trivial and the ominous, the low and the high, the ecstatic and the apocalyptic. To draw these worlds into alignment, DeLillo asks again and again: Where's the ball? The nuclear waste? The B-52s that patrolled the heavens during the Cold War? The secrets we try to keep from one another? Where does everything we value and everything we cast off and everything we forget go?

So posed, these questions seem almost childlike: they are the questions a child asks after losing a cherished object or a loved one. Where do we go when we die? What happens to our bodies after we're gone? By entitling his prologue to *Underworld* "The Triumph of Death," and then placing Brueghel's painting center stage in his narrative, DeLillo convenes his investigation of the ruins and the achievements of the twentieth century with an ominous vision of what lies ahead for us all. No matter how bright and important that ball game seemed at the time to those who were there and to those who read about it the next day and to those who, DeLillo later tells us, *felt* like they had been there, as the stadium emptied at the game's end on that day in October 1951, everything about that moment was already "falling indelibly into the past" (60).

As the novel zigzags across the next forty-plus years, characters come and go, move to the foreground, slip into the background, recede into the past, and disappear without a trace. There's the artist Klara Sax, who works with castoffs and goes to the desert to paint the mothballed bombers of the Cold War; Marvin Lundy, the memorabilia collector, who travels the world in search of Thomson's home run ball; Jesse Detwiler, garbage archeologist, who says that garbage is the cause of civilization because "it forced us to develop the logic and rigor that would lead to systematic investigations of reality, to science, art, music, mathematics" (287); Manx Martin, the con who steals the Thomson ball from his son and then sells it on the street; the Texas Highway Killer, whose "name used to be in the air, always on the verge of being spoken," who remains at large (807). There are chess masters and mobsters, drunks and thieves, names history hasn't yet forgotten—Frank Sinatra, Jackie Gleason, Lenny Bruce, Jane Mansfield—and the nameless, surging crowds.

Underworld's plot, to the degree that it has one, centers on Nick Shay, the eventual owner of the Thomson home run ball and, by the novel's end, an emeritus executive of Waste Containment, a global leader in the waste-hauling business. Over the course of the novel, we learn all of Nick's secrets—the mortal and the venial—and then DeLillo has to make a decision about where to leave this shadowy character. In the epilogue to *Underworld*, over which DeLillo hangs another recycled title, "Das Kapital," Nick Shay and Brian Glassic are sent to Kazakhstan to meet with Viktor Maltsev, who has a plan for making a killing in the post–Cold War economy: he wants to use nuclear explosions to destroy nuclear waste. Keenly aware of the dangers involved with his proposal, Maltsev wants to make certain his American visitors know what they are getting into, so he concludes the tour by taking them to a clinic he has dubbed the "Museum of Misshapens." As Shay and Glassic study the malformed fetuses stored in the pickle jars lining the walls of the room leading into the clinic, Maltsev explains that, during the earlier tests of atomic explosions, the mine shafts "they dug for underground detonations were not deep enough to preclude the venting of dangerous levels of radiation" (799). The miscarriages, stillbirths, and terminal defects are all the result of failures to test and properly dispose of the waste.

Maltsev then takes his guests into the clinic that cares for the survivors who were downwind during and after all these tests. Here, Shay sees blind children, children with cancer, a man with a growth beneath his chin that has "a life of its own, embryonic and pulsing"; he sees "disfigurations, leukemias, thyroid cancers, immune systems that do not function"; and he watches a game of follow the leader that involves limbless children and an eyeless boy (799–802). It is a nightmarish vision, one that shows how the nuclear waste left behind by the Cold War has transformed the imaginary landscape of Brueghel's *Triumph of Death* into a living reality. It is a vision that beckons us to see how the future is being inexorably shaped by an unacknowledged and unexplored past: "All the banned words, the secrets kept in white-washed vaults, the half-forgotten plots—they're all out here now, seeping invisibly into the land and air, into the marrowed folds of the bone" (802–3). Shay turns away from this horrific vision, goes back home, reconciles with his wife, and dedicates his time to something he can control: he begins rearranging his library. And this is where DeLillo discards Shay at the end of *Underworld,* standing "helpless in this desert place looking at the books" (810).

DeLillo turns the last pages of *Underworld* over to Sister Edgar, an aging nun who much earlier in her life had been one of Shay's grade-school teachers. She is, DeLillo tells us, a "fellow celibate and more or less kindred spirit" of J. Edgar Hoover's, sharing the former FBI director's aversion to filth and disorder, wearing latex gloves to protect herself from whatever she might come into contact with as she moves through the Bronx distributing food to the homeless and the dispossessed (826). But nothing can protect Sister Edgar from the violence of the world in which she works. She and another nun, Sister Grace, keep trying to make contact with a homeless girl named Esmerelda who lives in the shadows, always just out of sight. Just as Sister Grace begins to meet with some small measure of success luring Esmerelda in, they learn that they have run out of time. Esmerelda's body has been found. She has been raped and thrown from the top of a building.

How is one to make sense of the assault and murder of a discarded child? What story will satisfy? Sister Edgar falls back on her catechism: "The strength of these exercises, which are a form of perdurable prayer, rests in the voices that accompany hers, children responding through the decades, syllable-crisp, a panpipe reply that is the lucid music of her life. Question and answer. What deeper dialogue might right minds devise?"(815). Sister Edgar runs her mind across a set of answers to those questions, childlike and profound, that are always there, just beneath the surface of DeLillo's *Underworld:* "Who made us? God made us. Those clear-eyed faces so believing. Who is God? God is the Supreme Being who made all things" (815). And she draws hope, as well, from the miraculous appearance of Esmerelda's face on a billboard in the Bronx. Maybe it's just a trick of the light playing over the advertisement at sunset. Or maybe it's a real sign of God's grace. There are plenty of people to believe the latter option, people Sister Edgar joins who gather eagerly at sunset to wait for the subway lights to hit the billboard and for Esmerelda's face to shine through, luminous and reassuring. But then, the spectacle ends just as suddenly as it began. The ad on the billboard is torn down and replaced. Esmerelda's face no longer appears, and the miracle is over.

And what, exactly, does this prove? This is a question DeLillo poses directly to the reader: "And what do you remember, finally, when everyone has gone home and the streets are empty of devotion and hope, swept by river wind? Is the memory thin and bitter and does it shame you with its fundamental untruth—all nuance and wishful silhouette? Or does the power of transcendence linger, the sense of an event that violates natural forces, something holy that throbs on the hot horizon, the vision you crave because you need a sign to stand against your doubt?" (824). Nick Shay rearranging the books in his library. Sister Edgar "passing peacefully in her sleep" (824). DeLillo can offer no unambiguously reassuring answer to what lies on the other side of the underworld. Rather, having opened his meditation in euphoria and fear and then ended back in the same place, he is left only with his own ecstatic vision of what follows the release from the mortal coil, a vision, it should be noted, that could only appeal to those who have devoted their lives to stringing words together. After death has triumphed over Sister Edgar, DeLillo has her meet J. Edgar Hoover in cyberspace, where "[e]verything is connected in the end" (826). And then the writer, seated before his terminal, clicking through the hyperlinks, finds himself confronted with a word that "appears in the lunar milk of the data stream," a word that "spreads a longing through the raw sprawl of the city and out across the dreaming bourns and orchards to the solitary hills." And this word can do nothing more than novels can ever do: "all it can do is make you pensive" (826–27). In DeLillo's postsecular voyage through the underworld, what one finds at the end of the journey, after one has passed over the polluted waters, is this simple word: peace.

———————————————

This is a writing exercise.

First of all there would be the remains of the towers themselves, which together, empty, weighed approximately 1 million tons. Of that, 200,000 tons were steel. There were nearly 50,000 windows covering 600,000 square feet. (This will be particularly important later.) There were 12,000 miles of electric cable; 198 miles of heating ducts; over 100 elevators (D. Johnson).

Estimates immediately after the event as to the total weight of the ruins varied. John Skinner, executive director of the Solid Waste Association of North America, figured 1.25 million tons just for the trade center; another waste industry analyst went all the way up to 2 million tons; FEMA lowballed everyone with a wild guess of 450,000 tons, less than half of what the buildings weighed empty (J. Johnson 1).

But the buildings weren't empty, of course.

With over 1 million square feet of rental space, they were loaded down with desktops and laptops. Mobile phones, stationary bikes, answering machines. Executive chairs and white boards. Room dividers, carpet, ceiling tiles, fluorescent light fixtures, mirrors, urinals, sinks, showers, bathtubs, treadmills, family photos, trophies. Memo pads, post-its, appointment books, day planners, palm pilots. Floppy disks and hard drives, file cabinets and archives, file folders and reports: memories stored on paper, in bits and bytes, and on the cellular level.

Food, refrigerators, freezers, stoves, dishwashers. Toilet paper, tissues, forks and knives, plates, tablecloths, salt-and-pepper shakers, salad bowls, banquet tables, chairs with arms and chairs without. Raincoats, suit coats, pants, dresses, skirts, pocketbooks, wallets, watches, wheelchairs.

And there is more.

The wrecked fuselages of two Boeing 767s. Seat belts and seat backs. Inflatable life boats. Oxygen masks. Over-the-shoulder bags, carry-ons, electric razors, tweezers and pluckers, eyeglasses and contact lenses. All the paraphernalia for the care of tooth and gum.

This is an exercise without end.

———————————————

No one will ever know exactly what was released into the air when the towers collapsed. A week after the attacks, Christie Todd Whitman, director of the Environmental Protection Agency, declared the air in New York City and in Washington DC, "safe to breathe" (Moses). The accuracy of this assessment has since been called into doubt, though, as questions have come to light about: the EPA's measuring devices, the limits of testing only for substances covered by the EPA's Clean Air standards, and the wisdom of focusing exclusively on air quality in lower Manhattan (Garrett 22; Lioy and Gochfeld). Whatever faith one wishes to place in the EPA's initial determination, no one contests the fact that, when the towers fell, the combination of all that falling matter and the ferocious heat produced by the fires created a toxic cloud of unprecedented complexity. This cloud bore many things aloft, including finely ground particles of asbestos and "isolated fragments of ceiling tile, carpet fibers, paper, hair, and concrete pounded so fine that embedded crystals, formed when it hardened, came unglued" (Revkin). In the language of those who specialize in studying airborne toxic events, we are told that most of what settled in these smoky, gaseous clouds was in "the inspirable particle size range": the larger particles showed a preference for coming to rest in "the naso-pharyngeal and tracheo-bronchial regions of the respiratory system," while the "[f]ibrous materials with smaller agglomerated particles, and products of incomplete combustion . . . penetrat[ed] deeper into the respiratory system" (Lioy).

In other words, the heat and the crushing weight created a crucible of sorts for "weaponizing" the toxins in the building. According to a list drawn up by *Environmental Health Perspectives,* the toxins that were released when the towers fell included asbestos, which health officials were immediately worried about, since this known carcinogen was used in the lower sections of each tower before local building code restrictions prevented its further application. But there were also chromium and lead, a carcinogen and a neurotoxin, respectively, both found in computer and video monitors; benzene, released by the combustion of plastics; copper, which can damage internal organs; mercury, which can damage the central nervous system; polychlorinated biphenyls, which can cause reproductive and developmental abnormalities. Diesel fumes, dioxins, Freon, particulate matter, and sulfur dioxide. And then, of course, there was all that glass (Brinley 29). But the difference between all these finely ground particles and the finely ground particles of anthrax that soon after September 11 began making their way into the lungs of other unsuspecting people going about their business is this: weaponized anthrax kills quickly, whereas it takes anywhere from eighteen to thirty years for asbestos to begin registering its fatalities (Schneider).

Just as no one knows exactly what went into the air that day, no one yet knows what the health consequences will be for those who breathed the air around Ground Zero during the moments, days, and weeks that followed the fall of the towers. But studies are already underway to gauge the effect that this "witches' brew" of pollutants has had on the health of: the pregnant women who were in the area at the time; the firefighters and policemen who were involved in the search-and-rescue efforts; the more than two hundred ironworkers who put in twelve- to twenty-hour shifts for months on end to cut the wreckage into movable chunks; the six thousand to seven thousand people who were directly involved in hauling the garbage out of lower Manhattan and in to the Fresh Kills landfill; and even the search-and-rescue dogs who nosed their way through the ruins.[3]

What has already been documented is that many who live and work around Ground Zero and many of those who were caught in the wake of the toxic plume that fanned out from the wreckage over to Brooklyn until the fire was finally extinguished on December 14 have developed what is now called the "World Trade Center cough," a dry, nonproductive hacking cough which is "more syndrome than singular medical condition" (Ricks). Although crushed asbestos was initially thought to be the cause of the WTC cough, it is now believed that the respiratory ailment is brought on by inhaling "microscopic shards of glass, much of it coated with contaminants such as soot, bacteria, mold and human cells," along with highly alkaline pulverized concrete (Garrett, "Air"). While the lungs normally produce mucous to surround inhaled irritants so that they can then be expelled by means of coughing, the highly alkaline character of this particular toxic mixture, combined with the finely ground glass shards, causes the airways to constrict, trapping the contaminants within the host body. For some so affected, the cough can develop into reactive airways dysfunction syndrome, which is characterized by inflammation of the lungs, bronchial tubes, and sinuses; for others, it can evolve into asthma (Ricks). For the thousands of bodies so affected, there is a cough that produces nothing, the wreckage left inside.

According to a time line being developed to track the comings and goings of people at the World Trade Center on September 11, sometime between 9:30 and 9:39 firefighter Danny Suhr arrived and was making his way to the burning buildings with others from the Engine Company 216 in Brooklyn when he was hit and killed by the body of a woman who fell or jumped from the north tower.[4]

Accounts vary as to what happened next. Father Mychal Judge, chaplain for the fire department, appeared on the scene and either as he was administering last rites to Suhr or shortly thereafter he, too, was killed by falling debris. Judge's body was carried down the street to St. Peter's Church, last rites were administered, and the body was then transported to the morgue. Death certificate number 00001 designates Judge the first official casualty of the World Trade Center attack. Firefighters would later joke that this made it possible for Judge to get to heaven first, so he would be on hand when the other members of his flock who died on September 11 started to arrive in droves.

Almost immediately, there was a movement to have Father Mychal declared a saint. For this movement to succeed, though, someone would first have to pray to Father Mychal and he would then have to perform a certified miracle, which, for those who believe such things, would prove that he went straight to heaven and is at this very moment in a position to intercede for the faithful. Soon enough, a story began circulating about a boy named Mychal, born on Christmas Eve, 2001, whose damaged heart healed itself after the doctors' efforts had failed. While this story has all the signs of an urban legend[5]—the child's full name is never given, nor his exact location, nor the specifics of his heart problems—for those who support Father Mychal's canonization, there's no need to quibble over the details: "I know in my heart that Father Mychal is already a saint," one contributor to the Saint Mychal Web site declared. "He is in heaven, flying with the angels and with our Blessed Virgin. God bless him."[6]

It's instructive to stand such stories against the ones the hijackers told themselves as they prepared for their own deaths and the deaths of everyone else who would die along with them that day. They shaved off all excess hair, showered, put on cologne. They prayed for tranquility knowing, as Mohamed Atta put it in his final instructions to all the other team members, that "the time between you and your marriage [in heaven] is very short. Afterwards begins the happy life, where God is satisfied with you, and eternal bliss 'in the company of the prophets, the companions, the martyrs and the good people, who are all good company' [awaits]." As the moment to board the planes approaches, Atta advised, "Do not seem confused or show signs of nervous tension. Be happy, optimistic, calm because you are heading for a deed that God loves and will accept. It will be the day, God willing, you spend with the women of paradise." Having been told they would experience no pain after the first drop of blood had been shed, that there would be no death or judgment day for them because they were martyrs and not suicide bombers, Atta and the other men headed into the skies ("Atta Document"; Lelyveld).

And shortly thereafter the bodies began raining down.

———————————

The *Environmental Health Perspectives* list of contaminants present at the World Trade Center site includes one additional entry: biohazardous material, which arises from "blood and body parts [that] can transmit infectious diseases such as hepatitis and AIDS" (qtd. in Brinley). Given the nature of this calamity, biohazardous material of this kind didn't just fall from the sky, but permeated the site and was borne aloft in the smoky plume that rose from the wreckage in the longest burning structural fire in the nation's history ("Ground Fires").

The exact number of bodies lost when the towers collapsed has been subject to frequent revision. In the earliest moments of the attack, reporters spoke of the 50,000 people who worked in the two towers and there was a general hesitation to hazard a guess as to how many had gotten out before the buildings fell. Later that day, New York City's mayor, Rudy Giuliani, could only say, "We are talking about thousands of people, and I don't think beyond thousands we can be any more precise than that" (qtd. in Reilly). Reports followed that anywhere between 6,000 and 11,000 body bags had been ordered from FEMA for immediate delivery to the medical examiner. Initial estimates placed the death toll above 6,000, but in the months after the attack, this number moved steadily downward. On the first anniversary of the attacks, as the names of the 2,801 known missing and dead were read aloud, the count was again reduced after a duplicated name was discovered and three individuals listed as dead clarified their status as being among the living. Subsequently, the name of another person was blacked out from the list of "heroes of September 11" posted at Ground Zero when it was established that she had survived the attacks.[7] The number now stands at 2,793.

Who died? How? Where? When? These questions, central to any criminal investigation, cannot be answered with complete certainty in this case. According to the *Death Care Business Advisor,* the task of identifying the remains has "presented probably the most challenging forensic effort ever on U.S. soil": the number of bodies involved, the heat of the explosions, the massive impact of the collapse, the sprawling ruins, the time it has taken to sift through the rubble—all of these factors have impeded progress towards delivering buriable remains to the grieving families ("Identification"). "If a body burned at a very high temperature for only a few minutes before falling, tissue, hair and the pulp in the teeth might still be useful for identification": such was the degree of consolation that one of the forensic pathologists called to the scene could offer those waiting for proof that their loved ones were, indeed, gone (Dwyer and Altman 10). But it was clear to Dr. Charles S. Hirsch, New York City's chief medical examiner, as soon as he completed his initial tour of Ground Zero that, for many families, there would never be any conclusive evidence to turn over.

Later, Hirsch recalled his thoughts as he was emptying his pockets of the debris that had collected there during his first walk around Ground Zero: "If reinforced concrete was rendered into dust, then it wasn't much of a mystery as to what would happen to people" (Barry).

Despite Dr. Hirsch's personal feelings of foreboding, it has been his job as chief medical examiner to carry out, as he calls it, "the dialogue with the dead" that lies at the heart of any murder investigation. And so, in this case, he has assumed principal responsibility for overseeing the effort to recover and identify the human remains left behind in and amongst the dust and the rubble (Barry). Little more than a year after the attacks, Dr. Hirsch and his staff had positively identified 1,411 bodies, nearly 700 through genetic testing. There's no telling what else the 15,000 additional, as yet unidentified, remains will yield in the years ahead: as of this writing, for some victims, all that has been identified is a single shard of bone, a smear of cells; in another instance, though, more than two hundred pieces from a single individual have been recovered (O'Shaughnessy). The identification process, which had already cost $58 million by the end of 2002, continued with the goal, Dr. Hirsch said, of reuniting the names and the remains of 2,000 of the victims (Hotz). But by February 2005, the medical examiner's office had "largely ended its effort to identify the remains of those killed at the World Trade Center," leaving more than 1,100 victims unaccounted for, gone without a trace ("Effort").

During the more than nine months it took to remove all the wreckage from Ground Zero, the initial process of separating the human remains from the wreckage was fairly straightforward. First, the wreckage in Manhattan was broken up and loaded into trucks, then moved on to barges, shipped to Staten Island, and hauled off to the Fresh Kills landfill, which was reopened to handle the disaster after having been closed with great fanfare the previous July.[8] Once the debris had been reweighed, it was taken to a remote corner of the landfill, where FBI agents sifted through it first with machines and then by hand. Human remains were put on ice and returned to the medical examiner's on-site morgue, where they were then tagged, logged, and examined by a succession of experts: "the pathologist, the forensic dentist, the fingerprint analyst, the DNA specialist—all in search of something distinguishable, from an inscribed wedding ring to a set of genetic markers." From that point on, efforts were made to match DNA recovered from the remains with DNA taken from the toothbrushes, razors, and hairbrushes that belonged to the missing. When an identification was made, surviving family members were contacted and called in for a consultation. And when they came in, they often asked "whether their loved one jumped from a window" (Barry).

Even those who specialize in the business of death and disaster found discussing remains with surviving family members harder than at any previous time, in part because everyone involved had seen the towers fall over and over again on the news. A member of DMORT—the federal Disaster Mortuary Operational Response Team sent out to assist in processing casualties—used the following terms to describe what it is like to counsel the families of those who perished in the towers under these conditions: "We'll bring out the grid of the site, they'll be taking notes. And in a couple of minutes we're talking about this horrible, unthinkable event, and what happened to the bodies after they died. You kind of float out of yourself sometimes" (Barry).

These families are looking for stories that have an ending of any kind.

As it happens, the science of putting the dead back together again was also at the very center of the trial of America's own homegrown terrorist, Timothy McVeigh. When rescue efforts in the Oklahoma City bombing were abandoned and the Alfred P. Murrah Federal Building had been brought down by additional explosives, a left leg in olive-drab fatigues and a size 7½ combat boot was discovered in the wreckage. McVeigh's lawyers contended that this leg, which was initially determined to have come from a white male, belonged to the person actually responsible for the bombing. Subsequent tests revealed, though, that the leg in question actually came from a black female, one Lakesha Levy, who was a member of the Air Force, and was among those killed in the explosion. Not to be outmaneuvered, McVeigh's lawyers then argued that Ms. Levy must have been buried with the leg that belonged to the real bomber.

In order to pursue this line of inquiry, it was necessary to exhume Ms. Levy's body, reunite it with the appropriate left leg, and then have the left leg that was originally placed in Ms. Levy's coffin sent off to be reevaluated by the FBI. This gambit turned out to be inconclusive, however, since the exhumed left leg had been embalmed, which meant there was no way to extract usable DNA from the sample. This left the door open for the defense to maintain the innocence of their client, while the prosecution countered that the embalmed leg must have belonged to one of the other eight victims who was buried without a left leg (Thomas, "McVeigh Defense" and "2 Sides Agree").

The jury was presented with these opposing theories during McVeigh's six-week trial; they then considered all the evidence and convicted McVeigh of causing the death of 168 people. At his sentencing, in lieu of making a personal statement, McVeigh elected to quote former Supreme Court Justice Brandeis:

"Our Government is the potent, the omnipresent teacher. For good or for ill, it teaches the whole people by its example'" (qtd. in Thomas, "McVeigh Speaks"). After briefly pursuing the appeals process, McVeigh abruptly terminated all efforts to stop his execution.

At the appointed hour, while the families of those who had died in Oklahoma City crowded the teleprompters, McVeigh showed neither the remorse nor the suffering that his audience wanted. Having instructed his lawyers to pass out the poem, *Invictus,* which ends with the lines, "I am the master of my fate; I am the captain of my soul," McVeigh received his terminal injection without saying a word (Kennedy, Ingrassia, and Siemaszko).

When the time came, McVeigh's final act was to show the world his reading list.

———

How much are the lives of those who died at the World Trade Center worth?

For Kenneth Feinberg, speculating about such matters was not an idle activity, since it was his job, as the executor of the federal fund created to compensate families of victims of the September 11 attacks, to come up with an algorithm for determining the relative values of the lost lives. Distributing these monies—Feinberg and those who supported the creation of this fund believe— has been central to the project of addressing the suffering this event has caused. To gain access to Mr. Feinberg's fund and the financial closure it offers, though, claimants had to waive their right to file civil suits stemming from the attack, a requirement many of those affected were initially unwilling to accept.[9] Indeed, a year after the attacks, only fifty-two families had filed for compensation, with the average award offered being $1.57 million.

During this time, lawyers for the Cantor Fitzgerald firm, which lost 658 employees who worked on the upper floors of the north tower of the trade center, filed a brief claiming that Mr. Feinberg's terms for allocating compensatory awards were "unjust and illegal" ("September 11th Victims' Fund"). The problem, at least as the lawyers for Cantor Fitzgerald saw it, was that Mr. Feinberg's plan called for doling out equal awards to all victims with incomes above the ninety-eighth percentile of the national average, even though people in this category might have had very different incomes when they died. More than 250 of Cantor Fitzgerald's bond traders who perished on September 11 were in this elect, high-earning bracket and these individuals, the firm's lawyers argued, were discriminated against posthumously because the compensation fund placed "an artificial lid on payments to high-income employees" (Chen). The

Cantor Fitzgerald brief, which those closely involved in this matter referred to simply as "The Book," alleged that the surviving family members of one of their typical high-end wage earner's would be entitled to a five-million-dollar award, but would only stand to receive an award of roughly three million dollars under Feinberg's system.

Feinberg, faced with the unenviable task of passing judgment on just how far each of the victims fell financially, had to work with the flawed mandate Congress handed him, a mandate forged not by cool heads prevailing in times of strife, but by legislators overwhelmed both by the nation's grief and by the prospect of the potential collapse of the airline industry. Anticipating the sea of lawsuits that would follow in the wake of his work, Feinberg pointed to the unintended consequences that were set in motion by the rapid ratification of the Air Transportation Safety Act, which gave rise to the September 11 Victim Compensation Fund: "Are there no limitations? If somebody is earning $1 million a year, and you run the model, and they could, after offsets, get $10 million—should the taxpayer and this program subsidize a $10 million lifestyle and a $10 million tax-free award? Should 15 percent of the people get 85 percent of the money? That isn't what Congress intended. If Congress had thought this through for more than a few hours, I don't believe that's what they would have said" (qtd. in Belkin).

Predictably—and reasonably enough—the creation of the Victim Compensation Fund led people to ask if the lives of those who died on September 11 were somehow more valuable than those who died in Oklahoma City in 1995. Or those who died in the bombings of the United States' embassies in Kenya and Dar es Salaam in 1998. Or those who died in the anthrax attacks. Or those who died in the attack on the World Trade Center in 1993. Indeed, for a brief moment, it appeared that Congress was going to extend similar benefits to the surviving families of this larger class of victims but, ultimately, no action was taken, proving, as Representative Roy Blunt had predicted: "Some unlucky victims are more unlucky than others" (qtd. in Belkin). Insofar as the budget is concerned, there are those who died in the right place at the right time and there are those who didn't.

In the end, 97 percent of the eligible families accepted Feinberg's terms.

In the final weeks before the fund closed, Feinberg's office was swamped with last-minute claims from injured parties suffering from respiratory illnesses (Chen).

When the World Trade Center was attacked on February 26, 1993, a 1,500-pound bomb, concealed in a rented truck, was detonated on one of the lower parking decks. Six people were killed and more than a thousand others were injured. In the chaos that ensued, some people who were stranded on the upper floors on the towers headed out on to the rooftops, where they were transported to safety by a police helicopter. Subsequently, the fire department, which has no helicopters, agreed with the Port Authority's recommendation that the roof doors should be locked at all times for security reasons (Dwyer, "Investigating 9/11").

When the World Trade Center was attacked again on September 11, more than two hundred people who worked in the south tower tried to get out onto the roof. When they reached the 105th floor, though, they found they couldn't open the doors. Roko Camaj of ABM Window Washing, who was among this group, had a key to get out onto the roof, but the communications system which would have identified him to the people in the security office on the 22nd floor, who had the power to buzz him in, failed (Dwyer et al.).

When the towers came down, they destroyed, among other things, the city's Office of Emergency Management—the disaster command center that had been established, after the attacks in 1993, to coordinate citywide efforts to respond to natural and manmade disasters. Mayor Giuliani had insisted, over objections, that the multimillion dollar "high-tech, super secure emergency command center" be placed at 7 World Trade Center, a decision he later conceded had been a mistake (qtd. in Lipton).

So, add to the list of things amidst the rubble that made its way to Fresh Kills:

State-of-the-art communications equipment, rendered useless by everything that fell from the sky.

And the memorial fountain, carved of rose granite, meant to commemorate those who died in the 1993 attack.

It, too, is gone.

This is hard to believe but add, as well, *The Thinker, The Three Shades, The Burghers of Calais.*

Although *The Gates of Hell* was never definitively completed during Auguste Rodin's lifetime, this monumental project served as something of a lifelong companion for the sculptor and the source of two of his best known works: *The Kiss* and *The Thinker*. Originally commissioned in 1880 to serve as the entranceway to the new Decorative Arts Museum in Paris, which itself had neither been designed nor funded (and ultimately was never built), *The Gates of Hell* seemed misconceived from the start. There was, to begin with, the obvious question of whether or not Dante's *Inferno* provided suitable material for greeting future visitors to a museum meant to house elegant artifacts from the daily lives of the well-to-do.[10] And, although Rodin himself chose the subject matter, driven by the desire to have his own artistic achievements compared both to Dante's and Ghiberti's, he was never able to surmount the contradictions, perils, and ambivalences that came of having an artist so gifted at capturing sensuous and carnal pleasures devote his creative energies to representing humanity after the Fall, where those who give in to the pleasures of the body are doomed to eternal punishment. And so, although Rodin worked on his gates for more than seventeen years, he was never able to get this grand piece, with its representations of over 260 figures contorted in various postures of pain, all falling away, to cohere in any enduringly satisfying way.

The now famous seated couple tenderly embracing in *The Kiss* was originally meant to have its place in Rodin's gates as Dante's ill-fated lovers, Paulo and Francesca, but Rodin removed them from the evolving composition when he realized that his lovers could stand on their own as, among other things, a representation of the transformative and transcendent power of embodied love (Le Normand-Romain 42). And *The Thinker*, perhaps Rodin's best-known work, was originally intended to be Dante, the person responsible for bringing into being this vision of the layered realms of endless punishment awaiting those who betray their Maker. Now, variously known as *The Poet, The Creator*, or *The Thinker*, this tormented figure sits atop Rodin's monument and looks down with frustration, despair, and thinly veiled rage on what the sculptor has made: the weeping, terrorized masses; the suffering, writhing bodies, all struggling to get up and out, all falling inexorably back into the inferno (66).

Above *The Thinker*, there is no purgatory, no paradise, as there is in Dante's *Divine Comedy*. There is only more suffering. *The Thinker*, bent in thought under a frame of skulls, appears beneath *The Three Shades*, three identical, handless figures who stand atop the gates, heads bowed together. Originally meant to hold the admonition to "abandon hope all ye who enter here" that awaits those who descend into Dante's Hell, the slumped, dejected posture of these figures rendered Dante's words superfluous, so Rodin removed the sign. And then he removed the hands that once held it (76).

It's not clear if or when Rodin realized that this project wasn't ever going to come together. Up till the end of his life, he expressed dissatisfaction with the composition, its gaps, its incoherences; after 1900, he is said to have informed Leonce Benedite, who would eventually become the first curator of the Musée Rodin, "the Gates have too many spaces" (qtd. in Le Normand-Romain 28). However much Rodin may have wished to resolve the problems with *The Gates of Hell,* his growing success provided him with many other, more pressing projects that always seemed to demand his immediate attention. The first such distraction came in the form of a commission Rodin received in 1884 from the city of Calais. With the centennial of the French Revolution just five years off and the medieval walls of the old city on the verge of being dismantled to connect Calais to a large industrial suburb, the city planners wanted to produce a monument that would memorialize the historic sacrifice that six of the city's burghers had made to lift the British siege of the city during the Hundred Years' War. For this composition, Rodin chose not to represent the heroic moment when the six burghers volunteered to accept King Edward's terms. Rather, he depicts the six burghers complying with Edward's demand that they come out of the city "with their heads and their feet bare, halters round their necks and the keys of the town and the castle in their hands," heading off to certain death (qtd. in Butler 200).

The men are together, but they are alone, each contemplating what lies ahead. Their faces project resignation, fear, despair. Their bodies are ungainly things with overly large hands, the result of Rodin's evolving practice of assembling "limbs and bodies that had been designed separately, without worrying about the differences in the surfaces" (Barbier). Bodies are repeated. The same forearm, the same foot, show up on different figures. The men are different. The men are the same.

The city of Calais, having expected some noble rendition of the deaths of its heroes, refused to display the grouping at ground level, as Rodin had specified (Butler 295). They placed the *Burghers* on a pedestal, so no one would have to look any of these men in the eye.

Making our way back to Ground Zero, we note that, a quarter of a mile above Manhattan, on the 105th floor of the north tower of the World Trade Center, clients waiting to discuss their concerns about the bond market with representatives of Cantor Fitzgerald used to be able to gaze on selections from Gerald and Iris Cantor's private collection of Rodin's work. In fact, before Howard Lutnick wrested control of the company from founder Gerald Cantor's widow,

Cantor Fitzgerald's logo had been Rodin's *Thinker*. Cantor and his wife had spent more than thirty years amassing some 750 sculptures, prints, and drawings and then promptly began donating substantial pieces of their collection to museums around the world.[11] On September 11, up to one hundred examples of Rodin's work remained in the Cantor Fitzgerald gallery, including a small bronze cast of *The Thinker*, a full-size cast of *The Three Shades*, and a bust of Jean d'Aire from Rodin's *The Burghers of Calais* (Cosentino).

Improbably, workers picking through the wreckage of the north tower came across a severed foot and two headless bodies from *The Three Shades*, along with the bust of Jean d'Aire. While these fragments have since been turned over to representatives from Cantor Fitzgerald, the twenty-eight-inch bronze cast of *The Thinker*, which was last seen in a temporary headquarters the fire department had established near the disaster site, has disappeared again.

At some future date, we are told, Cantor Fitzgerald plans to use these recovered fragments from *The Gates of Hell* and *The Burghers of Calais* in a memorial for the victims of the September 11 attacks (Barry and Rashbaum).

———————————

On the day the towers fell, over eight thousand children attending schools adjacent to the World Trade Center were escorted to safety. One child, on seeing burning bodies falling from the sky, said, "Look, teacher, the birds are on fire!" (Hughes).

———————————

In Oklahoma City, once the ruins of the federal building were removed, the land was cleared and two "Gates of Time" were installed, the first representing 9:01 on April 19, 1995, the second 9:03. In between these gates, there are 168 chairs, a reflecting pool, a survivor tree, a search-and-rescue orchard, a children's play area (*Oklahoma City National Memorial*). In between these gates is everything that each moment holds.

There is much debate about what kind of memorial should be built on the land where the Twin Towers once stood. One plan imagines a tower going up on the site, with the top reserved for a memorial and the lower part for a cultural center. Another calls for a nineteenth-century-style garden, to set the space off from the bustle of hotels, malls, and businesses that will soon enough rush back into the area. And yet another calls for a subterranean monument, one that plunges eighty-five feet below ground level. In the end, it is this last version, which preserves the crushing indentation of all that falling matter, which has beaten out all the competitors (Wyatt).

It's a tricky business, though, this work of representing other people's suffering. When Eric Fischl's bronze, "Tumbling Woman," which depicts a nude woman falling helplessly through space, was installed in the Rockefeller Center a year after the attacks, it generated so many complaints that it was quickly covered over and cordoned off ("After Complaints"). And while Fischl initially apologized for having upset those who saw the sculpture, he later regretted having done so: "I hate this idea," he said, "that there are some people who have a right to express their suffering and others who don't. . . . It's not about necessarily witnessing firsthand that makes the experience. Picasso wasn't at Guernica when it happened; Goya wasn't there on the firing line. This is what a culture looks to art for, to put image, or voice, or context to a way of rethinking, reseeing, re-experiencing" (qtd. in Rakoff).

Not too surprisingly, artists of every stripe have been trying to find a way to process, represent, and perhaps even capitalize on September 11 and its aftermath. *The Guys* tells the real-life story of Anne Nelson, a journalism professor, who helps a fire chief write the eulogy he needs to deliver at the funerals for eight of his fallen colleagues.[12] *Bodies in Crisis,* a compilation of "ten dance poems exploring the emotional, political, and artistic ramifications of the September 11 terrorist attacks," was staged at the Edinburgh Arts Fringe Festival in the Summer of 2002, where one could also see a comic piece, entitled *Tina C's Twin Towers Tribute,* about a drag queen who is trying to use the attacks to revive her career as a country-western singer.[13] Plays, dances, spoofs, sculptures, paintings, poems, short stories, novels, songs, albums, benefit concerts: you don't have to rummage around long to find evidence of artists trying to fashion something new out of what the attacks left behind.

Perhaps the most notable artistic effort in the year following the attacks, though, was the production of the film *11'09''01*. Originally conceived by the French television director Alan Brigand as a way to get a sense of how this "universal catastrophe" was perceived and understood around the world, this project brought together eleven filmmakers from eleven countries. Each director was given an identical budget and told to produce and deliver a film that was 11 minutes, 9 seconds, and 1 frame long in time to be released immediately prior to the first anniversary of the attacks. And they were told, as well, "not to promote hate or violence or to attack peoples, religions or cultures" (Riding).

These clumsy constraints were seen as a way to level the artistic playing field by ensuring that the crews working in the eleven represented countries were all working with roughly the same materials. The results, as one would expect, are quite uneven, but two of the short films do stand apart from the rest. The first, directed by Idrissa Ouedraogo from Burkina Faso, follows a young boy named Adama who has been forced to quit school and sell newspapers because his mother is dying and his father cannot pay the school fees. One day, looking up from a paper announcing the promise of a twenty-five-million-dollar reward for the capture of the leader of Al Qaeda, Adama becomes convinced he has seen bin Laden walking the streets of the capital. Enlisting the help of friends from school, Adama sets out to capture "bin Laden." When the man they are following eludes them and boards a plane leaving the country, the boys burst into tears, crying "Osama, come back! We need you. We need that money!" The message, Ouedraogo has said of his light-hearted response, is that while he sympathizes "with the pain of the families and of the American people," he expects "in return the same wave of solidarity with Africa for malaria, AIDS, famine, thirst."[14]

Mexico's Alejandro González Iñárritu, who describes his short film as an abstract painting in black and white,[15] opens his piece with a darkened screen and a soundtrack that mixes murmuring, mumbling chants, and radio feedback: it is the prayers of the people of Chiapas mixed with sounds of that day. As the sound gets louder, the chanting mixed with a weather report, the screen remains darkened. Someone screams, "Oh, my God! Oh, my God!" over and over again and then there's a white flash on the screen and darkness again. Sounds of news reports about the attack, sirens, more radio feedback; another flash, this one a little longer. The cycle is repeated, the length of the flash of white increasing each time until the image becomes distinguishable. It is some black object moving at great speed against a white background. Then darkness again, more sound: news reports from around the world in many different languages, a woman leaving a phone message in a calm voice, saying, "Honey, I love you. We're having a little trouble on the plane." Another voice from a call-in show saying: "we should not only kill the people responsible for this, but their families and their friends. Everyone we can get our hands on." As the time allotted to the white images continues to lengthen, it becomes clear that the white background is provided by the light bouncing off the concrete of the World Trade Center Towers on that crystal-clear day and that the dark objects racing against this background are human bodies. The sound builds to a final crescendo, the screen is dark, and all we hear are the sounds of the buildings falling and the sirens wailing in the background and then silence. As the screen slowly resolves to white and the soundtrack resumes its murmured prayers, Iñárritu concludes his film with a question that appears in English and in Arabic.

"Does God's light blind us or guide us?"

When asked if he felt that film could be a "weapon for peace," Iñárritu answered candidly: "I would hope so, but unfortunately, the bureaucrats, the politicians, and those who hold power are not going to come see this type of film" (Iñárritu 17). And, indeed, there is no knowing how his short or any of the other ones would have been received by audiences either in England or in the United States. A prerelease review in *Variety*, which circulated widely, declared that several of the segments were "stridently anti-American," and that still others were "fiercely critical of the United States."[16] Subsequently, no distributor in either the United States or in England elected to bring *11'09"01* to the screen. Apparently, the idea that others around the world have suffered and continue to suffer is not something that can be voiced at this time.

This is our Hell.

———————————

On August 22, 1984, Alan Walker and Richard Leakey were taking Sunday off, when Kamoya Kimeu, a member of their archeological team, found a piece of skull embedded in the ground near Lake Turkana in northern Kenya. Although no one realized it at the time, Kimeu had led the team to what—after five painstaking years of brushing and sweeping, chipping and chiseling to move over 1,500 tons of sedimented material—remains to this day the fullest example of the skeletal structure of *Homo erectus* on record. The "hauntingly complete" set of bones that is now variously known as "Turkana Boy," "Nariokotome Boy," or just KNM-WT 15000, has come to occupy a central place in the debate about human origins and the definition of humanness (Walker and Shipman 28). Was *Homo erectus*, who lived in Africa as many as 2 million years ago and then disappeared between 500,000 and 250,000 years ago, human?

For Walker, the answer to this question could only be found by studying *both* the mind and the body of *Homo erectus*, because "the mind has to have a body to work on, and the body has needs and capabilities that set limits on what is possible" (122). But how could one know what went on in the mind of a boy who died more than 1.5 million years ago? All Walker had to work with were the mute bones and his own desire to get them to speak. He and his colleagues learned much about the boy and what his life was like as they studied his remains: they concluded that he may have died when he was no more than nine years old, perhaps of periodontal disease; that he had lost whatever body fur or hair his ancestors had possessed and thus may have relied on panting to generate heat loss in the dry, hot climate that was his home; that he was "tall and thin and probably black"; that "emotionally he may have been more like a twelve- or thirteen-year-old when he died, face down in the muddy, swampy patch"; that he walked upright, made tools, hunted, and traveled in groups; and, finally, that his skull showed evidence of housing a brain that had evolved to include "the Broca area," which governs speech (196–201).

What is it that makes us human? Walker kept returning to this question as he made his way across the topography of the boy's bones. He sent pieces of the boy out to other experts in the field: he wanted to know how the pieces fit together. Was the mind capable of taking full advantage of the body? Was the body capable of taking full advantage of the mind? As the pieces began coming back to him, the evidence began to mount that Nariokotome Boy had a mind-body problem all his own. From Ann MacLarnon and Gwen Hewitt, Walker learned that the narrowness of the nerve canal in the skeleton's thoracic region meant the boy lacked the means necessary for fine control of the intercostal muscles that coordinate inspiration and expiration during the breathing process (261–67). And from Marcus Raichle he learned that new PET scan technology revealed that "the Broca area" actually lies deep within the brain and "cannot make a detectable impression on the interior surface of the skull" (268). Suddenly, having assumed all along that the boy could talk, Walker concluded from these new studies that, regardless of what the boy might have been experiencing in his mind, he lacked the physical infrastructure required to create and control the range of sounds necessary for speech to occur. Thus, while it is certain that the boy and his fellow travelers could grunt and growl and communicate their feelings as animals do, it now appears that they could not speak because they lacked the neural network necessary to generate and control a wide range of sounds while exhaling.

Walker goes further, arguing that, even if the boy's thoracic cavity had been large enough to accommodate the neural network required to control the breathing process, the boy's brain lacked the neurological components required to generate "full language." And this, Walker believes, settles the question of whether or not the boy and his kind were, in the final analysis, human. Drawing on the work of Derek Bickerton, Walker describes the value of full language in the following terms: "The basis for full language . . . was a sort of mapping function, a means of representing the world internally. . . . The more complex this internal or mental prerepresentational system is—the more categories we can create for classifying the infinite number of items, sensations, and actions that we sense or think about—then the more distanced we are from the reality before us. . . . This distance has the advantage of freeing us from the tyranny of the present: it permits us to think about circumstances or events that are not occurring and may never occur. And, Bickerton notes, in order to achieve consciousness—in order to 'stand outside yourself' and look at (or think about yourself)—there must be somewhere else to stand. Without a detailed mental symbol that represents yourself, you cannot think about yourself in any complex way" (277). So defined, the essence of humanity is seen to reside in a complex of cognitive abilities concerning the representation of the self and the passage of time: to be human is to be able to step out of the moment, to be able to represent oneself to oneself and to others, and to be able to reflect on what has been and to consider what might be.

The paleoarcheologist, bent over the work table, slowly brushing away the dust, piecing together the bones, building an abstraction, imaging the possibilities, conveying the results to others: this is one example of what it means to be fully human. And working with this definition, Walker is drawn to a conclusion he never wanted to reach: the bones he had been studying for more than a decade were the remains of "an animal in a human body" (296). Walker closes his book, *The Wisdom of the Bones,* by describing his research as an effort to transport himself back to the time when Nariokotome Boy walked the African savannah. But when Walker pictures himself moving toward the boy, "preparing mentally to hail him and at last make his acquaintance in person, it was as if he turned and looked at me. In his eyes was not the expectant reserve of a stranger but that deadly unknowing that I have seen in a lion's blank yellow eyes. He may have been our ancestor, but there was no human consciousness within that human body. He was not one of us" (294).

If we keep digging through all the possible connections, from death and the shattered remains to art and language, driven onward by the image of falling bodies, we find, by chance, *Writing Down the Bones,* perhaps the best-selling writing guide of all time. Author Natalie Goldberg's goal is to provide her reader with nothing less than access to the creative potential and imaginative power she believes all humans possess. By getting her readers to "write down the bones," which she defines as finding "the essential, awake speech of their minds," Goldberg believes she is helping them to become more human. And to open these doors, Goldberg provides her readers with a set of exercises and routines that will help them give voice to their deepest hopes and fears. This is the defining practice for her and it all boils down to paying attention to details, expectations, disappointments, surprises: write about what is in front of you, be a tourist in your own town, be an animal, use loneliness.

And how does Goldberg feel when it is all over, when all the exercises have been gone through and her book is done? Does it all come together? In the epilogue to *Writing Down the Bones,* Goldberg describes feeling sad and scared that her project has come to an end. The final image she leaves us with is this: writing is to be understood as an "alone journey" and now that she's finished she doesn't know what to do, so she calls her father and tells him she wants to throw herself off the top of the Empire State Building.

And he says, "Do you have to pick such a high building?"

And she tells herself it's OK. There will be more books to write (169–70).

———————————————

No writer had more immediate access to Ground Zero than William Langewiesche, an investigative reporter for the *Atlantic Monthly*. While all the other reporters were standing in line trying to get press passes, Langewiesche was faxing the Office of Emergency Management, which had nominal responsibility for organizing the cleanup, and Kenneth Holden, the man at the NYC Department of Design and Construction who was in charge of all the heavy equipment on the site. Holden, as it happened, knew Langewiesche's work with the magazine and had read his books on flying; Holden pulled strings from the inside and Langewiesche ended up with an engineering pass that gave him "full access to every part of the site, as well as full access to the meetings and to the files."[17] Nine months later, when Ground Zero had been cleared and all the wreckage and remains had been hauled off to Fresh Kills, Langewiesche was putting the finishing touches on *American Ground: Unbuilding the World Trade Center,* a book that collects together three lengthy essays on the collapse of the towers, the flight of the airplanes, and the mining and excavation efforts that followed.

There is much about this book that has troubled reviewers: Michiko Kakutani described Langewiesche's account as "coldblooded," "self-congratulatory," and "weirdly voyeuristic." Rhonda Roland Shearer, director of the World Trade Center Living History Project and Marcel Duchamp scholar, has posted on the Web a thirty-three page long catalog of fifty-six factual errors and misstatements in Langewiesche's account as it appeared in the *Atlantic Monthly* and has called for "retraction, apology, and book-shredding" of *American Ground* (qtd. in Hagan). Firefighters around the country have protested the book's publication, objecting to a passage in *American Ground* that repeats a story told at the site about looting by a fire crew while the towers burned.[18] And one of the local papers in New York, *Newsday,* put together an entire multimedia unit on the controversy for schools to use: students are asked to read an article that describes the protest and includes a quote from a firefighter saying, "*American Ground* is a piece of trash that belongs in the Fresh Kills dump"; then they are to watch a video clip of a news broadcast on the protest; then they are to take a multiple choice test; then they are to write an editorial on the freedom of the press, making sure to show both sides of the issue, so as not to "seem dictatorial and closed-minded."[19]

This much hasn't changed.

Asked to describe the most lasting impression he took from the six months he spent following the effort to clean up Ground Zero, Langewiesche speaks of the kindergarten rooms at P.S. 89, which served as recovery headquarters. Here, amidst the miniature furniture, Langewiesche felt he saw a new kind of culture emerging, one where "full-grown men and women, including powerful executives and renowned engineers, sat around as if they were playing at being children again" (65). Here, "the high and the low were rubbing shoulders, and all were having to define themselves anew in life. Good solutions were being rewarded. But maybe more importantly, stupidities, mistakes, and bad ideas were being acknowledged as such, but people were not punished for them. It was quite surprising to see the level of intellectual maturity that was emerging spontaneously in this fantastic environment, with people sitting around at kids' desks and chairs" (qtd. in Stossel).

In this pragmatic space, there was, for some brief time, a sense of shared purpose.

There is no judgment day.

There is only what we choose to do to fill each moment as it passes.

5

THE ARTS OF COMPLICITY

> Admission to Harvard has never meant so much to so many. At
> a time when American parents seem palpably nervous about
> the nation they will bequeath to their children and when the
> mere fact of a college education has diminished in value as a
> ticket to success, the elite colleges—the Harvards, Yales, Stan-
> fords and Princetons—look more desirable than ever. Harvard
> routinely receives applications from more high-school vale-
> dictorians . . . than it could admit even if it were admitting only
> valedictorians . . . (Weber 46)

The year is 1996 and, unbelievably, James A. Hogue is up to his old tricks
again. Back in 1988, Hogue had wormed his way into Princeton by posing
as "Alexi Indris-Santana," a self-educated orphan with a hard-luck story and remarkably high SAT scores. For obvious reasons, university officials were not
amused when they discovered that the nineteen-year-old "Alexi" they had admitted was not, in fact, a ranch hand who read Plato under the stars while herd-
ing cattle in a canyon called "Little Purgatory," but was, rather, a twenty-nine-
year-old bicycle thief who had delayed his entry into Princeton for a year, not

because his long-lost mother was dying of leukemia in Switzerland, but because he was in jail. This being no laughing matter, the authorities at Princeton had Hogue thrown back in jail on the charge of "theft by deception" for having illegally received $22,000 in financial aid. Incredibly, as soon as Hogue was released, having served half of his nine-month sentence, he "resumed" his studies at Princeton in 1996, hanging around the library, eating in the dining hall, and telling people he was Jim MacAuthor, graduate student! Things seemed to be going quite well on this go-round until the hybridic, phase-shifting Hogue/Indris-Santana/MacAuthor was once again recognized by a real student, who brought the ruse to the attention of the authorities, who, in turn, promptly had Hogue put back in jail for violating his parole.[1]

Around the time Hogue was trying to pass himself off as a graduate student from Princeton, genuine graduate students at Yale were gaining national attention with their efforts to unionize in protest of their working conditions as teaching assistants. Reactions to the strike were quite varied, though shock and outrage made dependable showings throughout the profession's discussion of this development. The Modern Language Association weighed in with its now famous "Resolution 6" to censure Yale's administration and faculty for having threatened graduate student union organizers and all those who participated in the grade strike with academic reprisals, "including withheld letters of recommendation, disciplinary letters, academic probation, firing of teachers, denial of promised teaching jobs, or expulsion" (MLA, "Professional Notes," 542). After the MLA's Delegate Assembly voted to censure Yale's administration at the MLA's winter convention in December 1995, it was discovered that the resolution had been advanced by someone ineligible for membership in the MLA—another false student gumming up the works. Despite this procedural irregularity, the resolution was forwarded to the general membership for its consideration on the June 1996 MLA Special Ballot, accompanied only by statements from Yale faculty condemning the organization for trying to meddle in its affairs. While the debate about the resolution raged on for another year or so,[2] the strike itself collapsed shortly after the Delegate Assembly's supportive, but ultimately ineffectual, vote at the winter convention in 1995. Faced with the threat of losing their jobs in the spring semester and the university's unflinching insistence that they were "students, not employees," the striking teaching assistants at Yale submitted their grades and returned to work.

Those on the outside trying to break in, those on the inside trying to break out. It's an odd pair. Add to this another Ivy League story—this one from Harvard, where junior faculty in English are required to teach a sophomore tutorial once a year for prospective majors who intend to pursue an honors degree. In her article, "Pedagogy and Psychoanalysis: A True Story," Barbara Claire Freeman uses her experience teaching one of these tutorials as the occasion to consider the unintended consequences of having put together a course "that foregrounded connections between desire and language," and prepared students "to ask questions about relationships between gender and culture" (8). Standard enough work, to be sure, with the standard fare (Freud, Lacan, Foucault) as required reading. Things took an unexpected turn one day, though, when Freeman illustrated Foucault's discussion of the relationship between sexuality, discourse, and power with the following statement: "'How strange,' I said, 'There was no such thing as date-rape when I was your age, and I don't know if that's because it didn't happen or because it just wasn't discussed. Isn't it weird that language that looks as if it's telling the truth about date-rape may also produce it?'" (11).

A few days later Freeman found out just how "weird" this idea of language's productive powers could be when Teresa, her favorite student in the tutorial, asked to speak with her after class. Freeman says of this student that, in her class participation, she "translated my inarticulate stutterings into speech, heard what I could not articulate, and gave it back to me" (10). In her office, Freeman learned that, sometime after the class discussion on Foucault, Teresa had gone out on a date with a classmate she "had talked to a lot, but hadn't been alone with." She went to his room because she thought, "this is what people do here and it will be all right." And then she was sodomized by her fellow Harvardian. At the time, Freeman didn't think "about the proximity between the class's discussion of date-rape and Teresa's experience (or orchestration?) of it." Rather, she listened to her student's story, got her in touch with a trusted counselor, gave her a hug. In the process, Freeman realized that she'd "heard enough to understand why therapists—some of them anyway—love their work" (12–13).

Unlike the first two stories, the author of this third story, the "true" one, is determined to provide a happy ending. Teresa's rape, which Freeman's theory bids her to entertain as possibly an "orchestration," becomes a largely inconsequential event in itself, particularly when put in balance with all that it has made possible. After all, Freeman has learned about the appeal of therapy; she's had an experience that has helped her to think about psychoanalysis and the impossibility of pedagogical mastery; and, though she claims to have "no professional reason" for having written up the event, she's managed to improve her CV in the bargain. And Teresa? Equally good news! According to Freeman, her "therapy was short-term, but helpful; she has read this essay and is glad to see it published; we have become friends; most importantly, she is happy and thriving" (15). Here, as the house lights come up, teacher and student dissolve into one another.

When I read stories like these about the conflicting aspirations of administrators, teachers, and students, some of whom are also teachers-to-be, I am reminded of those primary-school projects designed to illustrate the contours of a magnetic force field, where iron filings, randomly spread across a sheet of paper, quickly form lines of force stretching from pole to pole as soon as the magnet is introduced beneath the page. In this instance, these stories illustrate the ways in which the allure of expertise serves both to organize the actions of all who enter the academy's social field and to produce, in turn, the academy's peculiar pathologies, its class distinctions, its tales of violation and success. The analogy isn't perfect, of course, but it rings truest in its ability to capture the helplessness of those caught in this field where, like those spinning, falling, frozen iron filings, no one seems quite able to pry themselves free from the power and the promise of an institutionally conferred pedigree. And like the disinterred creatures in George Romero's *Dawn of the Dead* who crowd the malls of America hopelessly searching for something to satisfy the insatiable hunger of the living-dead, Mr. Hogue, with his soul mates in the other stories not far behind, can't help but return to the site of his wounding, seeking to heal the sense of inferiority that seems to be his birthright. If only he could get a better disguise, forge some more convincing identification papers, become, in other words, less visibly out of place in the world of higher education, he wouldn't have to traffic anymore with the real frauds imprisoned by the tawdry desires of the marketplace. He could lift himself up into the ideal world, where rape is but an act of signification and union busting is deftly transformed by our best minds into an act of generosity.

I'm being deliberately outrageous here, indulging myself in the dominant discursive mode of the talk-show age—the polemic. Doing so is not without its amusements or payoffs, since whatever the polemic costs one in credibility is, presumably, immediately recovered with interest by the sweepingly persuasive force of a rhetoric that invites no response. This isn't the return I'm seeking, however. Rather, I have hoped, by opening in this way, to jar the ordinariness out of the question that will preoccupy me in what follows: Who, exactly, is it who might be said to have "false consciousness"? I hope, as well, to delay the obvious answers to that question. For, if we return to the examples discussed above, can we say that false consciousness resides with Mr. Hogue, the student impersonator who apparently believes that proximity to an elite institution might benefit him materially? Or it is the school officials who exhibit the signs of false consciousness in their steadfast insistence that the selective admissions process reliably separates those worthy of a higher education from those who aren't?[3] It's even harder to say who the mystified ones are in the case of the Yale strike. Is it the graduate students who were shocked to find that the administration and faculty, including those whose professional work focuses on questions of social and economic injustice, were willing to play hardball? Or is it those in power who have maintained that this is just a family squabble, that the graduate students who teach undergraduates are not employees, and that, in any event, "it is unreasonable for graduate students at this stage in their career to expect to earn a living wage"? (MLA, "Special Ballot," 4). And, with regard to the final case, is it the student—the one we are told is happy that her teacher transformed her date-rape into so much cultural capital—who now possesses false consciousness? Or is it her teacher, so eager to believe that the violence done her student is suitable material for some speculations about pedagogy and Lacanian theory?

When the problem is posed in this way, it may well seem as if the whole educational system is shot through with false consciousness and that everyone involved is crashing about in a mystifying haze they themselves have produced by believing in their own rank superiority. In effect, these news stories seem to conjure an apocalyptic vision of the world upside down, where teachers emerge as advocates of sexual violation, economic oppression, rigid social stratification. A world turned so far upside down that the students themselves are caught in the caterwauling inversion, tumbling thoughtlessly into the waiting arms of the academic and penitential institutions, which are, of course, only too ready to grind them up and then grind them down, profiting off their misery all the while.

Enough already.

The polemic may serve to get people's attention, but it is structurally incapable of delivering an argument that invites engaged response. While it amuses those who already agree with the speaker's point of view, everyone else has to just hunker down and wait for the blustering and chest thumping to come to an end so they can go on about their business as before. And for those who can't wait it out, if the windy rhetoric blows strong enough for long enough, they may well find themselves momentarily pried loose from their moorings and suddenly at sea in the nodding mass of fellow believers. The polemic is, thus, nothing more than a bully's rhetoric, a discursive act meant to force all present to acknowledge the bully's mastery of the subject at hand. In this case, that subject is the scene of instruction and our ways of telling the story of what goes on there. Much more frequently, though, the polemic is called on when the subject is global politics, economic theory, foreign policy, social justice. I will consider other uses of polemical juxtaposition shortly. For now it suffices to say that turning the world upside down as I have here may have helped to get false consciousness—that root concept for all liberatory pedagogues—back on the table for consideration, but it has done so at the considerable cost of making subsequent discussion all but impossible.

So, let me begin again.

LETTING THE STUDENTS GO

> Those truly committed to liberation must reject the banking concept in
> its entirety, adopting instead a concept of men as conscious beings, and
> consciousness as consciousness intent upon the world. They must
> abandon the educational goal of deposit making and replace it with the
> posing of the problems of men in their relations with the world.
>
> —Paulo Freire, *Pedagogy of the Oppressed*

For over thirty years, Paulo Freire's name and his writings have signified the brightest hopes of those who teach others how to work with words. Nowhere is Freire held in higher esteem than in the field of composition, where to invoke Freire's name is to declare one's allegiance to education as a practice of freedom and one's commitment to "revolution," "liberation," "conscientization," "problem-posing." And so, when scholars outside of composition wish to join in the field's discussions about the political consequences of teaching reading and writing, they turn, more often than not, to Freire's work to establish the sincerity of their interest in pedagogical practice and the depth of their belief that pedagogy and politics are inextricably intertwined. Citing Freire is, thus, a way of establishing one's credentials in the field, of showing one's true colors. We see this, for example, in Jane Tompkins's much discussed "Pedagogy of the Distressed," where Tompkins links her discovery of "a way to make teaching more enjoyable and less anxiety-producing" to a set of reflections prompted by Freire's insistence that "you cannot have a revolution unless education becomes a practice of freedom" (656, 653). We see this, as well, in bell hooks's *Teaching to Transgress,* where hooks identifies Freire as one of two teachers who has deeply influenced her efforts to enact a liberatory practice that "enables transgressions—a movement against and beyond boundaries" (12). Since Freire's death in 1997, such public testimonials have proliferated exponentially. Indeed, at the field's national conference in 1998, all presentations that reflected Freire's influence were identified in the program and a special session was convened to posthumously commemorate Freire's contributions to the teaching of writing. By 1998, Freire's status had risen to the point where he was declared by Kate Ronald and Hephzibah Roskelly, in their award-winning book, *Reason to Believe*, to be a romantic pragmatist in the tradition of Emerson, Thoreau, Dewey, and James!

What are those of us who teach writing to make of Freire's place in our profession's history? Why does his representation of the power of teaching hold such an appeal for so many of us? From a certain perspective, the answer to these questions is obvious. Freire has given teachers a way to see themselves as something other than the mindless functionaries of the state apparatus responsible for tidying the prose of the next generation of bureaucrats. His liberatory pedagogy offers a powerful critique of dominant educational practice, foregrounding the politics of teaching and the emptiness of equating education with vocationalism; it recognizes the interrelationship of word and world, language and power; it requires teachers to construct a teaching practice that is responsive to the students' needs and abilities. And, of course, Freire's well-known critique of "the banking concept" of education has succinctly captured all that is wrong with a teaching practice that has teachers deposit the oppressor's knowledge in the students in such a way that the students are sure to remain docile, unthreatening servants of the state. Freire's work has, in short, given weapons of resistance to those dissatisfied with instrumentalist approaches to education: it has offered a critical vocabulary; a philosophically grounded, politically defensible pedagogy; a vision of a better world.

When I entered graduate school in the mid-1980s, I was among those swept away by Freire's vision and the possibilities opened up by renaming the goal of our work in the classroom "conscientization." Having spent three years employed as a "learning skills specialist" on the margins of a major research university, I was only too well acquainted with institutional indifference and its consequences. I longed to work in the learning environment Freire described, where institutionally enforced passivity was eliminated and the teacher, as problem-poser, created, "together with the students, the conditions under which knowledge at the level of the *doxa* is superseded by true knowledge, at the level of the *logos*" (68). In such a place, where students were moved from *doxa* to *logos*, from belief to "true knowledge," the groundwork for radical social change was being laid.

But when I actually set out to take Freire's words off the page and put them into practice in the world, I ran into a set of difficulties that, in retrospect, seem all too predictable: many of my students resisted the "politicization" of the classroom; those who didn't seemed overly eager to ventriloquize sentiments they didn't believe or understand; and, at the end of the semester, no matter how spirited and engaging the discussions had been, the quality of the writing I received seemed, if I was honest with myself, to vary little from work elicited in other, more traditional classrooms. That there are problems involved in adopting Freire's pedagogy, which was originally developed to address the needs of the illiterate and dispossessed peoples of Brazil, to teach undergraduates in the United States is now widely recognized.[4] What I wish to consider here is a rather different matter, though: why is it that this image of the teacher as liberator of the oppressed has such an enduring appeal? Or, to put this another way, working in the spirit of Freire's own pedagogical practice, what can we learn by problematizing our community's most cherished self-representation? If we aren't in the business of liberation, uplift, and movement, however slow, toward a better social world, what exactly is it that we're doing in our classrooms?

LIBERATION AND THE OBEDIENT RESPONSE

Given the choice between the "mechanistic," "necrophilic," banking model of instruction and the life-affirming, consciousness-raising, history-transforming pedagogy of the problem-poser, it's not hard to see why so many of us have been swept away by the rhetoric of Freire's emancipatory practice and have continued to deploy it long after our own experiences have demonstrated its inutility. Of course, Freire long ago anticipated the possibility that his problem-posing approach would be accused of being nothing more than the banking concept in disguise, one that openly extolled the virtues of freedom while subtly enforcing a solidarity of vision. To counter such charges, Freire insisted from the beginning that the problem-posing approach had to "be forged *with,* not *for,* the oppressed (whether individuals or peoples) in the incessant struggle to regain their humanity" (33). Freire's commitment to a pedagogy that at every stage enacts a participatory politics creates a significant problem for him at the level of practice, for, as Freire himself puts it, "how can the oppressed, as divided, unauthentic beings, participate in developing the pedagogy of their liberation?" (33). That is, if one begins, as Freire does, by casting the oppressed as the faceless masses who have been deluded into accepting their own powerlessness, then "collaborating" with them seems positively counterproductive. After all, given *their* false consciousness, *their* "divided, unauthentic beings," *their* lust for material rewards over communal gains, what could *they* possibly have to contribute to the revolutionary project?

Freire's resolution to these seeming contradictions is straightforward enough, though not without its own complications. In order for the oppressed to participate actively in the creation of their own pedagogical apparatus, they must first realize that they have become host bodies for the oppressor's ideology and that they have molded their lives to conform to this ideology's image. To assist the oppressed in acquiring this insight, Freire sent teams of investigators to the communities that had been targeted for his educational project. These investigators approached the area "as if it were for them an enormous, unique, living 'code' to be deciphered" (103). Working in concert with local representatives, over time the investigators detected "generative words" and "generative thematics," revealing the contradictions that lie at the core of the target community's world of concerns. These words and themes were then codified in familiar images from the community and then "re-presented" to the learners for reflection. The learners would look at a picture of a well, say, and women carrying water bottles; they would decode the images; they would begin to speak of their frustrations about access to clean water in their neighborhoods; and, when the coordinator posed "as problems both the codified existential situation and their own answers," the learners would begin to make connections between the themes evoked by the images and their own positions of powerlessness (110). And, presumably, as the learners come to such realizations by having their "false consciousness of reality" posed to them as a problem or "through revolutionary action, developing a consciousness which is less and less false," they begin to liberate themselves from the oppressor's dehumanizing ideology (125).

One might think that turning to Freire's own examples of what his pedagogy looks like in practice would help to further clarify the differences between the banking and problem-posing methods. As it turns out, though, *Pedagogy of the Oppressed* provides only the briefest glimpses of what it means to be a student under the problem-posing system, devoting its attention, instead, to presenting the theory and the methodology that give rise to liberatory practice. Curiously, when the scene of instruction does surface in *Pedagogy of the Oppressed,* it seamlessly illustrates the smooth functioning of Freire's liberatory machine and the ease with which those in his system come to see the error of their former ways. Thus, for example, after Freire has argued that the oppressed internalize a logic of self-depreciation, he turns to one of his educational meetings to show how this logic can be exposed and dismantled. Here, we are treated to the following quote from an unidentified Chilean peasant: "They used to say we were unproductive because we were lazy and drunkards. All lies. Now that we are respected as men, we're going to show everyone that we were never drunkards or lazy. We were exploited!" (50). And, in another example, where workers in Santiago were asked to discuss two pictures—one of a drunken man

walking on the street and another of three young men talking on a street corner—Freire records the workers' open identification with and defense of the
drunken man. For Freire, this response proves the value of the problem-posing
method, which in this instance allowed the workers to say "what they really felt"
(111). Although the liberatory pedagogue might not be pleased to hear the
workers defending drunkenness, the liberatory pedagogue must accept the fact
that conscientization begins with the subjective perception of the world of lived
experience and only then "through action prepares men for the struggle against
the obstacles to their humanization" (112). Thus, in the first example, the Chilean peasants come to see that they never were drunkards, but rather were oppressed; in the second, the workers from Santiago have taken their first steps
toward changing their lives by objectifying and naming their own way of being
in the world. In both cases, it seems, the drunken consciousness is on its way to
sobering up.

Freire offers up these examples of spontaneous assent as illustrations of
the positive effects of his practice and we just have to take his word for it that
the workers in these learning situations were saying "what they really felt"—on
the assumption, perhaps, that the illiterate and downtrodden can only speak
without guile or nuance or that Freire, in some way, knows how to divine when
such authentic speech has occurred.[5] Of course, in order to maintain the essential distinction between the problem-posing and the banking pedagogies, Freire
must insist that those on the receiving end of his approach are free to come to
whatever conclusions they like because problem-posing leeches the power dynamic right out of the teacher-student relationship. While conceding that all
teachers have "values which influence their perceptions," Freire nevertheless
adamantly insists that the only value his teachers seek to share with the oppressed "is a critical perception of the world, which implies a correct method of
approaching reality in order to unveil it" (103). Given Freire's examples of the
ever-pliable peasantry and the force of his own argument, however, it is hard to
believe that the "critical perception of the world" he seeks to impart through
the problem-posing method is meant to produce anything other than a new
citizenry with a shared set of values. What else could the outcome be of teaching others ways to "unveil" reality, to shed their "false consciousness," to "cut the
umbilical cord of magic and myth which binds them to the world of oppression" (176)?

One reason that Freire's pedagogy has so much appeal is that it comes
armed with a rhetoric that overwhelms and neutralizes any effort to point out
this tension between an insistence on a collaborative methodology, where
people are taught not what to think but how, and a practice that, almost magi-

cally, produces people who know exactly what to think about injustice and how it should be redressed. Freire explains that those who resist his pedagogy with the complaint that they are being led by the hand to certain foregone conclusions respond in this way because they have begun "to realize that if their analysis of the situation goes any deeper they will either have to divest themselves of their myths, or reaffirm them" (155). Since divestment involves the painful process of renouncing whatever privilege it is that one has acquired, Freire continues, some choose instead to "reaffirm" their myths by accusing his pedagogy of "their own usual practices: *steering, conquering, and invading*" (155; emphasis in original). In other words, with this brilliant reversal, Freire argues that those who feel that they are not, in fact, free or equal collaborators in his venture are the ones most lost to "false consciousness"—they are, in effect, the bankers among us.

As Freire would have it, "well-intentioned professionals" are the ones most likely to fall prey to this way of thinking: they understand that following out his method of analysis would require that they "cease being *over* or *inside* (as foreigners) in order to be *with* (as comrades)" and they are afraid (154; emphasis in original). Borrowing a phrase from Louis Althusser, Freire then goes on to say that, although these professionals are "men who have been 'determined from above' by a culture of domination which has constituted them as dual beings," and despite the fact that they "are in truth more misguided than anything else, they not only could be, but ought to be, reclaimed by the revolution" (156). Althusser argues in "Ideology and the Ideological State Apparatuses" that it is precisely the function of schools to misguide professionals in this way: "the school (but also other State institutions like the Church, or other apparatuses like the Army) teaches 'know-how,' but in forms which ensure *subjection to the ruling ideology* or the mastery of its 'practice.' All the agents of production, exploitation and repression, not to speak of the 'professionals of ideology' (Marx), must in one way or another be 'steeped' in this ideology in order to perform their tasks 'conscientiously'" (128). In effect, then, these professionals—who include in their number, of course, university graduates and, more importantly, their teachers—are more deeply committed to their mythic and magical beliefs than the workers beneath them. And, were it not for Freire's calm reassurance that these professionals "not only could be, but ought to be, reclaimed by the revolution," one might be forced to conclude that these misguided souls might be better off dead.

Again, what puzzles me is why this vision of teaching and the accompanying visionary rhetoric that surrounds it should appeal to teachers, particularly teachers of reading and writing. Why, as a profession, would we be drawn to an approach that depicts professionals in such a negative light? Is it the institutionally marginalized position of composition instruction that allows us to see ourselves as somehow beyond the reach of Freire's critique? Do we imagine ourselves as standing outside the very system that employs us to instruct entering students in the language arts? Is there something about literacy work that makes its practitioners immune to the desires for advancement upon which hierarchical systems depend? Or is the vision of the teacher as liberator just a story teachers like to tell themselves about themselves—a way to make it from semester to semester that preserves whatever remains of the teacher's sense of self-esteem? In other words, is the appeal of the image of teacher as liberator itself proof that liberatory teachers are, in fact, filled with the very false consciousness that they're determined to eradicate in others?

"THE SEMIOTIC RICHNESS OF 'I DON'T KNOW'": PARODY AND COMPLIANCE IN THE CLASSROOM

When I first assigned Althusser's "Ideology and Ideological State Apparatuses" to undergraduates in an introductory cultural studies course I was teaching a few years ago, an entirely unexpected thing happened: the students loved it. Once they made their way through the echo chamber of his prose (the Ideological State Apparatus functions by ideology, it greases the wheels for the reproduction of the relations of production), they delighted in the work of enumerating the myriad ways in which the school system, as the prime example of an Ideological State Apparatus (ISA), had been designed to transform them into mindlessly obedient automatons. And, indeed, it was not difficult for us to see how the functioning of the Ideological State Apparatus, as Althusser defines it, made itself known in every aspect of the pedagogical encounter: the teacher stands, the students sit; the teacher speaks, the students listen; the teacher questions, the students answer; the teacher examines, the students are graded; the teacher has a name, the students are only numbers.

The following response captures the general analytic turn the students adopted in cataloging how fully the school system constrains student behavior: "from the start of school, educators constrain the student to calmness and obedience, and exert pressure upon him so that he may learn to conform to and respect conventions. In time, this constraint ceases to be felt and gradually gives rise to habit and instinct that render constraint [un]necessary. By the time the student reaches college, he instinctively remains quiet during lectures and unconsciously sits in a particular seat habitually without verbal suggestion of the professor" (Hong 6). Joy Hong, the author of this piece, went on to maintain that, after all these years of training in appropriate classroom behavior, students develop a repertoire for working against these constraints in socially accept-able—that is, in all but unnoticeable—ways. For proof, Joy cited informants who described sitting in aisle seats and at the back of the lecture hall so they could get out of class and away from their professors more easily. But even these slight gestures of resistance, Joy asserted, are captured by the dominant system: "though [the students] exercise power and control in seeking out their own or-der, they do it within the propriety that preserves and legitimizes the ruling ide-ology" (5). There is, it would seem, no way out—the forces of control are so powerful that the best a student can do is sit on the periphery in a mute act that further establishes the student's ultimate acceptance of domination.

To be honest, when I received this particular response, I wasn't sure whether Joy was putting me on or not. Having been asked, in light of our course work with Clifford Geertz and Janice Radway, to pursue an ethno-graphic study of some aspect of the culture of schooling, Joy seemed to have intentionally elected to focus on the most banal behavior she could find—why students sit where they do in class and why they tend to repeatedly return to those same seats during the rest of the semester. Over the course of her ex-tended analysis of this topic, Joy wavered close to parodying the kind of cultural studies we had been doing throughout the semester. So, for example, when she found that her informants didn't have much at all to say about why they sat where they did, Joy asked, perhaps mockingly, "Could I have overlooked the semiotic richness in the words 'I don't know' and 'habit'?" (2). Whether parodic or not, or both, Joy persisted in her analysis, finding a way to mine the "semiotic richness" she discovered (or fabricated) in her informants' inability to explain their actions. Perhaps inevitably, she concluded her analysis with the assertion that Althusser's description of the machinations of the Ideological State Appa-ratus did, indeed, provide the best account for the activity she had observed and for the ignorance of her informants.

Yet, as in so many student papers, Joy's argument continues on for a bit af-ter it reaches its formal conclusion, ending with a paragraph that implicitly calls into question the interpretive work that had taken up the body of the paper. Invoking Geertz, Joy declares: "in order to fulfill an insatiable desire for a world filled with significance, man seeks to interpret meaning and certainty in a world that, in reality, has neither." Though we can create quite elaborate symbolic sys-tems, Joy continues, the truth is that "[t]here is no absolute way of interpreting the world, for there will always be contradictions as we dwell between deter-minism and indeterminism, or view of man as reactor and actor" (6). And with this, Joy shows that her commitment to the Althusserian framework has been fleeting, at best. She has done the work required of her: she has produced a reading of some aspect of the culture of schooling; she has brought her understanding of Althusser, Antonio Gramsci, Raymond Williams, and Geertz to bear on her analysis; she has expressed, in suitably veiled terms, her doubts about the entire enterprise. And for some, no doubt, this final act would serve as evidence that the scales have not fallen from her eyes—that, in her heart, she still believes in the illusion of interpretive freedom, no matter what Althusser might have to say on the matter. For me, as Joy's teacher, to see in her concluding escape clause evidence of her "false consciousness" would be a mistake, however, just as it would be for me to find evidence of her enlightened status in her faithful rendering of Althusser's argument about the ways that ideology contains dissent. Either line of evaluative response shows, once again, that there's just no arguing with the "dialogic" theorists of false consciousness: they've got you coming and going.

BENEATH THE RHETORIC OF RELEASE

In *Domination and the Arts of Resistance,* James Scott offers another way of thinking about the actions of the structurally disempowered, one that sees social action not as the byproduct of false consciousness, but rather as the performance of a "public transcript" and a "hidden transcript." As Scott defines these two modes of discourse, the public transcript serves "as a shorthand way of describing the open interaction between subordinates and those who dominate"; it is a text that rarely fails to "provide convincing evidence for the hegemony of dominant values, for the hegemony of dominant discourse" (2). If the public transcript is, by definition, always available for inspection, the hidden transcript is, by contrast, a kind of discourse "that takes place 'offstage,' beyond direct observation by powerholders," and for this reason, Scott insists, "whatever form it assumes—offstage parody, dreams of violent revenge, millennial visions of a world turned upside down—this collective hidden transcript is essential to any dynamic view of power relations" (4).

It is Scott's provocative contention that, because the analysis of power has focused almost exclusively on the public transcript, it has only succeeded in generating ever more evidence that the disempowered willingly and thoughtlessly participate in the system that ensures their own subordination. Proof of this domination is always and everywhere ready to hand in the public transcript: it's on the news, it's in the libraries, it's in the critiques of mass culture; it's there to be ferreted out of the sales figures for televisions, VCRs, minivans, cell phones, home security systems; it's in our students' papers, which never seem to tire of mindlessly reproducing "original" arguments about the virtues of individuality, hard work, self-determination. Focusing exclusively on the public transcript, in short, supports the view that the subordinates are, in fact, mired in false consciousness. It also supports the corollary belief that it is the job of the well educated and the well connected to make sense of the world for those less able or less willing to do so for themselves. With his notion of a hidden transcript, though, Scott rejects both this "thick version" of false consciousness, which casts subordinates as actively believing "in the values that explain and justify their own subordination," and the "thin version" of false consciousness, which argues that subordinates comply with the social order because they have come to accept that it "is natural and inevitable" (72). Scott's contention is that subordinates are attempting to avoid any "*explicit* display of insubordination," so they reliably collaborate in the production of a public transcript that gives the impression that they have accepted the tenets of the dominant ideology, when in fact they have neither embraced this ideology nor resigned themselves to the fate this ideology has in store for them (86; emphasis in original). While the subordinates are on stage, we see them only "on their best behavior," doing what is called for in order not to put themselves in harm's way (87). Off stage, though, subordinates rehearse "the anger and reciprocal aggression denied by the presence of domination," jointly creating "a discourse of dignity, of negation, of justice" (37–38; 114). Away from the boss, away from the classroom, away from the oppressor's gaze, we all fantasize about alternative world orders.

Obviously, Scott is no easier to argue with than Freire. Where Freire argues that proof of one's false consciousness is revealed through the rejection of the Freirian model, Scott's sleight of hand is to maintain that proof of the hidden transcript's existence is to be found in its absence from the public transcript! Absence equals presence, no evidence equals evidence of hidden evidence! As Scott puts it, "the logic of infrapolitics is to leave few traces in the wake of its passage. By covering its tracks it not only minimizes the risks its practitioners run but it also eliminates much of the documentary evidence that might convince social scientists and historians that real politics was taking place" (200). Regardless of whether one finds this line of reasoning suggestive or solipsistic, it is important to recognize that the circularity of Scott's argument leads to an understanding of what constitutes a "real politics" that differs markedly from the understanding produced by the circularities in Freire's argument. For, unlike Freire, Scott insists that, in comparing the subordinate and dominant classes, it is "more accurate to consider subordinate classes *less* constrained at the level of thought and ideology [than the dominant classes], since they can in secluded settings speak with comparative safety, and *more* constrained at the level of political action and struggle, where the daily exercise of power sharply limits the options available to them" (91; emphasis in original). With this startling reversal, Scott relocates his version of false consciousness—that is, being more constrained at the level of thought and ideology—among the dominant classes. Indeed, as he sees it, one's freedom to think is *inversely proportional* to one's freedom to act as a political agent. The higher one climbs the social ladder, the greater the pressure to ascribe, in all phases of one's life, to the dominant ideology, the fewer opportunities to entertain doubts about or alternatives to that ideology. The lower one descends the social ladder, though, the more the pressure to hew the party lines and voice the ideological pieties declines, the freer one is to imagine other social arrangements and the less likely one is to be in a position to bring those utopian visions to pass.

For proof of his thesis that subordinates are freer to think about alternate social arrangements than their superiors, Scott points to the fact that, historically, subordinates have repeatedly given voice to imaginative renderings of a better time just over the horizon—renderings of a time when the current dominant system collapses and is replaced by a more just system. If one looks hard enough, one is sure to find in every cultural milieu depictions of the idea that, someday, the last shall be first and the first shall be last. This is because, as Scott sees it, subordinates have no difficulty *imagining* a "counterfactual social order," one that involves either "a total reversal of the existing distribution of status and rewards" or the negation of "the existing social order" (80–81)—this ability to generate hope for a better world is "part and parcel of the religiopolitical equipment of historically disadvantaged groups" (91). Thus, it is a mistake to think that the minds of subordinates have been so thoroughly colonized that they cannot conceive of or desire a better world. Rather, it is more accurate to say that subordinated peoples have no access to the channels of social power that might bring their visions of preferable social relations into being. And, following this logic, we might say as well that it is not that students have been so mystified by the Ideological State Apparatus of higher education that they can't see or understand how the system has been designed to deprive them of a sense of individual autonomy. It is, rather, that they are powerless to change the system and that they know only too well its ability to punish them for not complying with its demands. So they do what is required of them, slipping in enough of the hidden transcript to preserve their sense of self-respect: they write papers that lifelessly respond to the assignment; they contradict themselves, saying what they want to say and what they think the teacher wants them to say at the same time; they publicly announce their interest in the work at hand while manifesting no visible sign that their interest requires anything from them; they generate parody and compliance simultaneously. They hunker down and try to get by.

Of course, in making this analogy between subordinates and students, the oppressed and those paying individuals seated in our classes trying to earn their degrees in business, say, I have opened myself to the criticism that I am trivializing the manifest differences between the two groups. Freire, as has been previously noted, wasn't concerned with teaching first-year college students the nuances of academic prose or the virtues of the expository essay. His work was with illiterate peasants who were struggling to combat oppressive governmental policies. Scott, too, is generally more interested in forms of domination that carry the threat of physical violence, such as "slavery, serfdom, and the caste system [which] routinely generate practices and rituals of denigration, insult, and assaults on the body" (23). It would be foolish to equate the challenges Freire confronted in the field or the oppressive situations that interest Scott with the challenges that face those of us who teach the literate arts in the academy, since we work with individuals who have already found their way into the system, and who wish, at some level, to gain access to the material benefits that higher education is understood to promise. But in designating students as structurally subordinate, I have not meant to imply the general commensurability of systems of oppression; rather, I have meant only to point out that, by virtue of their subordinate position within the structure of the educational system, students, too, have their "hidden transcripts" where they store their reservations about what the schools are doing to them.

I have also meant to suggest that, however tempting it may be to describe our work as teachers as being pursued in the interests of "liberation" or "consciousness raising" or "resistance," the truth is that this rhetoric's appeal is so attractive because it covers over our more primary role as functionaries of the administration's educational arm. In the right setting, we can forget that we are the individuals vested with the responsibility for soliciting and assessing student work; we can imagine that power has left the room at the moment the student announces the insight, "we're going to show everyone that we were never drunkards or lazy. We were exploited!"; we can convince ourselves to accept whatever gets said at face value. The students, however, never forget where they are, no matter how carefully we arrange the desks in the classroom, how casually we dress, how open we are to disagreement, how politely we respond to their journal entries, their papers, their portfolios. They don't forget; we often do.

This is not to imply that no "authentic" interactions can occur within the space of the classroom or, conversely, that all interactions in that space are necessarily duplicitous, cynical, self-serving, or self-protective. I think it more accurate to say that we will never know, in any absolute and unqualified sense, if the work our students do is authentic or if that work reflects their achieved level of consciousness. Indeed, I would argue that the prevailing desire to reconstruct the scene of instruction as a site where authenticity is forged and layers of false consciousness are peeled away indicates a general commitment in our profession to imagining that the power dynamic in the teacher-student relationship can, under ideal conditions, be erased. Thus, Freire presents the recipients of his pedagogy as coming to their own conclusions, as learning to think for themselves. He doesn't linger over the fact that all this self-motivated thinking leads his students to think *exactly* what he would like them to think; he doesn't imagine that, possibly, his students are mouthing his pieties, silently collaborating in the production of the desired public transcript and then sneaking back home where they are free to question his lessons or to forget about them altogether. And Althusser condemns an education system populated by instructors who little suspect the coercive effects of their labor, but maintains that there are teachers who stand outside this system and work against its oppressive ideology. "They are a kind of hero," he tells us (157). Althusser doesn't think it possible that these seemingly benighted teachers might have reservations about the educational system, but know the material consequences of giving voice to their doubts. Nor does he entertain the idea that he, too, might have been captured by the very same ideology that draws people to the teaching profession, an ideology that forever casts the ideal pedagogue as someone who works against the system, is critical of its movements, is free of its impurities, is allied with science and reason rather than myth and folklore.

While Freire and Althusser thus struggle, in different ways, to hold out hope that the classroom can, under ideal conditions, contribute to the revolutionary cause, Scott argues that, historically, to the degree that the educational system has served to promote "radicalism," it has not been through the agency of the pedagogue, but rather because the classroom has served so often and so well as a scene of betrayal. The educational system regularly establishes the conditions for this sense of betrayal first by extending "the implicit promise of the dominant ideology (If you work hard, obey authority, do well in school, and keep your nose clean you will advance by merit and have satisfying work)," which, in turn, functions to encourage students to conform, to make sacrifices, and to develop often highly unrealistic expectations about what the future holds for them (107). And then, when those expectations are not realized—when a good job doesn't turn out to be waiting at the other end of all those years of smiling subservience—a general, almost palpable sense of betrayal spreads among those who formerly believed in the dominant ideology. (Think, for instance, of the prevailing mood among those about to enter the academic job market.) It is this dynamic that poses the gravest threat to hegemony, since the dynamic itself regularly produces individuals who have worked their way up through the system believing all the rhetoric about equality, liberty, opportunity, and merit, only to have those beliefs betrayed by a system dominated by glass ceilings, old-boy networks, off-stage agreements, and double-dealing administrators.

Momentarily swept away by his own rhetoric, Scott briefly entertains the idea that the potential for significant institutional reform resides in this untapped reservoir of betrayed individuals: "the system may have most to fear," he tells us, "from those subordinates among whom the institutions of hegemony have been most successful" (107). Perhaps this is an instance when Scott's own "hidden transcript" surfaces in his argument, a place where he can revel in the subordinate's familiar fantasy that raging against the machine constitutes, in itself, a meaningful political act. Scott quickly drops this detour into the roots of radicalism, though, and returns to his original concern—how one cultivates the arts of resistance when revolutionary transformation is out of the question. For my purposes, the value of Scott's work originates in this refusal to lead us once more down the path to revolution and to focus instead on the actual actions and experiences of those who labor under conditions of constraint. The classroom is, of course, one such place where the labor of others—both teachers and students—is constrained to meet the demands of outside forces.

RUPTURING THE PUBLIC TRANSCRIPT

Although Scott is, as I've already noted, generally concerned with more repressive forms of domination than those found in the classroom, he does invoke the teacher's mastery as an example of a particular kind of authority, one that "can tolerate a remarkably high level of practical nonconformity so long as it does not actually tear the public fabric of hegemony" (204). Thus, the teacher can lecture about the beauty of literature or the politics of literacy or the liberatory powers of the cultural studies paradigm, knowing all the while that the students aren't paying attention, aren't taking notes, aren't even listening. As long as no one actually stops the class to say it's all nonsense or to perform some other public gesture of contempt, the teacher's role as the ultimate arbiter of meaning is never really in danger. Any student who has made it to college knows these rules of behavior and knows, as well, the boundaries of permissible signs of disengagement (or learns them soon enough): eyes may close, pencils may doodle or be laid to rest, in some classes newspapers or laptops may be allowed to open, a crossword puzzle completed, a game of solitaire played, an instant message sent; heads down on the desk may even be ignored. Snoring, wearing headsets, audibly parroting the teacher's remarks are all ill-advised, as is—in most cases—openly contesting the teacher's point of view. The classroom can tolerate all manner of nonconformity, but every classroom has its limit, whether it be the expression of doubt about the virtue of the academic enterprise, unveiled speculation about the teacher's qualifications for running the class, or insistent disrespect for the methods of assigning and assessing the work the students produce. At some point, every teacher must enforce the boundary between the hidden transcript, where students regularly rehearse their misgivings about the education they're receiving, and the public transcript, where the virtues of the educational system are taken for granted.

The violation of this boundary can be quite shocking, but it is important to recognize that the shock arises not so much because the public revelation of the hidden transcript discloses unknown information, but rather because, in the act itself, the revelation threatens to "tear the public fabric of hegemony." Thus, if we take, for example, the frustrated student who suddenly "goes off" in class—announcing he's only taking the expository writing course because it's required, that he was graded more fairly in high school, that all this writing about culture has nothing to do with what he plans to do with his life—it is safe to say that nothing in the content of what the student has said can be construed as particularly surprising; rather, what grabs everyone's attention is the fact that the student has chosen to make this statement within his teacher's hearing. Or, to refer to an example from my own experience, when I summoned a graduate student to my office to discuss the open disrespect he had shown his peers in the required pedagogy seminar by reading through the course catalogue during their presentations, it wasn't the content of the graduate student's response that was shocking, but rather the fact that he chose to share that content with me. He said he really had no interest in the teaching of writing, but had come to the university to study literature. He told me he was taking the pedagogy seminar because it was what was required of him to be eligible for funding. And then he said, "All my most brilliant professors are truly mediocre teachers." We were both embarrassed, I think, by the fact that he made this final statement in my presence, and a silence opened between us. To quell such "revolts" we teachers often do what we do best: we start talking. Perhaps we are solicitous, perhaps not. Perhaps we invite the student to reflect on the assumptions that inform the stated critique, perhaps we tell the student exactly what those assumptions are and why we find them so pernicious. But the goal, more often than we care to admit, I'd say, is to restore order, return to the lesson plan, get the hidden transcript back offstage and out of sight.

One essay that seems to go out of its way to transgress the boundary that separates what can and what cannot be said about the culture of schooling is Richard Rodriguez's frequently anthologized "The Achievement of Desire." In this piece, Rodriguez, the son of Mexican immigrants, describes his increasing alienation from his parents as he began to excel at school, his growing embarrassment at their broken English, their apparent ignorance, their impoverished state. Mechanically devoting himself to his studies, Rodriguez rises through the ranks, goes to graduate school to study Renaissance literature, wins a scholarship to pursue research at the British Museum. To all outward appearances, he would seem to have realized the American Dream; inwardly, though, Rodriguez is consumed with doubt about what he has done and where it has taken him. He feels that he has betrayed his parents and that he has been betrayed by a system that has left him incapable of producing anything but "pedantic, lifeless, unassailable prose" (499). He is, in short, the very kind of person Scott would be willing to describe as having a thin version of "false consciousness"—one of those good willed people who "made sacrifices of self-discipline and control and developed expectations that were usually betrayed" (Scott 107).

When I first assigned "The Achievement of Desire" in my composition courses, I was surprised at the intense hostility students expressed in response to Rodriguez's reflection on the long-term effects of schooling. Far from seeing the assignment of Rodriguez's essay as an invitation to air their own critiques of institutionalized education, the students responded, as a rule, by accusing Rodriguez of being a traitor to his parents, his heritage, even his teachers. Doing well in school doesn't require that you sacrifice your integrity, the students said; indeed, many of the students went out of their way to make it clear that, as far as they were concerned, doing well in school was all but irrelevant to how they thought about the world, related to others, moved through the social sphere. Thus, in their own rush to rehearse again the lines about the virtues of education drawn from the public transcript, they transformed Rodriguez into a two-time loser: first, for betraying his parents and his heritage; and second, for allowing his education to play such a large role in his life that it fundamentally reshaped who he was and how he thought about himself and the world. As one of Rodriguez's more vocal critics put it: "The way in which he treats his parents angers me, he is so obsessed with his studies that he neglects his parents and his childhood. . . . This punk shows no love to his parents, and that is what I can't understand. . . . I see his parents in my mind. They are just like my parents, and I feel like hugging them and telling them that they are great parents. At the same time I feel like taking Rodriguez and wringing his neck."

It's hard to know what to make of such responses. For my purposes, though, reactions of this kind are of interest because, on the surface at least, they appear to articulate an instrumentalist theory about how schooling should function—that is, that schools should restrict themselves to providing "know-how" and that they should not disturb one's place in the world. And, at the same time, such responses voice a fear that schools do not, in fact, function in this isolated way, but rather produce (or reinforce) an estrangement from one's past, an uncertainty about one's place in the world, a resignation that what one must give up during the educational process can never be recovered. While Freire and Scott would agree that this fear of education's disruptive powers is well justified, Rodriguez concludes his essay by declaring that there is an abiding value to having been violated in this way: "If, because of my schooling, I had grown culturally separated from my parents, my education finally had given me ways of speaking and caring about that fact" (585). What many students and teachers can't forgive Rodriguez for is his public insistence that education inevitably alienates and empowers in these ways and that this is one of the appeals and transcendent values of scholarly work.

So, when confronted with this argument, the students put on a good show of being shocked that Rodriguez was attracted to something that created a buffer between himself and his family. They are less sure, though, about how to respond to Rodriguez's critical description of schooling. They are wary for good reason, knowing that to speak openly in class of what one loses through academic advancement (or of what one gains in the way that Rodriguez does) is to risk rupturing the public transcript about education's unquestioned virtues. And so, rather than have this piece of the hidden transcript of schooling make its way onto the public stage, the students collaborate in repairing the rupture and rise, in unison, to the defense of self-determination, freedom, individuality. They argue that being good at school need not change one in any substantial way; they insist that this son of immigrants could have had the best of both worlds; they declare that the rewards of a loving family far outweigh whatever benefits one might receive from mastering the scholarly apparatus. They lay it on thick. And, in the right context, everyone can sigh with relief that a catastrophe has been averted.

ON THE USES OF INSTITUTIONAL AUTOBIOGRAPHY

Between the poles of these two representations of schooling as either radically liberating and empowering or ceaselessly oppressive and instrumentalist, one finds a vast, unexplored territory—the fraught, compromised world where all of our classes are actually convened. While the preceding discussion has detailed the attractions and the perils of the rhetorics of liberation and violation most frequently deployed in analyses of the political consequences of teaching, I would like to conclude by suggesting that, in order for students to begin to imagine other ways of framing their experience of schooling and other ways of navigating the twisted paths bureaucracies cut through the social sphere, students must first be given an opportunity to formulate more nuanced understandings of the social exercise of power. And for this to happen, students must be provided with genuine opportunities to discover the virtues of discursive versatility, by which I mean opportunities to acquire the skills necessary to speak, read, and write persuasively across a wide range of social contexts. Lest this sound like a refurbished but thinly disguised call to embrace a curriculum based on the rhetorical modes, let me make it clear that I am interested in promoting: (1) ways for students to acquire a fluency in the ways that the bureaucratic systems that regulate all our lives use words; (2) a familiarity with the logics, styles of argumentation, and repositories of evidence deployed by these organizational bodies; and (3) a fuller understanding of what can and cannot be gained through discursive exchanges, with a concomitant recalibration of the horizon of expectations that is delineated by our sense of what words can and cannot do when deployed in the public sphere. Were I a polemicist, I might say what I am after is a pragmatic pedagogy, one grounded in "the arts of complicity, duplicity, and compromise," the very same arts that are deployed, with such enervating effect, by the host of social, bureaucratic, and corporate institutions that, together, govern all our lives.

But if Scott is right in positing the existence of a hidden transcript that runs alongside the public transcript, it would seem that there is little need for inaugurating the pragmatic pedagogy I am calling for. After all, according to Scott's theory, everyone already has a sensitivity to context and learns, through the process of familiarization, where and with whom it is safe to speak openly and when discretion is the better part of valor. The goal of a pragmatic pedagogy, though, is not to create discursive versatility where none existed before; it is, rather, to build on the discursive versatility that our very humanity bestows upon us. Thus, with regard to the classroom, the goal is not to teach the students that there is a difference between the literate practices valued in the academic and domestic spheres: undergraduates are already well aware of this differential valuation and its consequences. (Rodriguez is hardly exceptional in being able to detect this difference the moment he entered primary school.) The problem is not that students are unaware of the conflicts between these competing spheres, but that, within the space of the classroom, their very sensitivity to the differing contexts manifests itself, more often than not, either as silence or as open assent to the teacher's position. And, as every teacher who has heard the exasperated plea, "just tell me what you want and I'll do it," knows, when the students set out to conform to what they believe are the teacher's expectations, more often than not they simultaneously convey the impression that what a teacher finds most pleasing is the fully compliant, obedient, perhaps even unthinking student. As Scott explains, all students have been taught the consequences of not assuming this pose: "One deserter shot, one assertive slave whipped, one unruly student rebuked; these acts are meant as public events for an audience of subordinates. They are intended as a kind of preemptive strike to nip in the bud any further challenges of the existing frontier" (197).

Of course, as teachers, we too are subject to the demands of this classroom drama, which forever requires that we measure up to ambient expectations about what it means to teach and to be an authority on one's subject. Thus, we are quick to cover over our own ignorance, talk over our own confusion, hide our own doubts about the rewards of learning because, if we act otherwise, we would risk rending education's public transcript by exposing the highly credentialed person at the front of the room to be nothing more than a fraud. Under such learning conditions, it is hard to know what the lasting lesson is meant to be, beyond sustained instruction in the ways educated people are supposed to carry themselves in public. This is, to be sure, an important lesson, but it's one that's all about the deadening effects of formal compliance—a lesson that leaves no room for thinking about the range of permissible forms of action that can occur within this flexibly bounded, inevitably permeable space.

By providing a forum for teachers to discuss what actually occurs in their classrooms, the field of composition studies has helped to show that there are other roles for the teacher to occupy besides unquestioned master and final arbiter of meaning. The discipline's abiding interest in reconsidering how power and authority are distributed and conferred in the classroom reflects a genuine desire on the part of the majority of its members to be seen as working to undermine an overarching system that is hierarchically organized ("We'll sit in a circle," I say), status-conscious ("Please, just call me Richard"), exclusive ("Everyone's opinion is valued here"). Similarly, the waxing and waning of the discipline's debate about whether composition instruction should introduce students to academic discourse or help them articulate and generate insights about their personal experiences reveal a constitutive ambivalence in the workforce about what it means to write in the academy: when you teach composition, we keep asking ourselves, are you working for the system or against it? This ambivalence about the status of our work is easy enough to understand. After all, since composition is traditionally situated on the margins of the academy, in the borderland of remedial and basic instruction, it is regularly staffed by people who know firsthand how casually and quietly the bureaucratic system of higher education parcels out economic injustice. Why prepare students to produce work that is valued by such a system? Why not teach them to resist, to intervene, to dismantle?

I don't believe that these two activities are mutually exclusive—that preparing a student to succeed in business, say, is incompatible with the project of teaching a student to think about the effects of discriminatory hiring practices. In the current fraught environment, though, I've stopped trying to convince teachers and teachers-in-training about the "merits of complicity" through argument. With the seductive rhetorics of liberation and resistance in the air, I've learned that it isn't long before the conversation produces charges that pursuing such a course requires selling out, cashing in your ideals, kissing up to the man. To circumvent this thoroughly familiar exchange, where the principled work of education in this corner squares off against the mercenary interests of the business world in that corner, I've designed an assignment that asks teachers-in-training to write in the entirely unfamiliar (and perhaps, even, nonexistent) genre of the institutional autobiography, a genre which, as I have sought to demonstrate here, unites the seemingly opposed worlds of the personal—where one is free, unique, and outside of history—and the institutional—where one is constrained, anonymous, and imprisoned by the accretion of past practices. In this genre, one still considers the conventional questions that reside at the heart of the autobiographical enterprise: questions about how one has become the person one has, overcome the obstacles one has, achieved what one has. The overriding goal, though, is to locate one's evolving narrative within a specific range of institutional contexts, shifting attention from the self to the nexus where the self and institution meet. So inflected, the questions that drive the institutional autobiography become: What experiences have led you to teach, study, read, and write in the ways you do? What institutional policies have promoted or inhibited your success? What shape and texture has your life in the institutions given to your dreams of release?

When I first assigned this writing task in a graduate seminar a few years back, the students, not too surprisingly, weren't sure what to produce and I couldn't really say what I wanted them to hand in, since I didn't really know what I was looking for and I couldn't predict what it would look like before I found it. We had watched the film *Dangerous Minds* and critiqued Hollywood's fascination with producing classroom narratives of conversion and redemption; we had noted the prevalence of this narrative at our own conferences and in our journals where, as one student put it, we tend to tell stories about the teacher-hero who, after some initial difficulties cutting through the bureaucratic red tape, gets down to the business of "liberating right, left, and center." Critiquing the master narrative was easy enough. The challenge lay in figuring out how to work within and against its constraints simultaneously, so as to acknowledge without overstating the influence of past teachers and one's own work in the classroom. Although the students had no models for how to do this at their immediate disposal, they were not working in a vacuum. I encouraged them to return to the archives—their own personal archive, including the papers, notes, and other pedagogical paraphernalia they'd saved over the years, and the public record, including transcripts, graduation requirements, and professional correspondence—to unearth material evidence of past practices. I also had the students read a set of texts that focus on the institutional constraints that shape the business of higher education: Ian Hunter's *Rethinking the School*, Robin Varnum's *Fencing with Words*, Howard Tinberg's *Border Talk*, and David Tyack and Larry Cuban's *Tinkering Toward Utopia*. Then I stood back and waited to see what would happen.

One of the teachers responded to the assignment by recounting how the course of her professional life was changed when the governor of South Dakota decided to commit the state's educational system to technological innovation. She was a part-time instructor working on the fringe of her home institution at the time this change was announced, surrounded by tenured faculty who were understandably reluctant, in the early 1980s, to learn about computers and computerized instruction. This teacher volunteered to give technology a try and slowly made her way to what appeared to be a permanent teaching position in her home department. Her victory was short-lived, though, for, as her school's needs and requirements shifted in the late 1990s, this teacher was informed that she would need to show progress toward the doctorate to maintain her position. Neither wholly the victor nor the victim in this process, this teacher concluded her institutional autobiography with this observation: "I know I am a better teacher than I would have been if technology hadn't interfered. That technology, forced into my teaching career by the bureaucracy, pushed me to 'see' writing courses and writing itself in a new framework. That new framework emphasized my lack of knowledge in a subject I was struggling to teach and forced me to read, research, and realize how much more I needed to know." Though this teacher had begun the course by describing herself as working in a state educational system that was ruled by bankers and business-men, by the end of the semester, she had revised her story so that it could account for the relative freedom she had experienced while working within a system governed by shifting and arbitrary requirements.

This isn't an ideal story, of course, with the kind of happy ending we've come to expect from teacher narratives. The direction of the state educational system that employs this teacher continues to be determined by the whims of corporate culture; this teacher finds her classes filled with students who are driven by an interest in financial success that she does not share; and this teacher's ongoing employment is contingent upon her upgrading her credentials—a requirement that has led her to move away from her family while she completes her coursework in the graduate program that best meets her needs. Focusing on the disruptions and disappointments caused by this shift in governmental funding priorities and local employment practices may be personally cathartic, but experiencing this catharsis does not, in itself, do anything to alter the fact that the most pressing problem confronting this teacher is how to construct an inhabitable and hospitable life within these constraining conditions. There are those who would use this situation to raise, once more, the call to overthrow the system. And there are many more who would say that the teacher has no choice but to roll over and take it. The truth, though, is that none of us knows for certain what lies ahead for this teacher, her institution, or the state she works in. We don't know what will happen. All we know for sure is that the future will be like the past insofar as it will ceaselessly demand of us all that we continue improvising solutions to problems we never imagined possible.

Far from being rendered powerless by the requirement that we persevere in the face of uncertainty, those of us who teach are actually very well positioned to assist our students in acquiring the skills necessary for persisting in the ongoing project of navigating life in a bureaucracy, by virtue of our years of experience making our way through this frequently capricious and indifferent system for distributing social privilege. And what we can teach our students is how to work within and against discursive constraints simultaneously—thereby helping them to experience the mediated access to authenticity that social action allows. Having our students develop this kind of discursive versatility won't serve to demolish the barrier that will always separate the public and the hidden transcripts, nor will it necessarily produce supporters of the kind of social justice Freire envisions. Rather, the more modest goal of the pragmatic pedagogy I've outlined here is to provide our students with the opportunity to speak, read, and write in a wider range of discursive contexts than is available to them when they labor under the codes of silence and manufactured consent that serve to define the lived experience of subordinates in the culture of schooling. If, through this process, the students learn how to register their reservations about academic practice in ways that can be heard as reasoned arguments rather than dismissed as the plaintive bleating of sheep, if they learn to pose their questions about the work before them in ways that invite response, and if, finally, they learn how to listen to and learn from the responses they receive, they may well be in a better position to negotiate the complex social and intellectual experiences that await them just beyond the classroom's walls. There is no knowing if the students will, in fact, end up in this better position, but this is the goal. It is only the polemical rhetoric that surrounds the discussion of pedagogical practice that would lead us to expect that any other, more definite outcome could be guaranteed.

EDUCATING CHARLIE
FRAUDULENCE AND THE LIBERAL ARTS

When I was a student at St. John's College in the early 1980s, one joke making the rounds went like this: name the three most famous people to graduate from the college since it was founded in 1696. After a suitable pause, which the respondent dutifully filled by staring blankly into space, the punch line was delivered: Francis Scott Key, Francis Scott Key, and . . . Francis Scott Key.

Even at the time, this was considered a poor attempt at humor. But for the small community of students who attended the college, telling the joke was less about being funny than it was a way for us to publicly express our shared anxiety about the uncertain path we'd taken by enrolling at the "Great Books school," a school without electives, majors, or grades, just four years of reading classic texts from the fields of philosophy, math, science, and the language arts. And so, what the joke did was divide the world neatly in two: there were those students at all those other colleges who were thoughtlessly preparing themselves for future careers in business or biochemistry or just killing time haphazardly racking up credits in the cafeteria-style elective system, and then there

were the students at St. John's, who were going to college for all the right reasons—students who were pursuing Truth with a capital T; students for whom
learning was its own reward; students who were becoming the kind of well-
rounded generalists the world really needed, if it only knew. While those other
students might be pursuing Great Fame, Great Fortune, or some other tawdry
form of Greatness, those of us who'd elected to spend our college years studying Plato and Aristotle, Kant and Hegel, Euclid and Einstein, Lavoisier and
Mendel, Shakespeare and Tolstoy were after something much greater, something not of this world: wisdom.

Many years later, when this idea of using a reading list to cut the world up
into the wise and the foolish, the sincere and the mercenary, no longer made
sense to me, I began researching the history of the Great Books program to
learn what initially had led people to place so much faith in the liberal arts.
Early on in the process, as I was working my way through the papers and personal correspondence of Scott Buchanan, the man responsible for bringing the
Great Books curriculum to St. John's in 1937, I was still trying to get a handle
on the dramatis personae of the liberal arts education movement when I
stumbled across an entry for a letter from Charles Van Doren, dated October
30, 1959. Having just seen Robert Redford's feature-length film *Quiz Show,* I
could provide a broad-stroked summary of Van Doren's role in the most noto-
rious television scandal of the twentieth century: English professor from Columbia University wins fame and fortune as unbeatable contestant on the game
show *Twenty-One* in the mid-fifties; is eventually revealed to be a fraud who
was fed the answers ahead of time by producers eager to use his good looks and
his intellectual pedigree to boost their ratings; resigned from Columbia, fled the
public eye in disgrace, presumably never to be heard from again. Why would *he*
write to Buchanan?

As I waited for the folder containing Van Doren's letter to be delivered to
my carrel in the archive, I wondered why, at the very moment Van Doren was
being called to testify before the congressional subcommittee investigating deceptive practices on the television game shows, he would choose to write the
former dean of St. John's College. I wasn't thinking about the joke we used to
tell at school about famous alumni. I was just trying to get the facts to line up.
When the folder arrived, the mystery only deepened: there was a copy of Van
Doren's twelve-page confession, which he would read to the congressional subcommittee three days after posting his package to Buchanan; and there was a
brief cover letter where Van Doren wrote that he wanted Buchanan to have the
statement first, "Not for pity, nor for sympathy, nor for justification. Just because this is the true story," a cover letter that closed with the utterly enigmatic

observation, "I have the feeling that you may be the only person so far who understands why I did it. But my dad always said you were the wisest man in the world."[1]

It didn't take much sleuthing to figure out that Charles Van Doren had graduated from St. John's College in 1946, when Buchanan was still serving as dean, but this fact didn't shed much light on the statements in the cover letter. Why would Buchanan, who created an undergraduate curriculum devoted to the search for Truth, be the one to understand why Van Doren lied about his actions for so long, to so many people, under so many different circumstances? Not too surprisingly, when I returned to watch *Quiz Show* again, I found that the film makes no mention of Van Doren's relationship to Buchanan or to the college, even though a detailed summary of Van Doren's educational past is provided at one of the film's most dramatic moments. During the scene in question, Herb Stempel, the sweaty, nasal-voiced, working-class quiz show champ who was unseated by the witty, urbane, handsome, and more marketable Van Doren, is in the process of testifying to the congressional subcommittee about the advanced coaching he received from Dan Enright and Albert Freedman, the producers of *Twenty-One*. Stempel describes their requirement that he dress the part of a struggling member of the working class; their directions that he breathe heavily into the microphone while searching for the answers; their instructions about how many points he should wager at each point during the game; and, finally, their insistence that, after a series of stage-managed ties with Van Doren, he was to suffer a humiliating defeat by failing to know the answer to a question that anyone in the audience could have shouted out at the time: which film won the Academy Award for best picture in 1955?

Stempel concludes his testimony by charging that, since the producers of *Twenty-One* fed him answers ahead of time while he was the champ and since they had fixed his own inglorious downfall, the obvious conclusion was that Van Doren himself must have been in on the deception. Angrily rejecting this last accusation, Representative Peter Mack of Illinois responds by booming out the following catalogue of Van Doren's educational accomplishments: "Charles Van Doren is a professor at Columbia University, [has] a master's degree in astrophysics, a Ph.D. in literature, hails from one of the most prominent intellectual families in this country. Isn't it just possible Mr. Stempel that you got the answers and he didn't?" The ferocity of this response strikes Stempel dumb. How can he, a working-class Jew, convince Mack and his colleagues that they must question the honesty of a gentile who has such impeccable credentials and comes from such a family?

By this point in the film, the audience knows that Representative Mack is wrong to assume that the well-educated, well-connected Van Doren is innocent, so it's probably overkill to point out that Mack also doesn't have his facts quite right: Van Doren was awarded his master's degree in mathematics, not astrophysics, and he didn't earn his Ph.D. until two years after he had defeated Stempel on *Twenty-One*.[2] Such minor historical details are no more relevant to this film's project than is the information that Van Doren received his undergraduate education at St. John's College or even the fact that a survey of the testimony actually made before this committee reveals that this dramatic exchange between Representative Mack and Stempel never actually occurred.[3] Redford's got more important things to do than worry about such trivial matters as the historical record: he wants to tell the story of the unlimited power of the mass media and the destruction of the little guy, of big business versus the fragile family structure, of lies and deceit against eventual truth and integrity, and he's not above embroidering on the facts, creating composite characters out of many actual agents, and playing fast and easy with the time line if it helps sharpen the critical edge of his exposé on the deceptive practices of the television industry.

Perhaps fittingly, the most succinct assessment of this conflict between the film's message and its method comes from Dan Enright's assistant, Albert Freedman, who is depicted in the film as being unable to understand big words and who simulates masturbating when Van Doren voices moral reservations about participating in the deception. After watching *Quiz Show*, Freedman observed: "Ironically the film is fixed. It is even more rigged than the show it portrays" (Bernstein).[4] While the film's willful distortion of time, character, and the sequence of events certainly opens it up to such criticism, I would argue that the most significant problem with the film is not that it takes such liberties with the historical record, but that it does so in order to deliver an indictment of contemporary culture that can only seem the oldest of old news. Indeed, according to Jeff Greenfield, it was Redford's decision to put the Van Doren story to this use that caused it to fail at the box office: "To tell today's audience that powerful institutions and people lie is not compelling. It isn't that we fear confronting our loss of innocence. It's that it bores us" (qtd. in "Enigma").[5]

There is another, less familiar story that the quiz show scandal might be used to tell, though, one that involves that other powerful, manipulative institution lurking on the margins of the film—higher education. For me, the question to ask about this scandal is not, "What are we to make of a society where even our most highly educated citizens fall prey to the media's corrupting influence?" Rather, I want to ask, "How can Van Doren's fall assist us in reassessing the virtues attributed to the study of the Great Books, in particular, and to the literate arts, more generally?" I propose to disrupt the view of the modern university and its employees as having ever been outside and above the demands of the business world, and so to promote a vision of higher education that builds upon and embraces what I have referred to in the previous chapter as "the arts of complicity."

EXPLICATING CHARLIE'S INEXPLICABLE SUCCESS

> Nothing is more human than education. . . . Animals have instincts, but men have arts; and the intellectual arts are those that free them to be themselves. College, where the intellectual arts are encountered, makes more difference in a person than anything else ever does; it turns the child into a man.
>
> —*The Autobiography of Mark Van Doren*

Although Paul Attanasio, the screenwriter for *Quiz Show*, didn't feel that Charles Van Doren's attendance at St. John's added anything to the story he and Redford were putting together on the corruptive power of the media, it is clear from the passage above that Charlie's famous father, the poet and literary critic Mark Van Doren, considered the college experience *qua* experience to be the single most important event in anyone's life story. Given his belief that college "turns the child into a man," it should come as no surprise to learn that Mark Van Doren decided early on where his two sons should have this formative experience. In fact, although Charlie was but eleven years old and his brother John nine at the time that Scott Buchanan and Stringfellow Barr founded the Great Books program at St. John's, as soon as Van Doren learned that Buchanan, his longtime friend, had settled in Annapolis,[6] he fired off this enthusiastic letter of support to the new dean: "I am very much excited about St. John's. I am sure it will go, and I have no doubt that it is exactly the place you ought to be. Charlie and Johnny are set to go there to college if you will have them. Can they apply so early? Mortimer [Adler] brought us a copy of your 'New Program' and we read it with enlightenment no less than admiration. Now that will be education; and where else will there be any?"[7]

Although Charlie, at eleven years old, was obviously too young to start reading Plato, by a curious twist of fate, the bombing of Pearl Harbor made it possible for him and his brother John to enroll in the college much sooner than expected. With students leaving in droves to join the war effort, Barr and Buchanan were desperate to find bodies to fill their classrooms, so they lowered the age of admission to fifteen and added a summer session so that the youngest entering students could fit their college education in before they were eligible for the draft at the age of eighteen (Smith 62). With this shift in requirements, Charlie entered the program in 1942 at the age of sixteen and his brother John followed the next year at the age of fifteen. It was not long before Buchanan was able to inform the senior Van Doren: "reports still continue that Charlie is one of our best talkers."[8]

In *The Joy of Reading*, published in 1985, long after the quiz-show scandals of the 1950s had faded from public memory, Charles Van Doren credits Buchanan with having taught him "an amazing thing: not everything, not even in the best books, can be understood, even by the best readers," and he adds that the college curriculum Buchanan designed taught him he "could read any book" (4–5). Van Doren quietly passes over his stint on *Twenty-One* in this account of how he came to his lifelong love of learning. But, as *Time* reported in the February 1957 issue that featured Van Doren on the cover, "Some of [Van Doren's] classmates at St. John's College in Annapolis, famed for its 'great books' course and its cloistered devotion to scholarship, say that Van Doren's quiz wizardry flies ironically in the face of what the college and Charlie himself stand for" ("Wizard" 45). To be sure, it was puzzling: here was a man who had learned no book could ever be fully understood but who had somehow managed to master the book of the world, displaying an encyclopedic knowledge that seemed to span all categories—from ancient history to geography to baseball to opera. There were, however, those who saw no necessary contradiction between Van Doren's training in the eternal verities and his uncommon knowledge of truly obscure facts. For this group, which included faculty at the college, *Time* reported, "Van Doren's mind comes through on TV not as a card-index file but as a reasoning instrument that explores a memory clearly embedded in taste" (45).

In retrospect, it is hard not to find such assessments comical, exposing as they do a naked desire to lend some legitimacy to Van Doren's success in an arena that *Time* itself referred to as "the crassest of lowbrow entertainments" (44). But to get lost in the multiple amusements and ironies that such assessments afford is to miss what such interchanges reveal about the contradictions inherent in the academy's efforts to produce and regulate the circulation of cultural capital. By presenting Van Doren's mind as "a reasoning instrument that explores a memory clearly embedded in taste," the faculty at St. John's were participating in the struggle to explain Van Doren's uncommon ability, as *Time* put it, "to whip up a doting mass audience for a new kind of TV idol—of all things, an egghead" (44). And in this struggle it was not just Van Doren versus whatever contestant the producers came up with; it was, as *Time* framed the contest at the cultural level, Van Doren "the Renaissance Man" against Elvis "the pelvis," the thinking man versus the dancing man, the mind versus the body, the wisdom that accretes over time versus the acrid smell of instant gratification. Thus, in order to recuperate Van Doren's accomplishments in this tawdry sphere, explanations for his success had to be generated that highlighted his distinguished heritage, his impeccable educational pedigree, his transcendent quality of mind.

This world of inheritance and cultured dispositions is exactly the world Charles Van Doren was born into: his father, Mark Van Doren, was a Pulitzer Prize–winning poet and a professor of English at Columbia University; his mother, Dorothy Graffe Van Doren, was a former editor for the *Nation* and a novelist of some renown. The home Charlie grew up in was populated by various intellectual luminaries of the time: Thomas Merton, Sinclair Lewis, Edmund Wilson, his father's brother Carl (another Pulitzer Prize–winner), and Mortimer Adler, the philosopher who served as Robert Maynard Hutchins's right-hand man during the effort to reform undergraduate education at the University of Chicago and who had authored the classic how-to manual for the culturally insecure—*How to Read a Book*. As family friend Clifton Fadiman put it, "The Van Dorens represent a tradition of people that is almost dead now, like Thoreau and Emerson. They have their roots in the 19th century. They are content and confident in themselves" (qtd. in "Wizard" 46).[9] But as culturally rich as this environment was, it alone could not confer on its members a lasting sense of legitimacy because, as Pierre Bourdieu has argued, cultural legitimacy cannot be permanently secured through inheritance alone, but must be constantly reasserted through the perpetual manifestation of the right kind of disposition—"the taste for old things," which includes, of course, a taste for old books and the ancient ideas they hold (Bourdieu 71). The Great Books program Buchanan and Barr had established in Annapolis was the ideal place for the Van Doren children precisely because the college would help them perfect their taste for old things while protecting them from that dark triad of *worldly* dispositions: vocationalism, specialism, and professionalism.

While the college served this useful purpose for all parents who wished to pass on to their children the cultural patrimony of the ages, Buchanan and Barr were bitterly disappointed to discover that, of their own friends and colleagues, all of whom were vociferous public supporters of the Great Books program, not one could be enticed to come to Annapolis and actually help them run the college. And so, as administrators of a cultural institution for conferring legitimacy, Buchanan and Barr found themselves in the unanticipated position of struggling to find teachers who could handle the broad demands of the Great

Books curriculum—teachers, that is, who could legitimately tackle the entire curriculum, from Plato to Hegel, Euclid to Einstein, Archimedes to Huygens. This was one of the difficult lessons the two administrators were to learn during their stay in Annapolis: that it was one thing to argue that all students should receive a liberal arts education; it was quite another to expect adults who had embarked upon other lives, other careers, and other worldly engagements to set aside these commitments to answer the call to staff courses in unfamiliar areas, read admissions applications, and spend the remainder of their days discussing the same handful of books over and over again.

This lesson was not long in coming. Just a year after Buchanan became dean of the college, he was pleading with Adler to come to Annapolis, arguing that the addition of such a stalwart supporter of the integrated study of the liberal arts "would push us over the top by next June. I even think we could all leave then and the thing would go on: I mean Winkie [Barr], you and I. I suspect we have more important things to do, and could get the right kind of administrators to carry on."[10] But Adler could not be persuaded to leave the security and the luxuries that his position at the University of Chicago afforded: "There is no question in my mind about my past or character up to this time. I have followed Mammon; I have been Machiavellian. Fame and riches, ease and success, comfort and acclaim, these have been what I have set my store by; and on the side I've had a little respect for the truth; and when everything else has been going well, I have worried inconsequentially about my soul."[11] Years later, aware of how his own actions in this instance and in others might appear to conflict with the public position he had staked out on the transcendent value of studying the Great Books, Adler offered the explanation in his "intellectual autobiography," *Philosopher at Large,* that he was "emotionally immature" during the twenty-two years he stayed at the University of Chicago and that his behavior at the time should be seen as the byproduct of "a defect in my own makeup rather than in the educational theory I had gradually developed" (7). Whether this is the most fruitful way to account for this disjunction in Adler's public pronouncements and his private actions will remain an open question for the moment. What is certain is that, for whatever disparate reasons, all the leaders in the national discussion of the Great Books curriculum—Robert Maynard Hutchins, Richard McKeon, Alexander Meiklejohn, and even Mark Van Doren—responded in the same way to Buchanan's personal invitation that they come and be a part of the St. John's faculty: however flattering it was to receive such an offer, life at the little college in Annapolis held little lasting appeal.[12]

Indeed, by 1942, just as Charlie Van Doren was commencing his studies at St. John's, Buchanan was writing to the elder Van Doren to express his growing fatigue with the administrative demands of running the college and his hopes of finding some way out. Buchanan suggested that he and the elder Van Doren shed what he termed "the Columbia and St. John's academic smell" by capitalizing on a proposal Alexander Meiklejohn had made for the establishment of an "institute for training teachers in international education" that drew on the resources of the mass media to promote the study of the great books.[13] By 1946, the year of Charlie's graduation, Buchanan's distaste for life at the college in Annapolis was complete: both he and Barr resigned and set off on an ill-fated journey to establish a new college in Massachusetts and, when this failed, they turned their attention, reasonably enough, to the problems of establishing a world government.[14]

THE UNDERSIDE OF "THE INTELLECTUAL LIFE"

While there's nothing in the consultable record to account for why Charles Van Doren placed his trust in Buchanan on the eve of his confession before the congressional subcommittee, the best we can do is assume that Van Doren felt Buchanan—either by virtue of his learning, his experiences, or his own past actions—was particularly well positioned to appreciate just how difficult it is for those who have committed themselves to the life of the mind to acknowledge the allure of worldly things. What we do know is that, in Van Doren's statement, he acknowledges that, by participating in the deception and then by publicly denying it for so long, he betrayed the trust both the public and his colleagues had placed in him as a professional educator. As Van Doren tells the story, originally he had been convinced to play along with the con by Freedman's argument that, just by appearing on the nationally televised program, he "would be doing a great service to the intellectual life, to teachers and to education in general, by increasing public respect for the work of the mind through [his] performances."[15] Throughout the four months he spent on the show, Van Doren struggled with this justification, before concluding that his success "was really giving a wrong impression of education. True education does not mean the knowledge of facts exclusively." To correct the audience's persistent misunderstanding of what the real fruits of a true education were, Van Doren "wrote articles trying to express this feeling, but few were interested."

Van Doren refrains from providing a full explanation of why he was persuaded by Freedman's argument that his success on a television game show would somehow change public perception of education for the better: he says only that he does not wish to "bore this committee by describing the intense moral struggle that went on inside" him as he thought this through. Conceding that his actions harmed and disillusioned many, Van Doren concludes by noting that he did manage, for a brief time, to channel some of his success toward the good of the nation. After having racked up $129,000 in winnings on *Twenty-One,* he signed a contract with NBC for $50,000 a year to appear on their morning news show and "talk for 5 minutes every morning about some subject which [he] considered interesting and important."[16] Van Doren used these precious five minutes to speak about subjects ranging from science to poetry to history to famous people and when he spoke about poetry he did so, he says, "as I would to a Columbia class." With a national audience focused on him, Van Doren continues, he used the television to generate that taste for old things: "I think I may be the only person who ever read 17th-century poetry on a network television program—a far cry from the usual diet of mayhem, murder and rape." Thus, even as Van Doren bares his soul by confessing his complicity with the national network's deceptive practices, he labors to preserve the marks that distinguish him both from the masses and from the business world, those two groups whose denizens have little interest in "true education" or in being treated to a bit of old poetry along with their morning coffee.

As it turns out, there's no question that people did, in fact, admire Van Doren's accomplishments: one letter to the editor in *Time* nominated him for the Man of the Year Award; and *Time* itself reported that one in four letters to Van Doren thanked him "for taking the curse off studying" ("Wizard" 49).[17] But, surely, the game-show format itself offered a particularly bizarre vision of the rewards for studying, since in this world of isolation booths and perpetual examinations, little boys and little girls around the country were being told— knowledge is money, so get cracking because now it literally pays to learn! In fact, what the quiz show offered, in effect, was an opportunity to see the familiar world of education turned upside down, for here the average person (the housewife, the cook, the shoemaker, the military officer) could reveal him or herself to be uncommonly talented and receive in exchange not what education usually offers—a grade, a degree, the promise of a bright future, a pat on the head—but something much more valuable: immediate material wealth!

The most common explanation for the pleasures generated by such spectacles is the assertion that viewers who are taken in by this imaginary world are cultural dopes who have been brainwashed by the media to embrace the religion of consumerism. However, as we saw in chapter 5, one reason to reject such appeals to false consciousness is that, as James Scott has argued, historically subordinate groups have spoken freely offstage, in "the hidden transcript," about "a total reversal of the existing distribution of status and rewards," a world where the first shall be last and the last shall be first (80). The quiz show offers a vision of just such a world: in this imaginary world, what you're worth is what you've put inside your head, not who you know, where you were born, who your parents were, or where you went to school. Gone is that other world—the one ruled by ambiguity, injustice, and the undeserved privilege that comes through the accident of birth—and in its place is a utopian democratic meritocracy. Here, your worth is a direct measure of a tangible quantity, producible on demand—your ability to answer factually based questions in the time allotted. And so, although those who enjoy the spectacle of the quiz show may well be powerless to disrupt the circulation of power, prestige, and material wealth in the real world, it doesn't necessarily follow that they are incapable of imagining a different world of social relations. This, at any rate, is one way to explain the incommensurate pleasure that quiz-show fans experience when one of the contestants reveals, after much lip biting and brow mopping, that he has exactly what his examiners want and he's had it hidden away deep inside all along.

If Scott's theory can account for the broad appeal of the quiz-show genre, can it also explain the audience's attraction to Van Doren, whose weekly successes, in Scott's terms, reinverted the quiz show's world upside down and reestablished the primacy of the well born, well educated, and well connected? One could argue that Van Doren's appearance in this "lowbrow arena" played well to that other imaginative sensibility Scott attributes to the members of subordinate cultures—namely, the desire "to negate the existing social order" (80–81). Seen through this prism, the very fact that Van Doren elected to compete on *Twenty-One* could be read as proof that this blue-blooded New Englander wasn't, in any fundamental way, different from "the culinary Marine captain or the opera-buff shoemaker" who had won vast sums on the *$64,000 Question*; Van Doren just happened to be better at the game than they were. He was, as *Time* put it, "an agile Jack-of-all-subjects," the equivalent of a knowledge handyman ("Wizard" 44). And, if Van Doren's appearance on the show served both to legitimize quiz shows and to flatten out essential distinctions between the classes, the scandal surrounding his involvement in the deception provided one final delicious reversal, confirming, as it did, what subordinates record in their hidden transcripts all the time, but rarely allow themselves to speak aloud in public: the whole system is rigged to advance the fame and fortune of those already in power.

Scott's argument gleefully invites such open-ended speculation about the thoughts and motives of subordinates, but such speculation is unlikely to be received as compelling evidence that Van Doren's deception was anything less than the world-shattering event it is represented to be in media histories. A more convincing argument—at least within the academic community—would draw on actual statements viewers made at the time, but this is the very kind of evidence the archive is least likely to preserve, save in the predigested and predetermined form of editorials of outrage and despair over the media's betrayal of the public trust. The archive does contain one surprise, though: a remnant of the hidden transcript that lay just beyond Van Doren's public declaration of contrition. Two months after testifying to the congressional subcommittee, his contract with NBC terminated, no longer an employee of Columbia University, Van Doren wrote Buchanan to say: "I very much want to make up for what I have done. By that I don't mean make up to men. To hell with men. Only a few of them deserve it. I mean to scholarship, philosophy, learning, whatever. I want to bury myself completely in a long, important job. I want to be anonymous. I may not, of course, always feel this way."[18] And with this response to his public humiliation and to his own suffering, Van Doren turns the vision of the selfless educator on its head and returns us to the very question with which we began: in seeking this brand of scholarly anonymity, in seeking solace in ideas rather than in human community, is Van Doren departing from or moving toward the ideals of the liberal arts education?

MAKING THE PITCH FOR THE GREAT BOOKS

As it so happens, Mark Van Doren himself addresses this very question about the ultimate aim of the liberal arts education in a promotional film he narrated for St. John's in 1954. Produced with monies provided by Paul Mellon's Old Dominion Fund, *The St. John's Story* was meant to introduce prospective students to the college's singular approach to education: according to Richard Weigle, who served as president of the college from 1949–1980, from the time *The St. John's Story* was released in 1954 until the time it was taken out of circulation in 1959, the film bore "the major burden of recruitment" for the college and was seen by "about a quarter of a million persons" (42). It's a remarkably ambitious work, unique in the genre of promotional films for its effort to capture and give drama to that very activity so central to the quiz show producers and yet so hard to capture visually—the mind at work on a problem. Unlike the quiz shows, though, where the concern was to offer a vision of the mind at work reproducing facts on demand, the makers of *The St. John's Story* faced a dual challenge: first, they had to come up with a way of dramatizing, in just under thirty minutes, the mind latching on to an idea, wrestling with it, and then joining in the Great Conversation; then the filmmakers had to find a way to make such a story appealing to high-school students who were thinking about which college to attend.

The filmmakers tackled these interrelated problems by providing a whirl-wind tour of one student's journey through the four-year program, beginning with the culmination of the educational experience at the college—the public defense of the senior thesis—and then working backwards. In a lucky twist of fate, it turns out that William Barrett, the film's main character, has written his thesis on a topic which couldn't be more fitting for our purposes here: "Political Facts and Natural Law." But before we are brought in to witness Barrett's defense, it is Mark Van Doren's voice we hear over the opening shots of the campus and its environs: "About a century ago, John Stuart Mill, the philosopher and economist said, 'Men are men before they are lawyers or physicians or manufacturers and if you make them capable and sensible men, they will make themselves capable and sensible lawyers or physicians or manufacturers.' This is the tradition of the liberal arts at St. John's. This means learning to think, to analyze problems, make judgments and express ideas." Once again, we are treated to a vision of a college that defines itself over against those schools primarily concerned with vocationalism or professionalism; and we are presented, as well, with what has become the most familiar defense of liberal education— that, by training people "to think, to analyze problems, make judgments and express ideas," the liberal arts produce "capable and sensible" people who can, in turn, train themselves to be whatever they please. The liberal arts, in other words, generate independence of mind and a hearty self-reliance.

Barrett's thesis, as he presents it to the three faculty members who have convened to examine him, touches on this very subject: "My thesis is about the statement, 'might makes right.' Many people accept this statement as a political fact. To show that they are wrong, I have to show that 'might makes right' is not a law of human nature. There are many kinds of laws and they are not all the same: there are civil laws and scientific laws; laws about the way things are and the way things ought to be." This is hardly an original thesis to tackle, which is precisely the reason why it appears in the film, for it captures the essence of a college community committed to contemplating perennial questions about the nature of Man: is Man innately good or can he only be deemed so within a given political system?[19] Anticipating the possibility that members of the projected audience might respond to this opening scene by wondering why *anyone* would bother with such broad questions, the scriptwriters interrupt Barrett's defense and flash back to a time when Barrett himself doubted the utility of pursuing such an education. In this flashback, Barrett enters the dean's office and declares his intention of dropping out of the program. Frustrated with the mandatory rituals of introspection, the eternal questions, and the obsession with language at the college, Barrett asks the dean: "What's it all got to do with me? I've got a life to live." At this point, the elder Van Doren's voice returns to the film, speaking over the image of the dean and Barrett locked in the conversation that will eventually convince the lad to remain at the college a bit longer: "Barrett had a life to live and he couldn't see what training his mind had to do with living. There is no simple convincing answer the dean could give. For Barrett, there seemed to be no connection between understanding Plato's arguments and doing one's job, between the mathematics of Copernicus and finding one's place in a democracy. The connection is there. To develop the mind means to exercise it in the broadest way, to train it in imagination, in mathematical accuracy, in powers of analysis and expression. The value of a broad liberal arts education is enormous, but sometimes this is hard to explain."

The difficulties the filmmakers run into here in trying to show how one comes to understand this concept which is so hard to explain—namely, the ongoing relevance of a liberal arts education—are difficulties that hamper *any* effort to visually represent the experience of education. Learning or becoming engaged in a discussion or getting lost in thought never produces the kind of visual spectacle that a quiz show delivers with such ease—money piling up, lights going off, curtains opening to reveal that fabulous new car. In *The St. John's Story*, these difficulties are worked through by recapturing the discussion that helped Barrett find his way back to the seminar table, where the Great Conversation is always ongoing. It happens, of course, in a flash: one minute Barrett is staring off into space while his classmates rattle on senselessly about Machiavelli and the next he can't restrain himself from pouncing on a student who has suggested that Machiavelli is simply being realistic about the way the world is. When Barrett snarls, "But maybe Machiavelli is only looking at half the facts. People don't always have to act like a pack of wolves. They know what human rights are. And they can learn to respect them, can't they?" Mark Van Doren's voice intones that our lost student has once again found his place in the college and a thesis to boot. It's hardly a fine-grained depiction of engaged, thoughtful discussion, but it's the best the medium can do with the impossible job of transforming an essentially internal, private act of connection into an external, dramatic event that the viewing audience can enjoy.

The film concludes its pitch for the liberal arts by returning to Barrett's public defense of his thesis, which is winding to a close. Barrett's examiners would like for him to speak to the issue of what dangers education might pose for a democracy:

Q: What kind of a safeguard does a democracy have against tyranny?

B: Well, it seems that education is the only safeguard.

Q: Isn't education itself subject to tyranny? Wouldn't it be possible to set up an educational system that would enslave people?

B: Yes it would. I was thinking of an education that would teach you to think for yourself.

Q: Then education can be bad?

B: Yes, when it pretends to teach you what you ought to think. I don't mean that a good education is easy, but it's the only safeguard that a democracy has, because it must teach its people to think clearly and act impartially.

Q: Our time seems to be about up.

Relying on language that in another context might be termed vacuous and insubstantial, the film thus concludes with its declaration of faith in the power of education: to protect democratic freedoms; to produce an active and aware citizenry; and to ensure that a bedrock of common culture is there to be found beneath the appearance of the citizenry's multiplicity and difference. This was surely intended to be a rousing send-off for high-school students watching the film at the tail end of the McCarthy era. And so, although Barrett never does get beyond reciting these familiar pieties about what constitutes a "good education," the "heavy propaganda" of the film, as Buchanan might have termed it,[20] leaves little doubt that the liberal arts education is the only safeguard a democracy has.

BURYING CHARLIE

It would be hard, I think, for any professional educator to claim to have escaped the capture of some version of this story about why what we do is important: this is, after all, our "common sense" about the value of teaching. Just beyond this comforting story of education's central importance, though, we have Van Doren's embrace of a brand of scholarship which seems to have nothing to do with this noble fight over democracy, citizenship, and the cultivation of "capable and sensible" people, but rather is an avenue to anonymity and social insignificance, a way to disappear from the scene of culture into the sense of security that only the world of texts can offer. In this moment, when Van Doren declares "to hell with men," how do his family, his teachers, and his protectors— all public supporters of the vision of education espoused in the film—respond to his desire to disappear from the scene of instruction? Is this a time to "teach Charlie a lesson"? Or is it time to have Charlie teach us a lesson about the nec- essary and inevitable disjunctions that exist between the rhetoric that buttresses liberal arts education and the actions of those involved in propounding its mission?

Perhaps the best place to begin to answer these questions are with Buchanan's response to Charlie's confession of guilt. The archive contains no record of Buchanan's having ever responded directly to the letter where Van Doren cred- its him with being "the only person so far who understands why" he partici- pated in the deception. What the archive does contain, though, is a letter from Buchanan to Harris Wofford,[21] written just weeks after Van Doren's confession, where Buchanan offers a fairly candid appraisal of what the affair has revealed about Charlie's character: "It is doubtful that Charlie can put himself together again, or as Steve [Benedict] said, 'for the first time.' Put another way, it is doubtful that Charlie has any internal machinery for comprehending what he and the gang did, or what he has to do to compensate for it. As he says, he loves persons so much that he cannot bring himself to do what is best for them and himself when it hurts them immediately, as early exposure in this case might have done."[22] Despite this dark assessment of Charlie's "internal machinery," Buchanan joined the effort to see if they could put Charlie back together again. When the scandal broke, Buchanan was ensconced at Robert Maynard Hutchins's Santa Barbara think tank, the Center for the Study of Democratic Institutions, where he, Adler, and Hutchins had discussed for more than a year how "to rescue Charlie from the TV monster." Although they'd been hoping for some time to install Charlie as one of the main editors of the *Encyclopedia Britannica,* this idea stopped being feasible once Van Doren had confessed to his role in the deception, so they all "agreed on one rather rough term, namely that what Charlie needed was to be temporarily 'buried.'"[23]

Because William Benton, part-owner of the *Encyclopedia Britannica* and longtime associate of Hutchins, was not keen on having Van Doren work for the company, fearing the bad publicity, Hutchins and Adler "invented the end-run," finding a way to have Charlie work for Hutchins "writing essays on the whole new *EB* enterprise," with the money coming from a special fund the *Encyclope- dia Britannica* gave to Adler—a strategy that had as "one intention being to let Benton learn" about Charlie's talents. Buchanan was clearly uncomfortable with this arrangement, but calmed his own fears with the thought that: "everybody has to learn his way through the dark wood, and Charlie along with the rest of us has a lot still to learn. The delicacy and deviousness of this arrangement will be a way of learning in many ways." With the arrangements for Charlie's "burial" thus concluded, Buchanan closes his letter to the elder Van Doren with a startling revelation that emerged from the planning session: "There is one thing about Bob [Hutchins] that has impressed everybody: from the very start he has said that he can well imagine himself doing everything that Charlie did, quiz show, NBC, and all up to the grand jury, and he probably would have done that too if he hadn't had a training in law. This shocks his worshipful staff, but they now know he means it. In his very typical style, the other day, he remarked that whenever he had thought of writing his autobiography, all he could find to say was the title, My Life is a Fraud."[24] This is a remarkable confession from Hutchins, who had insisted years earlier, in his nationally acclaimed jeremiad, *The Higher Learning in America,* that, with the establishment of a "real university" with "a real program of general education," it "may be that we can outgrow the love of money, that we can get a saner conception of democracy, and that we can even understand the purposes of education" (118–19). Against these now familiar claims about the transcendent value of a liberal arts education, Hutchins's admission that his own lifelong pursuit of such an education had not, in fact, inured him to the appeal of the material world and his conclusion that, as a consequence, his own life had traced out a path of fraudulence is positively bracing, for it opens up the possibility of imagining a rather different project for education—one where this distance between the rhetoric of recruitment to the humanities and the actuality of human motivation is allowed to collapse and a more humane, more productive account of the human condition might rise in its place.

BENTON'S FOLLY AND THAT FAMILIAR HEADLONG PLUNGE INTO THE ABYSS

As the evidence mounts, with Charles Van Doren, Mortimer Adler, Scott Buchanan, and now Robert Maynard Hutchins all confessing to feeling like frauds, despite or perhaps because of all their years spent promoting the revivifying powers of the Great Books, it will pay to take one final turn through the field to see how it came to be that Buchanan, Hutchins, and Adler were in a position to bury Charlie at the *Encyclopedia Britannica* and bestow upon him the gift he desired and the resolution that was essential to all concerned—his burial in the realms of the anonymous. In order to pursue this final line of inquiry, it is necessary first to return to events at the University of Chicago early in 1935, where Hutchins and Adler had initiated their efforts to redefine the undergraduate general education curriculum.[25] One unintended consequence of these efforts to put important books on the undergraduate reading list was that Hutchins found himself called before the Illinois Senate to address charges initiated by the department-store magnate Charles Walgreen that the University of Chicago was subjecting its students to communist influences by requiring them to read the *Communist Manifesto* and other suspicious works in order to graduate.

While Hutchins was successful in alleviating the senate's fear that the university had become a breeding ground for the Red Insurrection, he also felt that the damage done to the university's reputation was substantial, so he asked William Benton, a classmate from his Yale days and a newly retired advertising magnate, to come study the problem of modern university public relations. Although Benton had no intention of staying on once his work was done, his report was so well received and his influence so immediately felt that he eventually agreed to spend six months each year serving as one of the university's vice presidents, a decision that ended up profoundly shaping the university's financial future. Benton's fund-raising powers were nothing short of magical: less than a year after Hutchins had appeared before the senate, Benton had convinced Walgreen to donate more than half a million dollars to the university, a portion of which went towards establishing the Charles R. Walgreen Foundation for the Study of American Institutions.

Benton's biggest coup, though, came two days after the bombing of Pearl Harbor when he commented, during a lunch with General Robert E. Wood, chairman of Sears, Roebuck and Company, that it seemed "rather unsuitable for a mail-order house to own the *Encyclopedia Britannica,*" particularly in wartime (qtd. in Hyman 247). When Wood agreed, Benton suggested that the general donate the encyclopedia to the university, which, after a significant pause, Wood said he would do. In the following year, Benton worked tirelessly to find a way to transfer the encyclopedia to the university, ultimately putting up his own money to cover the anticipated cost of running the company for one year and becoming owner of two-thirds of the company's stock with the university holding the other third. If the company didn't prove to be profitable after one year, Wood agreed to take it back; if it did, the university had the option of buying one-third of Benton's stock, thereby becoming the major holder. And thus, on January 14, 1943, Benton and the university found themselves in the curious position of owning that monument to the sweep of the British imperial gaze, the *Encyclopedia Britannica.*[26]

Although no one knew it at the time, this chain of events put in place all the essential pieces necessary for the emergence of the project to collect together and publish a bound set called *Great Books of the Western World*. Benton (who had once sought the assistance of a psychologist at the university to cut his sleeping time down to five hours so that he could get more done in a day) realized the need for such a handy collection when, in the fall of 1943, he and his wife enrolled in what was known as the "fat cats' course," Hutchins's and Adler's Great Books seminar for the trustees and other businessmen. As the story goes, Benton found the process of trying to find the books at the library or the local bookstore too time consuming and asked Adler and Hutchins to put together a complete set under the aegis of the *Encyclopedia Britannica,* which seminar members could then buy at one fell swoop. When sales executives at *Encyclopedia Britannica* pointed out that many of the books on Hutchins's and Adler's reading list were already readily available, for much less than they would cost through the *Encyclopedia Britannica,* and that a comparable venture, Dr. Eliot's "five-foot shelf," the *Harvard Classics,* was doing quite poorly, Benton realized that he needed a trick, a gimmick, "some kind of allure that will induce people to take the great books off the shelves and actually read them to find out what they want to know" (qtd. in Hyman 287).

The gimmick Adler came up with was soon known as either the *Syntopicon* or "Benton's Folly," depending on who was speaking: "an index of ideas, great ideas. . . . [A]n index," according to Adler, "that will help the average reader learn about topics in which he is especially interested" (qtd. in Hyman 287). As Adler tells the story, the idea for an index that would catalog and cross-reference the great ideas of Western thought had occurred to him when he was writing *How to Think about War and Peace.* In researching the book, Adler found passages in the Great Books that he had not attended to carefully in previous readings and this led him to conclude "that the only way the great books could be thoroughly mined involved reading them again and again, each time with a different specific question in mind" (Adler 237). In the interests of "thoroughly mining" each great book and of constructing a twenty-five-century long conversation between the books, the *Syntopicon* was born. By the time it was completed, its two volumes of meticulously cataloged cross-references had consumed over half of the two million dollars expended on the entire fifty-four-volume set of *Great Books of the Western World.*

While Benton's commitment to publishing a set of the Great Books was unstoppable in 1943, as time passed, he was forced to consider abandoning the project by the steadily increasing cost of collating the *Syntopicon* and by the suddenly precarious state of the encyclopedia business, which had suffered from declining sales once the war ended and people had begun to spend their

disposable income on refrigerators, automobiles, and other more physically re-
warding purchases. But Benton was a remarkably canny businessman who
knew that the success of any business venture depended on creating a market,
so he wasn't going to give up without a fight: he himself had become a major
stockholder in the Muzak company in 1939 and is credited with getting that
company to move into the business of selling, as he himself defined it, "music
that is *not* to be listened to" (qtd. in Hyman 214). In this case, the solution
Benton came up with required that Hutchins and Adler assume the burden of
creating a market for the fifty-four-volume set of *Great Books of the Western
World:* specifically, in order to keep the project going, Hutchins and Adler
would have to drum up five hundred benefactors who would commit to buying
one complete set of the books for five hundred dollars apiece, which, in turn,
would generate the quarter of a million dollars required to cover the initial
printing costs.

At the *Great Books of the Western World* publication party in New York on
April 15, 1952, held for all those who had helped Hutchins and Adler reach
their sales target, Hutchins had this to say about what the successful launch
signified: "This is more than a set of great books, and more than a liberal education. *Great Books of the Western World* is an act of piety. Here are the sources
of our being. Here is our heritage. Here is the West. This is its meaning for mankind, for here before everybody willing to look at it is that dialogue by way of
which Western man has believed that he can approach the truth" (qtd. in
Ashmore 336–37). If publishing the Great Books was an act of piety, it was an
act performed by a very small, select sect, with beliefs impossible to determine.
Certainly, by 1952, Hutchins and Adler held few illusions about the number of
people who were genuinely interested in taking part in the Great Conversation.
In fact, as Hutchins and Adler well knew, it wasn't simply the market that was
hostile to this product; there were those intimately involved in the project itself
who had grave doubts about its integrity.

As early as 1946, Buchanan had informed Adler that he felt those seriously
interested in advancing the mission of the liberal arts education had to cut all
ties with the *Encyclopedia Britannica:*

> As long as [the *Encyclopedia Britannica* is] a commercial firm, I
> don't think we can safely work with them, except as suppliers of
> books on a commercial basis. The Great Books project is my
> convincing point against them. I am now quite horrified at the job
> of selecting books that we did, and wish I had stuck to my resigna-
> tion. . . . You are doing a crazy job in the Index, and you can't

control it now because they have spent so much money on it. . . .
The burden of selling the books has given your activities in adult
education a fever that also horrifies me.[27]

Within months of writing this letter, Buchanan's critique of the project had
mushroomed to the point where he informed Hutchins: "Mortimer [Adler] has
played a trick on us and on himself in his index project. He is packing all the
apparatus and aids for readers that we disapproved into his index, which is neither scholarly nor an interpretive aid. It is simply Mortimer getting his staff to
blow up to a monster his own bogus tricks of research, scissors and paste mixed
with his to-day's current position in philosophy. I asked him who could or
would use his index and he said people like himself and again he was not concerned. The people who are like him will be disgusted and angry, if they ever
look at it."[28]

For those who did go ahead and purchase *Great Books of the Western World,*
the volume entitled *The Great Conversation* was there to introduce them into
what was imagined to be a lifelong project of self-education. Hutchins begins
this volume with the proclamation that the multivolume set of books was offered neither in an "antiquarian spirit" nor to take "tourists on a visit to ancient
ruins." Rather, those who plan to make their way through the collection must be
prepared to accept the fact that what lies ahead won't be entertaining in the
conventional sense of the word: "We have not thought of providing our readers
with hours of relaxation or with an escape from the dreadful cares that are the
lot of every man in the second half of the twentieth century after Christ. We are
as concerned as anybody else at the headlong plunge into the abyss that Western civilization seems to be taking. We believe that the voices that may recall the
West to sanity are those which have taken part in the Great Conversation" (xii)
Reading these books, thus, is understood to offer possible salvation for a modern world confronted with the horror of imminent global holocaust. Throughout *The Great Conversation,* Hutchins returns again and again to this theme,
stressing that industrialization is the force responsible both for bringing Western civilization to the edge of the abyss and for making education available to
the masses through the provision of increased leisure time.

"But what," Hutchins asks in horror, "if the time that is gained for life off
the assembly line is wasted, as much of it is today, in pursuits that can only be
described as subhuman? What if the man as he works on the line has nothing in
his head?" (22). It is with just such an audience in mind that the editors have
organized the Great Books series: the collection has no scholarly introductions
nor any other orienting apparatus nor is it be mangled by the "classical dissec-

tors and drillmasters" (29). The series editors have stepped out of the way so as to ensure that the reader, just off the assembly line and ready to fill the emptiness in his head, might approach the books in a pure and natural state. "Since we hold that these works are intelligible to the ordinary man, we see no reason to interpose ourselves or anybody else between the author and the reader" (xxv). Granted this unmediated relationship to the Great Books, the "ordinary man" would be free to find a place to speak within the Great Conversation and to begin to feel "a member of the species and tradition that these books come from" (30). In this way, the books might be able to draw the reader back from the abyss so that he could participate in revitalizing the dialogue that leads to truth.

Here, too, we run into the same reception problem we encountered earlier: there's no way of knowing what kind of readers actually ended up purchasing the series, what their motivations were, or how they used the books once they got them into their homes without embarking on a very different kind of study than the one taken up here. The available figures suggest, however, that while the series sold well in its first year, sales declined dramatically thereafter until the *Encyclopedia Britannica* began to market the series door-to-door on the installment plan.[29] Even so, by the early 1960s, the series had ceased to be a profitable venture for reasons that had to do, according to Adler, with the "generally iconoclastic and anti-retrospective atmosphere" of those revolutionary times (228, 259). While the series continues to be published by the *Encyclopedia Britannica*, having been expanded to include contributions by contemporary writers on twentieth-century philosophy and religion, social science, and imaginative literature, with an asking price just shy of two thousand dollars, the mass appeal of this now sixty-volume series is undoubtedly severely restricted.

Contracted on a whim, overseen by a coterie of thinkers whose educational theories committed them to a disdain for worldly things, produced in response to a need that announced itself in no clear or visible way, *Great Books of the Western World* survives to this day as the expression of a strange and contradictory piety for books and ideas—an offering, if you will, for a benighted citizenry Hutchins himself had described years earlier in *The Higher Learning in America* as a "faithless generation [who] take no stock in revelation" (97). In a certain way, it seems almost humane that this is where Charlie would end up being buried, among the fellow travelers who worked at the *Encyclopedia Britannica* and at Hutchins's Center for the Study of Democratic Institutions, all of whom could find no other way to resolve the tension between their stated belief in the utterly transformative power of books and their actions as embodied, contingent beings moving through the real world. From another vantage point, though, Van Doren's consignment to the world of ideas seems a much crueler punishment than was meted out to the other central players in the quiz-show scandals: by the early 1970s, Dan Enright and Jack Barry were back out in the open and on the air with *The Joker's Wild* and *Tic Tac Dough*, while Van Doren was just emerging from the shadows as a ghostwriter who had spent nearly two decades working for Adler and Hutchins. His name appeared on the dust jacket of the 1972 revision of Adler's *How to Read a Book;* he slowly rose through the ranks to become a vice president at the *Encyclopedia Britannica*; he published books on subjects ranging from the history of knowledge to the joys of reading; but his name remains forever linked to the fraudulent acts he committed over a few weeks in the mid-1950s.

Forty years after Van Doren resigned his position as assistant professor in the English department at Columbia University, he was invited back into the light of day by the class of 1959 to speak at their reunion.[30] He accepted the invitation and delivered a talk on living a good life. He gently suggested that a happy life was largely dependent upon "good fortune" and that having a life one could judge at the end to have been happy required accepting the justice of Apollo, who "was—is—the handsome stranger with a smile on his face who promises us whatever we desire and then betrays us." When he completed his talk by urging his aging former students to avoid the despair that comes from descending into the underworld and scorning the gods, a strange and perhaps beautiful thing happened: "the entire audience rose to their feet as if they were one person and gave him a thunderous ovation. The audience's response brought tears to Charles Van Doren's eyes." Forty-five minutes later, the question period completed, where no one asked anything that "might have been considered tastelessly personal," Van Doren was gone, leaving behind at least one observer who could only think of "the thousands and thousands of students who were deprived of his wisdom and inspirational capabilities" by his precipitous fall from grace.

THE EDUCATOR'S ROLE IN THE PUBLIC SPHERE

In 1959, the same year Charlie Van Doren appeared before the congressional subcommittee to publicly confess his guilt, Daniel Keyes published a short story in the *Magazine of Fantasy and Science Fiction* entitled "Flowers for Algernon." Keyes subsequently expanded this story into a novel: it is now in its fifty-eighth edition, has been made into an Oscar-winning movie, and remains a perennial favorite on the high-school reading lists. The story concerns another Charlie, one who also found himself at the mercy of a set of professionals concerned with the business of making people appear "smart." This Charlie—Charlie Gordon, to be exact—is a young man with an IQ of 70, who has been selected to participate in an experiment that will double his intelligence. He is also a vehicle for delivering Keyes's completely straightforward critique of the medical profession's relentless pursuit of omnipotence. As Dr. Nemur, the physician in charge of the intelligence-enhancing experiment puts it, he and his team have "taken one of nature's mistakes and by our new techniques created a superior human being" (143). Here, it is the panoply of medical professionals, rather than the educators, who are endowed with transformative powers by virtue of their expert training: the neurosurgeon, the psychotherapist, the testers and evaluators, the peekers and the pokers. But their powers are limited: although they succeed in giving Charlie brief access to higher order thought, eventually Charlie's mental abilities begin to erode and he slides back down the other side of the bell curve. His fall is so complete that, by the end of the book, he is back in the position of being the helpless victim of the culture industries' mass-produced fantasies: he buys pornographic magazines, which give him funny dreams. "I wont buy them any more. I saw in one of those books they got magic powder that can make you strong and smart and do lots of things. I think mayby Ill send away and by some for myself" (270). Within a few pages, to our great relief, I suppose, Charlie dies.

If the rhetoric deployed to bolster the study of the Great Books musters visions of civic responsibility in a democracy and the transcendent values of education, the rhetoric Keyes draws on offers a relentlessly sentimental counternarrative, one where the professionals, the technocrats, and the teachers are all to be viewed with suspicion: they are not the agents of change that they seem to be, but rather the mere instruments of corruption, denying the intrinsic value of human life as they seek to extend and advance their puny careers. I'm tempted to say that there's a certain timelessness to the appeal of this popular version of how larger institutions interact with the weak, the isolated, the downtrodden. One can find a variation on this theme of distrust and suspicion in Lewis Gilbert's 1983 film *Educating Rita,* where Dr. Frank Bryant, an alcoholic English professor, finds himself responsible for tutoring Susan Rita White, an enthusiastic but untrained adult student. Rita's from the working class, but she's disaffected with the life that stands before her and she has dreams of bigger things: as she says, "The masses—it's not their fault, but sometimes I hate them."

To escape the fate of the masses, Rita decides to enroll at the Open University, which relies on the mass media to deliver its educational product—its lectures are broadcast over the BBC, its lessons are delivered through the mail, and its tutoring sessions are held on campuses across the country. It is Rita's "native" charm and her essential earthiness that captures her tutor's fancy and he watches, somewhat helplessly and then in horror, as the educational process he has helped to set in motion deprives his favorite student of all that is original, honest, and admirable about her: her accent disappears; her naive candor is replaced by a knowing sophistication; her sense of poetry's power gets redirected into an increased awareness of the egregious gaps in her reading background. By the story's end, we are, I gather, meant to feel some regret that Rita has been seduced by Bryant's lectures about poetry, that she embraces the very system he disdains, that her success in the academy transforms her into a different sort of person than she was initially.

The problem with such responses to the master narrative about the liberatory powers of the liberal arts education is that, in countering the promise of redemption and rebirth that is said to come through sustained contact with the Great Books, these alternative stories offer a vision of education and professionalism as exclusively the province of corruption and decay: both the master narrative and the counter-narratives, in effect, pivot on representing the student as essentially either the lucky benefactor of the educational process or its unwitting victim. Historicizing Charlie Van Doren's role in and response to the quiz-show scandals, however, upsets this easy opposition, since he appears to have oscillated between the poles of victor and victim, alternately responding to the calls of the mind and the calls of the body as the context seemed to require. In this respect, Hutchins's admission that he, too, would have fallen prey to the offer of easy money and instant fame provides a refreshing example of shared vulnerability we all have, regardless of our educational training, in a world of infinite possibility. Hutchins reaches the wrong conclusion, though, about the significance of this admission and the realities of the human situation when he elects to describe his own life as that of a "fraud." On the strength of Scott's analysis, we might just as well say that all cultural interactions are fraudulent, that we all collude in the ceaseless production and reproduction of a public transcript that we all know, in our private moments, to be an elaborate theater for preserving the status quo.

To deploy the charge of fraudulence in this way—that is, to take it to the furthest extreme and find everyone and everything fraudulent—serves the dual purpose of evacuating the charge of its damning power, while also exposing its limitations as a term of critical inquiry. That is, since the tensions between the public and the private, the mind and the body, the ideal and the pragmatic are irreducible and unresolvable, seeing every human action as tainted with fraudulence is neither productive nor useful. While such a cynical account of human affairs may be reassuring in some dark way, all it really does is relieve one of the responsibility of engaging in the endlessly frustrating and humanizing work of fabricating evanescent solutions to the ever-evolving social, political, economic, and personal challenges that ceaselessly confront us by virtue of the fact that we are embodied, thinking beings sharing the same living space. With this in mind, I would argue from the vantage point of an educator interested in reform that "fraudulence" becomes a useful analytic term for investigating what occurs in the academy only when the disparity between the public and private transcripts is not openly acknowledged, with the result that the public transcript is treated as *the* account of how things truly are.

Dorothy Van Doren's account of what it's like to live with an eminence of such stature that he is known, even to her, simply as The Professor, provides a particularly eerie vision of just how crippling it can be to insist that there is some pure distance that separates the learned from the power and appeals of the material world. *The Professor and I,* published just prior to the revelation of Charlie's involvement in the quiz-show scandals, commences its account of the quotidian experiences of the nation's literati with The Professor and his wife traveling to various friends' houses to watch Charlie's weekly exploits, which The Professor and his wife must do because they—none too surprisingly— don't own a television set themselves. As Charlie's winnings mounted, The Professor found it increasingly difficult to watch the show fearing that, in the excitement, he "might die or something," so, after two months of enduring this torture, The Professor heeded his son's advice that he spare himself the agony. While Dorothy was able to watch "the amazing total mount" a bit longer, eventually no one in the family could stand the suspense, so they would sit in some other room while emissaries, watching through their fingers, would report on Charlie's successes (2–3). By the end of this introductory chapter, though, The Professor and his doting wife have achieved a rather different relationship to the box: finding themselves in possession of a television set Charlie had received from one of the quiz show's sponsors, The Professor soon became "in a mild way, an addict. And an addict not of the super, the egg-head type of program, although we catch a few of those, but of mysteries, westerns, crime stories, true stories, and a quiz or two. He is lost" (8). As the curtain closes on this domestic scene, The Professor is planted before the set, watching wrestling, of all things, and confessing "shamefacedly" to his wife that he "just wanted to see what it was like" (9).

As The Professor gets sucked into the set, joining everyone else in that "headlong plunge into the abyss that Western civilization seems to be taking," it's worth pausing to reflect on one source of this continued *public* insistence that, under the best circumstances, the educator does not respond to the calls of the material world, even when there's a mass of private evidence that points to the vulnerability that results from exaggerations about the extent and permanence of such spiritual transcendence. In that greatest of all fantasies about a rationally ordered state, Plato's *Republic,* Socrates' belief in the transformative powers of education leads him to make his famous call for state supervision of "the makers of tales" on the grounds that the state must regulate which stories get to be told and which people are allowed to mix with each other. Including his interlocutors in this thought experiment, Socrates declares that: "We'll persuade nurses and mothers to tell the approved tales to their children and to shape their souls with tales more than their bodies with hands. Many of those they now tell must be thrown out" (377b).

As Socrates and the others pursue their project of building a city in words, the power of the imagination is consistently cast as the greatest threat to the smooth workings of this well-ordered polis—a problem which is solved by the expulsion of the poets, the Sophists, and all who would use language in ways that allow for ambiguity or deceit . . . by turning out, in short, the entire entertainment industry of ancient Greece. And throughout this discussion, Socrates constantly engages in the paradox that has been the central preoccupation of this chapter: he argues about the tremendous dangers that poets pose to the city and yet, through his repeated citations of their work, demonstrates his deep familiarity with the very material he most disdains. Of course, resolving this paradox is easy enough within this system of thought: the guardians of society —those gold-souled leaders of the tribe—just aren't susceptible to the lures and attractions that so effortlessly ensnare those folk with souls of a lesser order.

In light of the foregoing discussion, one could say that Socrates' argument is simply the public transcript of the dialogue and that the participants know going in that all this talk about justice, politics, and the production of good citizens is of absolutely no consequence. It is something they've all agreed to engage in—accepting the various twists and turns in the logic, the moments of embarrassment and the moments of insight—with the understanding that, in the end, they'll all go home and continue living as they always have. It's just a way of passing the time. So, yes, by all means expel the baser pleasures, they agree; expel all those things we enjoy, because they pose a danger to *lesser* people; we'll be fine because we take our pleasure in the highest things alone: the use of the mind and its ways with words. One could also say that Charlie Van Doren is, as we all are, the true inheritor of such lessons and that his story offers a particularly vivid example of the consequences of such a fraudulent pedagogy, where hypocrisy is silently transformed into the highest virtue. This is not all that education does nor all that it might do, but it is safe to say that educators will never escape the domination of this alluring vision of the transcendent importance of the mind working in isolation from the world as long as those engaged in the business of educating others insist on representing themselves as liberators and protectors of culture, clinging all the while to rhetorics that proclaim their mysterious abilities to judge the "quality of mind" of others.

The dangers posed by these more familiar definitions of the educator's mission are many, but I want to close by discussing the most central one at this time. For those who study the job market in higher education, it is clear that we are at the twilight of the profession as we have known it: the declining tax base, the rise of animosity for education as a kind of "social engineering," the steady replacement of tenured lines with temporary workers, the encroachment of total quality management and outcomes assessment, and the public cries for tangible evidence of the "products" of education have all served to change what it means to be a teacher in the academy and what it means to be a graduate student training for entry into this profession. While there are those who, in the wake of these changes, deplore the disappearance of students who embark on the adventure of advanced study purely out of their love for and devotion to learning and while there are still others who lament the public's intrusions into our discussions about what should be taught and why, I find it hard to mourn either the passing of these ways of imagining the business of higher education or the decline in this rhetoric's power to capture and mesmerize higher education's clientele. Perhaps the hard economic times that are unquestionably ahead for the academy will occasion a reconception of the opposition of the world of thought and the world of work, disrupting the fiction that those involved in the business of education are pure lovers of learning and replacing it, instead, with the possibility of a classroom environment where what gets discussed is not simply education's public transcript, in all its haughtiness and mastery, but the hidden transcript with its accounts of lived experience's refusal to conform to any totalizing, rationalistic system. By smudging, interrogating, and peering across the boundary separating these two realms, it is possible, I believe, to lessen what Bourdieu calls "the symbolic violence" of the educational process. Furthermore, by practicing the interrogative pedagogy grounded in the arts of complicity I have advocated here, it becomes possible to do the very thing which none of the figures in the preceding discussion could manage— that is, to work against the profoundly antidemocratic vision of education embodied in those rhetorics which openly embrace teaching's civilizing mission while saying under their breath, "To hell with men."

7

SPEAKING WITH THE DEAD

In the room where my father is lying on what will shortly turn out to be his deathbed, the attending respiratory technician asks me what I do for a living. Unable to hear over the sounds of the percussive massage she is giving my father, I have her repeat the question. Upon learning that I am an English teacher, she giggles and says, "Uh-oh, I better watch my language."

Believe it or not, I think my father would have enjoyed this incongruous scene. On one hand, you have the well-educated son who is powerless to ease his father's physical torment. On the other, there's the nurse who is well accustomed to witnessing the body's final decline, the one who knows from experience that what matters most to English teachers is whether subjects and verbs agree, that infinitives aren't split, that the apostrophe finally sits down in its appointed place. In his own writing, my father delighted in telling stories that recreated such uncomfortable encounters, stories where different experiential registers would bang into one another and no one would ever really quite know what was going on or why everyone was so upset and angry. He was also forever recording the confused silences that follow the well-intended but misguided efforts to establish a connection across these divided worlds. The weeping audience member, lost in her private sorrow. The reassuring pat on the hand by the concerned but confused friend at her side. The comforting observation that there's no reason to be so sad: the skull in Hamlet's hand isn't real. It's just a play. It's just a play.

Though I am neither a poet nor a fiction writer, I, too, have an abiding interest in such disjunctions because, for me, they dramatize the clash of cultures that serves as the pivot point for any potentially transformative educational experience. In this particular instance, as I see it, the drama in the intensive-care unit reverses the quintessential student-teacher interaction. Under normal circumstances, this encounter involves a student who feels, for whatever reasons, the need to hand in a paper that contains some dark truth—a divorce, a rape, a suicide attempt—and a teacher who scribbles in the margins "more detail, please," "this description of your father's death would be more moving if only you could spell better," "very sad, but doesn't address the assignment." On this occasion, though, it is the teacher and his father (also a teacher) who are overwhelmed by the world and the ravages of time and it is the student who finally gets the chance to say, in effect, "it is all very well and fine to be moved by an experience, but when the chips are down an appreciation for formal correctness is the hallmark of the educated person." And so, to those with a certain turn of mind, this exchange enacts a delicious moment of cultural revenge: across the text of my father's dying body, the student gets to scrawl, "Now, you watch your language!"

My example is extreme, of course. (Mine always are.) To some it may even seem absurd or offensive. For what it's worth, I can only offer the assurance that it doesn't reflect what I wanted to be thinking about during the final hours of my father's life. Regardless of my intentions, though, before I knew it I was envisioning education as the wound that never heals, hoping that peace would come in whatever form, and smoothing out the peaks and valleys in my voice so my father would relax and cough on command.

What is it that makes someone want to become an English teacher? This is a question that annually confronts new teachers in a graduate seminar I offer called "The Teaching of Writing." Because most of the students who enroll in the course have come to graduate school to pursue their interest in literature or theory, film or criticism, gender or politics, they are surprised to find out just how difficult and time consuming the work of reading and responding to student writing turns out to be. Many of the graduate students in the seminar have been drawn to teaching by the alluring image of the academic at the podium lecturing with authority, the figure at the center of the bracing give-and-take of class discussion, the one who waits patiently for the embers of thought to burst into flame. Movie houses are forever telling this story about pedagogy's amazing powers of conversion. There's always some alienated group of students abandoned by the system just waiting to have their cynicism and contempt slowly eroded by the mysterious elixir of the new teacher's unorthodox methods and her dreamy visions of how liberating education can be. The students always gain access to some higher level of understanding. The blind always learn to see.

I love this story. Like its daytime cousin on the small screen, the genre of the schoolhouse melodrama offers similar emotional rewards to its knowing viewers, who understand that no matter how bad things look for our innovative teacher, there's never reason to give up hope. Before long, fans of this genre know, there will be reason enough to rejoice, because nothing can stop the delivery of that final scene. The students have to take to their desktops and recite "Oh Captain, My Captain," the teacher must be convinced not to quit by students who use poetry to tell her how important she has become to them, the governor must show up for her music teacher's retirement party ready to play her clarinet. For those willing to wait, there's sure to be the performance of some spectacular act of homage to the teacher's lasting importance. There just has to be.

The truth though, which becomes clear enough to the new teachers in my seminar after their first few weeks of trying to teach composition to real students in real classrooms, is that this cinematic version of teaching has about as much to do with the actual work of soliciting, assessing, and responding to student writing as the version of romantic love on *Days of Our Lives* has to do with the actual work of generating and sustaining a lasting relationship. For those people who have always been good at school, this encounter with students who just can't seem to find their feet in the textual world, students who don't know the conventions for building a coherent paragraph, let alone a cogent argument, students who haven't read much and don't seem to feel somehow unfinished or incomplete as a result—well, let's just say, it's a shock. All those years distinguishing themselves from their peers, all those courses where they were required to scale the heights of literary theory, all that time spent mastering the rigorous regime of self-problematization: all of this, just to be sent back to work with the very kind of student they have labored so hard to get away from? Isn't this an incredible waste of human resources? Shouldn't cleanup work of this kind be somebody else's job?

In *Work Time: English Departments and the Circulation of Cultural Value*, Evan Watkins argues that graduate students are lured to the teaching profession by the promise of theory. In his example, people become English teachers so that they can research the frontier myth in F. Scott Fitzgerald's fiction and present their findings to audiences who share in the belief that such work is important. These people don't become teachers, he says, to read and grade hundreds of student papers about *The Great Gatsby*, to sit on departmental search committees, to write letters of recommendation—in short, to do any of the tasks that take up the vast majority of a teacher's actual work time. Arguing along similar lines, Cary Nelson has called the Modern Language Association to task for its failure to communicate a more accurate representation of what it now means to enter the profession of English studies. Here is the ad Nelson satirically suggests publishing to announce what really awaits those contemplating a life in the teaching profession working with words: "Come and teach marginally literate business majors how to write! Help students increase their earning power! Loans available to help cover your expenses! Good job performance ratings will have no effect on plans to terminate your employment!" ("Lessons" 21).

Here again we find a collision of differing experiential registers. Even as Nelson offers a much-needed critique of the MLA's refusal to come to terms with the realities of the marketplace and the actual content of a teacher's professional life, he can't help but be repulsed by the very kind of work that the members of my seminar—and graduate students throughout the profession—are regularly required to do and, if they are lucky enough to land a job after graduating, can pretty much count on doing for the rest of their careers. This is Nelson's Kurtzian moment, for the horror he imagines is a world where the noble English teacher is forever compelled to move among the "marginally literate," forever lost to the menial work of teaching others to write, forever vulnerable to an indifferent employer who extracts labor without regard to its human consequences. However much one might agree with Nelson's analysis of the inequities in the academy's labor practices, it is hard for me to share in his panic at the thought that teaching the literate arts might largely entail working with non-English majors or that the ultimate goal of such labor might be nothing more than assisting students in improving their social position.

It is not difficult to imagine a preferable world, one where students come to college to learn how to work collectively on solving the major problems of the twenty-first century. But back in the world that we have, the learning situation that prevails—the one that Nelson finds so distasteful—is the one that composition teachers must find a way to live with every day: students are required to take expository writing courses and that they are so required is understood by everyone involved to be an expression of the institutional belief that all students must be proficient writers if they are going to advance through the system. From the institutional standpoint, there's nothing personal about this peda- gogical relationship. Students must attend; teachers must be present; papers must be solicited, assessed, returned. And, regardless of what actually happens during this process, instruction *must* be said to have occurred.

Of course, my denuded description of what the teaching of writing actually entails doesn't make for any better ad copy than the ones provided by Nelson or Watkins; mine just reflects what getting into the teaching business "on the ground floor" looks like from the institutional perspective. However disap- pointed and frustrated the new teachers in my seminar may be to find them- selves engaged in such impersonal work, my project is to help them see the value in teaching their students to use writing as a technology to think with rather than as a tool for succinctly recording the thoughts of others or as a weapon for fending off other points of view. I try to show, as well, the intellec- tual merits of such work—the excitement and rewards it offers—even as I illus- trate how demanding it is to do the job well. As part of this project, I ask the new teachers repeatedly to write about what made it possible for them to excel in school. I want to denaturalize their own scholastic success so that it may be- come for them an object of study; I want them to consider the role that open- ended forces like contingency, chance, and luck may have played in getting them admitted to one of the nation's best English programs. Unless they learn about their own ways of learning, I tell them, they won't be well positioned to recognize, understand, or respond to the many other ways of learning that stu- dents bring with them to the classroom.

To this end, I assign Bourdieu's "Aristocracy of Culture," so the new teach- ers can familiarize themselves with his description of how educational systems create, hierarchize, and naturalize arbitrary distinctions among people. One of the implications of Bourdieu's analysis is that the educational system has inter- nal as well as external effects: the system doesn't just churn out credentialed in- dividuals, it produces people who, because they have done well in school, actu- ally end up *feeling* smart and people who, because they have done poorly, find that they can never quite forget the experience of having once made their in- choate thoughts subject to public evaluation. ("I better watch my language.") Bourdieu helps the new teachers to see that what happens in the classroom is an education in silence as much as it's an education in expression. I also assign Mike Rose's *Lives on the Boundary,* in which the new teachers learn about Rose's long journey back to the world of ideas thanks to an unexpected confluence of caring teachers, interested friends, determination, chance.

In response to these reading assignments, the new teachers provide me with their own literacy narratives, which make almost no mention of important teachers, family members, or other role models. Their responses record instead a certain talent for schooling, a drive to succeed, a preternatural love of learning, a history of good grades stretching out over the horizon. And, from a few, I receive intimations of how isolating academic success can be, passing references to a desire to avoid situations where the limits of one's understanding might be exposed, veiled confessions of doubt about how much longer the facade of one's brilliance can be kept in place, and shadowy expressions of a yearning to return to some earlier time where reading was more pleasurable than it is now. In general, though, there is a frank expression of disgust with "the personal," with Rose's reliance on autobiography, with the idea that experience might be used to interrogate prevailing theories of any kind—be they literary, pedagogical, cultural, or historical. I read these responses but, because I've forgotten where I am and where my students are for the moment, I don't understand them. Rose has written about the importance of teachers and teaching, about the necessity of having a community of learners, about the central role that chance has played in determining his place in the system. The new teachers have responded by writing about the invisibility of teachers, the loneliness of learning, the pleasures of knowing the right answer without ever having been told how to get to it, their sense that their own success was, in some way, foreordained.

This clash in expectations is, actually, a good place for us to begin thinking about the desire to teach both as the expression of a relation to culture and as a cultural byproduct. The new teachers' responses to *Lives on the Boundary* can be seen as illustrating Bourdieu's central thesis—namely, that the social fact that there are those who are good at school and those who are not is forever susceptible to being misrecognized as proof that nature, not culture, determines who occupies what position in the social hierarchy. And, as long as the new teachers in the seminar are trapped by this act of misrecognition, the central task of the course—understanding how one has come to know what one knows—can never be of more than marginal interest to them. That is, for those new teachers who cannot generate an interest in investigating the movement of the self through the institutions, the history of one's own experience of the educational process is only the empirical detritus that trails after the trajectory of one's inevitable rise through the academy's merit-based system. Submerged within this logic is the assumption that teaching itself can never be more than an act of authentication of this inevitable rise. The teacher can wave her arms, generate new curricula, redesign the classroom to her heart's content, but the only thing that's really happening underneath all the pedagogical pyrotechnics is, as everyone knows, a "natural" separation of those who can learn from those who can't.

I find this a bizarre belief for teachers to hold—namely that, in some absolute sense, teaching is impossible. This is not to say, though, that maintaining this belief is senseless or that it is without reason or use. To the contrary, those who embrace the view that teaching is impossible take considerable solace in this belief at those times when the students, refusing the teacher's bait and sinking into silence, leave in their wake the heartfelt suspicion that all this work with words and received wisdom is irrelevant. The belief that teaching is impossible is also flexible enough to rescript those moments of apparent success in the classroom as moments of recognition—as those times when the eyes meet across the room and the secret society of true learners discovers a fellow traveler in its midst. The belief that teaching is impossible may be a bizarre one for teachers to hold, in other words, but it is—like all beliefs—functional, producing a self-confirming reality. It serves to give the chaos of social life some coherence; it establishes the worth of the individual; it provides relief from the overwhelming sense of powerlessness that institutional life effortlessly provides. It is not, however, a promising foundation upon which to build a pedagogical practice whose goal is to ensure that all students are provided with ample opportunity to master the arts of using reading and writing to foster meditative, deliberative, and speculative thinking. For those who wish to lay such a foundation, for those who believe that there is both an art and a lasting value to creating evanescent institutional spaces where teaching and learning can happen, the place to begin is not with the concession that teaching is impossible, but rather with the introspective project of retracing the histories of individual learners as they move through the educational system; histories that are inevitably idiosyncratic and generic, ideopathic and predictable; histories that envelop, shape, and define teachers and students alike. The place to begin is with mapping the path of one's encounters with culture and her defenders.

This is my story. But it is not my story only.

Though it is not typically read in this way, T. S. Eliot's "Tradition and the Individual Talent" is, among other things, a quick sketch of an educational program for producing writers of the highest merit. To achieve greatness, Eliot tells us, "the poet must develop or procure the consciousness of the past and . . . he should continue to develop this consciousness throughout his career" (28). It's a curious sort of blueprint, to be sure. How exactly might one "procure the consciousness of the past"? Where does one go to acquire this commodity, sensibility, or experience: the library, the art museum, the university? By the end of the sentence, Eliot seems to have recognized the shortcomings of this installation model of consciousness and returned instead to the idea that this consciousness is developed through the poet's commitment to a lifelong regime of education. When the poet embarks on this endless project, Eliot continues, "[w]hat happens is a continual surrender of himself as he is at the moment to something which is more valuable. The progress of an artist is a continual self-sacrifice, a continual extinction of personality" (28).

What would it be like to take this idea seriously, I wonder? If one were to embrace this pedagogical program meant to generate poets of the highest caliber, what kind of life would follow? And, if the program failed to deliver on its promises, what kind of life would it leave behind? What would happen to those who were unable to realize the disciplinary dream of "a continual extinction of personality"?

My mother met my father at the University of Chicago, where they where brought together by friends who felt these two deep admirers of Chancellor Robert Maynard Hutchins's curricular and institutional idealism were made for one another. My father introduced himself as Warren C. Miller. When we were children, we would ask my mother what the "C" stood for: she didn't know and Dad wouldn't say, no matter how much we teased him about it. What little we did know about my father's past we pieced together from his short stories and his second unpublished novel, *The One Best Alternative.* We gleaned that there was never any money, a mother who died in an insane asylum, war experiences that couldn't be discussed. We were raised on the New Critical belief that the biographical facts of an artist's life were irrelevant, that it was the work alone that merited attention. So, for the longest time, we never pressed for more information.

After my father died, my mother discovered that the name she had been calling him throughout their married life was not, in fact, the one he had been provided with at birth. According to his original birth certificate, which we found secreted away in one of his many file cabinets, my father was first named Ben Miller, apparently after the man identified on the certificate as his father, one Benjamin Miller. Benjamin Miller abandoned his wife before Ben Miller was born. As far as my father had been able to recall, he never saw this man. A shadowy figure appeared on the porch, once, and handed his mother some papers. That was all.

The file cabinet contained another surprising document. When my father was two years old, his name was changed from Ben Miller to Chappy Warren Miller, his father's name replaced by one belonging to a favorite uncle. However much this change of names may have helped to relocate my father in the world of known entities and caring individuals, it wasn't long before his name once again became a reminder of some tragic absence. When my father was twelve years old, his Uncle Chappy cut into a live wire at the Texas Oil Company; the current entered a hand, taking out a piece big as a half-dollar, exited the forehead, taking out a similarly sized piece, and left behind the black and blue remains. On the overnight drive to the funeral, Dad fell asleep as his mother and his aunts argued over whether what had occurred had been an accident or was payback for Uncle Chappy's philandering ways. When the time came, Dad did as instructed: he bent over the coffin; he kissed Chappy Coles good-bye. Inside, he wondered about the wax that had been used to conceal his uncle's wounds. He vowed never again to attend a funeral.

At the onset of the Second World War, the official documents record that it was Warren Chappy Miller who enlisted in the army and that, when his tour with the medical corps in the European theater was completed, Warren C. Miller was the man who returned. Thus, in an act that was both self-preserving and self-creating, when the opportunity arose, my father left the name of Chappy behind and everything it signified—death, poverty, the rural world, powerlessness, manual labor, the depression, his ill-fated family. And then, with the help of the GI Bill, my father escaped Port Arthur, Texas, the stench of its oil refineries, and God knows what else; he was free to enroll at the University of Chicago, to embark on adventures with the Great Books, to travel in the world of art and ideas, to commune with others who shared his deep love of literature. To one way of thinking, his time line begins here.

The sequestering of one's past, the invention of a new self. Is this what the continual extinction of personality entails? Or are these actions better understood as the component pieces of a strategy for surviving one's personal history, a life-saving strategy that in this case just happened to mesh all too well with an aesthetic pedagogy designed to rescue art from the ignorant masses? "Poetry," Eliot tells us, "is not a turning loose of emotion, but an escape from emotion; it is not the expression of personality, but an escape from personality" ("Tradition" 30). To pry emotion from the self. To shed all idiosyncrasies. To shroud local history in darkness. To leave the body and its past behind. There must be a kind of salvation in this, I think, some profound sense of relief that one experiences upon being released into what Eliot termed "tradition" and Hutchins called "the Great Conversation," that roiling dialogue amongst the Great Books that presumably has gone on and will continue to go on for all time.

———————————

At the university where I am now employed, each year a series of distinguished authors and poets is invited to give a reading and, if they so choose, to sit in on some classes where their work is being studied. A few years back, a well-known essayist was part of this program and it was arranged to have him contribute to my graduate seminar's ongoing discussion about how best to respond to student essays. I was curious about how our guest would handle this task. How does "a master of the form" teach others how to work within the form? How does one of the greats teach those who are just starting out? Our guest did not disappoint.

One of the new teachers introduced a student paper that he felt showed promise and then proceeded to describe the trouble he was having responding to it. The problem, the teacher explained, was one of engagement: beyond writing "good point" in the margin a couple of times and concluding with an end comment that read, "NICE WORK!," he didn't know quite what to say to the student. His hope was that the other seminar members would be able to help him find some way back into the paper so he could provide a response that went beyond expressing a kind of empty enthusiasm.

Before the new teacher had finished reading the first paragraph of the student essay aloud, our guest interrupted him. "The problem here is that this student has no mind," he said. "You can see it right off from the dreck she's writing about. Alice Walker? A second-rate hack if there ever was one! And look at her syntax, the way she wears this language like it's a hair shirt!" Our guest was enjoying himself immensely, drinking in the shocked reaction he was accustomed to having his pronouncements receive in what he most assuredly would have termed "these politically correct times." Delighting in the fact that the ensuing tidal wave of objections to his dismissive reading had succeeded in shifting attention away from the student essay and back to him, where he felt it properly belonged, our distinguished guest invited us to consider those time-honored questions at the core of the canon wars: who is or isn't a great writer; who can or cannot become one.

"My job," he told me happily after class, "is to provoke."

Provoke what, though, I wondered? The self-styled Great Writer encounters the student text and he experiences feelings of revulsion; he declares aloud his disgust; he throws thunderbolts down from on high. And those who watch can't help but conclude that teaching writing is impossible, that it is work too low by far for the high-minded.

When I was fifteen, my mother received a fellowship to do research in southern France for a scholarly article she was writing on the poet La Cepede. During those six remarkable months, my younger brother and I were liberated from the public school system and our parents took on the unenviable task of being our educators. At home in Florida, I had been an indifferent student, bored by school and unable to hide it, lowering the bar of expectations semester by semester, cutting what corners and what classes I could without drawing undue attention to myself. My parents divided up my courses: my mom got French and algebra two; my dad, world history and the section of tenth-grade English I would be missing—how to read poetry. We worked together out of an anthology entitled *Six Centuries of Great Poetry*. Dad would assign a set of poems for me to study and I would spend hours in the always empty library on the top floor of the foundation looking up archaic words, trying to get images to rise from the references and the allusions, the rhyme and the meter, doing my best to understand what it means to build an argument in a poem. My father was remarkably patient: he would take me through the poems line by line, pausing over a word, a line break, an image, spurring me to speculate about the decision involved and its consequences. Away from my friends and all I was familiar with, without quite intending to, I fell in love with the pleasures of close reading and the sense of community this activity produced.

We spent the greatest amount of time with the metaphysical poets. My father loved George Herbert in particular, so we devoted days to "The Collar," until I finally figured out that the collar around the poet's neck signified that he was both a representative and a prisoner of his faith. Dad got the most enjoyment, though, out of John Donne: he was both infinitely amused and deeply moved by the way Donne violently yoked together the most heterogeneous of ideas, as Johnson put it. The flea as a vehicle for delivering an invitation to the conjugal bed? Sure! Graphic descriptions of human decay as a prompt for a sexual liaison? But of course! The reliquary as an image of the magnitude of one's carnal love? Why not? I did not know it at the time, but one thing I was learning during these exchanges was a version of what my father had learned from reading Eliot's essay, "The Metaphysical Poets": "When a poet's mind is perfectly equipped for its work, it is constantly amalgamating disparate experience; the ordinary man's experience is chaotic, irregular, fragmentary.

The latter falls in love, or reads Spinoza, and these two experiences have nothing to do with each other, or with the noise of the typewriter or the smell of cooking; in the mind of the poet these experiences are always forming new wholes" (64).

When Peter Ackroyd set out to write Eliot's biography, his efforts were severely hampered by the Eliot estate, which refused him permission to quote from Eliot's unpublished work or correspondence. Apparently, Eliot never wanted such a book to be written. It's the art that matters, not the artist, remember. This seems to continue to be a matter of principle long after the artist was put to rest and a memorial for him placed in Westminster Abbey's Poet's Corner.

We do learn from Ackroyd's biography, however, that one of Eliot's nicknames was "The Undertaker," an allusion to the poet's detached manner while moving about in the social world. Indeed, for a time, Eliot is said to have worn a slightly green face powder to affect a cadaverous appearance. But this was just theatrics, Ackroyd insists: it made Eliot "look more modern, more interesting, a poet rather than a bank official. He was too intelligent not to realize the effect which he had upon others—that slightly chilling and aloof quality of which we have read descriptions—and this was one way in which he mitigated it" (136–37). We learn as well that Eliot's family disapproved of his first wife, Vivien: his sister Charlotte said that it was not a "eugenic" union (144). The marriage slowly deteriorated as Vivien's mental health declined. After ten years of living with The Undertaker, she had grown increasingly unstable and had "reverted to infantile terrors of loneliness; it was a loneliness compounded by the fact that her husband spent much of his time away from her" (149).

Afraid that he might never again be able to write poetry, Eliot began to assume the role of editor and lecturer. In 1926, he planned a trilogy to be entitled, "The Disintegration of the Intellect," which was to include three scholarly books—*The School of Donne, Elizabethan Drama,* and *The Sons of Ben* (156). This project was never completed.

Eliot did, however, become a British citizen. He converted to the Anglican religion. He cut himself free of his wife. He started over again. In my end is my beginning.

When Robert Maynard Hutchins graduated from Yale Law School in 1925, he was promptly asked to join the faculty. Two years later, at twenty-eight, he was appointed dean of the law school. Two years after that, he became president of the University of Chicago. On this occasion, he thought it a good idea to take an inventory of what he knew. At thirty years old, he had "some knowledge of the Bible, of Shakespeare, of *Faust*, of one dialogue of Plato, and of the opinions of many semi-literate and a few literate judges, and that was about all" (qtd. in Ashmore 98). As Hutchins tells the story, when he revealed this list to Mortimer Adler, Adler warned him that unless he "did something drastic he would close out his educational career a wholly uneducated man" (98).[1] To repair the faults in Hutchins's education, Hutchins and Adler agreed to set up a Great Books seminar at the University of Chicago for a select group of first-year students to discuss the masterpieces of Western civilization—a seminar designed to save these students from the prospect of a similarly unsatisfying inventory of what they knew when they reached the age of thirty. Though this project, according to Adler, "was originally designed to initiate the education of Hutchins and continue the education of Adler, it had much more far-reaching effects" (129).

The most far-reaching effect of this project was the conviction it gave rise to in Hutchins that *all* undergraduates should spend the first two years in college studying the Great Books. To make this happen at the University of Chicago, Hutchins tried to build a core of faculty who supported reforming the curriculum along these lines. After bringing Adler to the university, he enlisted the services of Scott Buchanan, Stringfellow Barr, and Richard McKeon, putting them all to work on the newly formed Committee on the Liberal Arts. A funny thing happened, though, when these men convened to design their curriculum devoted to the Great Conversation. According to Buchanan's correspondence, despite the members' common interest in the Great Books, the "meetings were discontinued when it appeared that civil conversation to say nothing of intellectual discussion and reading of texts was impossible."[2] After just two meetings, the group split apart, and Barr and Buchanan were left with the meaningless task of cochairing a memberless committee. Buchanan passed the time writing Hutchins a series of position papers on the lasting value of the liberal arts, the first of which argued that "the only available medium which is adequate to the intellectual salvation (education) of the American student is the great European tradition."[3] Early on in Buchanan's argument, approving references to "Tradition and the Individual Talent" abound.

Hutchins racing the clock to become educated. A committee of like-minded men committed to the Great Conversation unable even to speak to—let alone learn from—one another. The wound that never heals. The unexamined life.

————————————

Scott Buchanan and Stringfellow Barr could see that they had no future at the University of Chicago and thus departed at the earliest opportunity. In 1937, they became the dean and the president, respectively, of St. John's College. When Buchanan and Barr arrived, the college was in bad shape, having recently lost its accreditation because the outgoing president had awarded a degree to a student who hadn't fulfilled the requirements for graduation. The college was also on the brink of financial collapse because the board had squandered much of the college's meager endowment in real estate speculation. Shortly after Buchanan and Barr took over, the college ran into even graver trouble. First, the rush of young men to enlist in World War II threatened to drain the admissions pool dry and then the Naval Academy made an opportunistic grab for the college's property on the pretext that it needed the land to train more combatants for the war effort. Against these considerable odds, Buchanan and Barr nevertheless prevailed, putting together a viable structure for an undergraduate education entirely devoted to the study of the Great Books that has outlived them both.

When I enrolled at St. John's in the late 1970s, Buchanan and Barr were long gone, but their program was thriving. I wrote home about the momentous experience of reading the first book of Euclid. I had given up hope of ever learning geometry while in high school: when I was in tenth grade, the football coach who was charged with teaching this material to me and my fellow classmates handed out his worksheets, spoke of angle-side-angle, and then would stretch out atop the bookcases that lined the back of the room to get some relief from the heat and the tedium. And I, in my turn, quite dutifully put my head on the desk and let it all pass me by. At St. John's, though, I had another shot. We spent weeks on Euclid's definitions: What does it mean to say that "a point is that which has no part"? How can something that has no parts be anything at all? Isn't a point just nothing, a line a collection of nothings, the movement from A to B a fiction? We methodically worked through the proofs, unknowingly making our way toward the climax of the first book, the Pythagorean theorem. We saw how a set of assumptions and a collection of working definitions was all one needed to construct and then map a conceptual universe. After working for months to get to the place where we could derive the proof showing that the square of the hypotenuse is equal to the sum of the squares on the sides of a triangle, we read the *Meno*, the Platonic dialogue in which Socrates gets a slave boy to figure out the Pythagorean theorem just by asking him a few questions about a diagram drawn in the sand.

Socrates is making an argument about how the ideal forms are there in us all, just waiting to be brought out; he is showing that it is through the art of the dialectic that we come to remember these forms and pull them to the surface. Behold the illiterate slave boy, with no knowledge of geometry, utterly unacquainted with Euclid's *Elements*. Behold his teacher who, with nothing else at his disposal but a stick, some sand, and the right set of questions asked in the right order, is able to show that the slave boy knows more than he thinks he knows. It's a great trick. There's no better stage prop than the handy slave boy eager to do his master's bidding. And I, for one, was completely taken in by the con.

I wrote home to share my excitement and my father wrote back, sharing his memories of studying the *Meno* at the University of Chicago and his own thoughts about this idea that we have the forms buried away inside us, ready for the finding if only we'll look hard enough. He said he felt scars represented memory on the cellular level, that they were a lasting record of the body's injuries as it moved through time. He told a story about scar tissue that had swelled suddenly after decades of peaceful coexistence on the palm of his hand. While washing dishes, the skin softened. He massaged the painful area, worrying it until it released its treasure—a filament of fine spun glass from a childhood accident in a stock room. The wound had been imperfectly cleaned. The flesh had closed around evidence of the mishap and then it had held on with all its might.

Years later, I would think about the scars on my father's wrists, the scars on his throat, the scars on his chest near his heart, and I would wonder: what is it that they remember? And I would wonder as well if there was any way to exorcise those memories, any way to deprive them of their mysterious powers.

St. John's is a small college with a total enrollment hovering around four hundred students. After awhile, with everyone having read the same books, in the same order, and then having had the same discussions about those books, it begins to feel like the world is closing in around you. There were jokes that the training we were receiving was not so different from the one the cadets at the Naval Academy across the street were subjecting themselves to. We, too, felt the extinction of personality; we, too, disappeared into a homogenous culture.

One night, a woman asked me if I wanted to get off campus for a couple of hours. She had some shopping to do, a car. It was a beautiful night, clear and crisp. I had a lot of reading to do. She insisted. She was in all my classes. We could talk about our homework during the drive. It wouldn't take long and we would come back refreshed.

I didn't have to be asked twice.

We drove out to a pharmacy, where she picked up a prescription. We stopped at a liquor store, where she bought some champagne. I don't remember much else about the drive, save that when we got back to campus, I started to take my leave in the parking lot and she stopped me with a question. It was a special night, she said. An anniversary of sorts, a celebration. Did I want to join her? I slapped my books, said "another time," and headed to the library.

She went back to her room and celebrated alone.

That weekend she was discovered by a concerned hallmate and, a few days after that, the papers carried her story. It had been the anniversary of the night she had murdered her mother. At her memorial service, friends who knew her from the psychiatric ward where she'd served out her time broke down when they spoke about how hard she had tried to conquer her demons. One of our teachers praised her courage. Back at school, a friend said that it was just like the *Oresteia*. The Furies won't tolerate matricide, so sooner or later they were going to get her. There was nothing anybody could do to stop them.

Those Greeks. They have an explanation for everything.

———————————

Against the prevailing notion that education is an exclusively salutary experience, Gayatri Spivak has suggested that it be considered an "enabling violation." When I was a student in one of her seminars, Spivak used her own trajectory through the educational system to illustrate what she meant by this oxymoronic formulation: a Brahmin educated first at Oxford and then at Yale, a woman who, on the strength of her command of the most complex French theorists, has worked her way up to an endowed chair in the Ivy Leagues, Spivak owes her own vaunted position in the academy to the British colonial legacy in India, the injustices of the caste system, an emerging academic market for those who can theorize the work of decolonization and postcolonialism. India. Britain. France. The United States. The realm of ideas. Soon enough and sure enough, the educated person feels at home nowhere.

When I came up against this idea in graduate school, I felt a strange sense of release. For a while, I was drawn to the poststructural notion that one doesn't speak, but is spoken by a range of discursive practices. It all sounded so good to me on paper, but when I tried to move from applying these ideas to other works I'd read and sought to interpret my own experience through this critical frame, I came right up against a paradox: what if it turns out that you have been spoken by the silence of another? That is, what if, in the process of cataloging the voices that have shaped what you think and the institutional practices that have shaped the ways you think, you discover an overriding sense of placelessness, dark spaces of unknowing, avenues of feeling and being in the world whose genealogy you have no hope of tracing out? Instead of finding realms of possibility or interstices of relative freedom, all you find is a world of dead ends.

Frustrating discoveries of this sort need not lead to paralysis, though. Such silences can be taken as an invitation to speak back, as an opportunity to disinter the past, and even as the occasion to refashion the future. Given my career choice, my own response to this silence was predictable enough. I wrote home and, at the age of twenty-nine, I finally asked my father to tell me about his life prior to the University of Chicago.

Who knows how long Dad had been waiting for somebody to make this request? All I know is that he made the fulfillment of this assignment his final major writing project. Just a few weeks after I sent my request, my father's memoirs began to arrive in typed, single-spaced, hand-corrected installments. As I read through each chunk, it appeared to me that my father had set out quite methodically to report everything he could remember about growing up in Port Arthur from the moment he was born—the many moves necessitated by his family's poverty; the comings and goings of aunts and uncles during this time; his overriding sense of having been a burden to everyone. His memory was phenomenal: he knew the addresses of everywhere he had ever lived, no matter how briefly; he could place what for others would only have been floating childhood recollections in specific times and locations; he could recall the names of friends and family with whom he had not communicated in at least thirty years. Having struggled for so long to keep on writing in the face of his looming anonymity, of contending with the repeated rejections of his second novel, he suddenly had a focus and an audience. When he concluded the first major section with the words "End of Part I," the manuscript was nearly two hundred pages long.

When he was in the midst of this project, it seemed like nothing would stop him from seeing it through to completion. And, in fact, he only allowed his first suicide attempt, which occurred over Labor Day weekend in 1990, to briefly interrupt his writing. The next, newly minted installment arrived in October with no cover letter and no mention of the events that had preceded it. By March of 1991, though, the impetus to keep going had dissolved and Dad took a break from the project. The next section, which would have covered his adolescence, was never written. The final installment he wrote describes his mother's decision to leave Village Mills, a town that had been all but abandoned once the sawmill at its center had laid the environs to waste. And it concludes with this memory: "I looked forward to living again in Port Arthur with excitement and happiness. I plunged into helping to pack. I couldn't wait to get back to where I felt I belonged."

In *The Academic Postmodern and the Rule of Literature,* David Simpson laments what he sees as academic postmodernism's turn "against theory." The return to storytelling and the renewed interest in conversation, lived experience, and expression are all signs, he says, that "speech and presence are very much back in style," despite the deconstructive efforts in the 1970s and early 1980s to disrupt such work (72). There's an essential phoniness to all these plain-speaking academics that Simpson feels moved to expose: "the energy with which the habit of speaking personally is now taking over professionalized academic discourse suggests, I think, a weariness with professionalism itself, but also a revival of a particular kind of literary professionalism"—namely, a professionalism that presents itself as an alternative "to the respective reifications of science, history, and philosophy, and to the whole culture of specialization and divided labor by which modernization has been achieved" (76). One way that Simpson seeks to counteract this movement is by refusing to take part in it: while others may be swept along by the cult of autobiography, he resists the instincts of the herd on principle; if necessary, he alone will remain untainted by the baubles of the academic marketplace. Alluding to those who don't have his powers of restraint as "the bearers as well as the fools of our common history," Simpson declares: "But I am not going to tell you my life story in this book, and if I am everywhere in what follows, as I must be in serious as well as trivial senses, then it will be in disguise" (14). Whether the unexamined life is worth living remains open to debate. For Simpson, though, there is no doubt that the examined life of mere mortals is not worth reading.

I agree with much of Simpson's critique of the cult "professional antiprofessionalism," where a reliance on personal experience is deployed as proof of one's essential earthiness—that one is in the institution, but not of it. His decision to steer clear of this kind of discursive action is understandable enough: he's got more important things to do with his time than fall into the navel-gazing work of recounting the violations and epiphanies of his past. And, as Simpson points out, his undergraduates hardly need instruction in this genre— they are, after all, "far readier to talk about themselves and how they feel about a text than to try to understand it by way of impersonal, technical vocabularies" (80). But, if one values something in those impersonal, technical vocabularies, as Simpson and I both do, it is still possible to imagine responding to the kind of classroom Simpson describes by embarking on a project that involves finding ways to assist the students in learning how to break down the opposition between the personal and the academic, lived experience and the world of ideas, local history and global events, the teaching of writing and the teaching of reading. Simpson, though, doesn't consider what it might take to get students or the profession to turn back toward theory and history; indeed, he doesn't even gesture in the direction of such pedagogical considerations. Instead, he concludes his book with a critique of "the urge for solutions" (162). Dissatisfied with the "virtual stampede into autobiography" (82), Simpson has chosen to respond with, as he puts it, the "traditionally professional solution" of writing a history of how this problem has surfaced in the academy over time (165).

It is worth wondering about the rhetorical efficacy of this move. That is, what are the odds that those masses stampeding their way back to autobiography are going to pause on their way to read Simpson's valuable analysis of how "the personal" figures as a form of cultural capital in the academy at this historical moment? How many will trouble themselves with his assertion that recounting personal experience is now the officially sanctioned way to lay claim to being transgressive, oppositional, anti-institutional, authentic? Simpson knows that the chances of his attracting such an audience are slim to none: he has no illusions about the likelihood that his bid to historicize this struggle will actually alter the course of the debate or that his argument will convince others that the kind of scholarly labor he advocates is capable of producing "emancipatory knowledges" (165). In short, Simpson has a writing problem and he doesn't know how to solve it: he can't produce an argument that is going to convince anybody except those who already agree with him. How to end? How to end it all? It is the perennial problem of the composition classroom; it is the problem that haunts everyone who writes.

Conceding that the problem of the academic's return to autobiography cannot be "solved," at least not by way of traditional scholarship, Simpson concludes with a discussion of academic quest novels, focusing on A. S. Byatt's *Possession*, which he considers to be "the masterpiece of genre," because it does the best job of dramatizing the idea that "[i]f we just go deep enough into our narrow little specialties, we will emerge into satisfied citizenship of the world" (172). Simpson confesses that, quite against his will and despite the protections afforded by his critical apparatus, even he was possessed by the novel and its alluring vision of the creative process. "Editors, critics, and theorists of all genders, sexual preferences, and generations are captured by the spell of authentic passion and by the power of writing to bring it back to life. It is hard not to be possessed. It is hard not to want to speak with the dead" (174). Nevertheless, Simpson feels that this desire to bring the dead back to life must be exposed for what it really is: "the desire for irresponsibility, for not being (perhaps criminally) responsible . . . and the desire for the confirmations of the local habitations of body, touch, and voice . . ." (176). The novel pulls him one way, his critical training pulls him another; he shuttles back and forth between thinking and feeling, refusing to give in to the desire to speak with those who aren't here.

On December 21, 1988, a bomb stowed in the cargo hold of Pan Am Flight 103 exploded over Lockerbie, Scotland. Bodies began to fall from the sky. Unlike the bodies aboard TWA Flight 800 out of JFK, which exploded eleven minutes after takeoff on July 17, 1996, and plunged into the Atlantic Ocean, the bodies from Flight 103 landed in open fields, crashed through rooftops, went to pieces, and disappeared. Houses and people on the ground were vaporized in explosions produced by the rain of debris. Steven Flannigan, having snuck over to a friend's house, returned to find a vacant, smoldering lot where his parents, his sister, his childhood had been (Emerson and Duffy).

Suse Lowenstein, a sculptor and the mother of Alexander Silas Lowenstein, one of the thirty-five students from Syracuse University on Pan Am Flight 103, has since invited other mothers of the victims to her studio to assist her in memorializing the lasting effects the bombing has had on the families who have been left behind. She asks the mothers to recall the moment when the news was broken to them. She asks them to return to that time, to react as they did then, to assume whatever posture grief imposed. The women become models of agony. The result is an homage to the victims, which Lowenstein has entitled *Dark Elegy*.[4]

This piece was recently installed on the quad in front of the building where I teach. From afar, the larger-than-life figures, placed in concentric circles, seem to be involved in a tribal celebration. Some of the figures have their arms stretched to the heavens, others sprawl on the ground: all of them are nude. *The Rites of Spring*, I thought, when I first saw it out my window. Upon closer inspection, though, the fact that the figures are suffering comes into focus and the error of my initial response becomes clear. People pause to read the explanatory plaque, to peer into the faces of these crushed women, to sit at their feet. Life goes on around the installation, as it must.

I am moved not so much by the figures as I am by the larger narrative involving real terror, real death that these figures memorialize. The artist has used her art to preserve the moment of shock, that instant when the magnitude of the mother's or the wife's or the sister's or the friend's grief overwhelms the forces that separate the public from the private: naked and broken, these women hold tight to their pain. It is a sign of their love, a testament to their loss.

Embedded in each figure, hidden from view, is some memento of the lost loved one. With the passage of time, as the figures decay and break open, these objects—a photograph, a lock of hair, a shoestring—will be exposed for others to puzzle over. The private will again become public. It is a gift, of sorts.

Perhaps because the events this installation alludes to are too horrifying to contemplate head-on for long, I find myself wondering about something else: where are the men, the fathers, the sons, and the husbands of those who fell from the sky? Why has their grief been kept from view? The piece seems to reinstantiate Woman as an essentially maternal being: she who grieves. Or perhaps that isn't it at all; perhaps the absent men are meant to evoke the absence of Lowenstein's son Alex? I make another bid for the piece, but now I can see only what my years of schooling have trained me to see—namely, what isn't there, what has been excluded. A friend explains to me that it is not the case that male grief is unrepresentable; it's that this is not something males allow themselves access to in public. Rather, they keep it inside or they head to the mountains. Or they get their hands on a gun and make the news. Or, in the case of public figures, there are those examples of strategically deployed lachrymose moments where, on command, the orator reaches for his hankie, daubs an eye, regains composure, and shoulders on.

I learn later that Lowenstein did, in fact, open her studio to the men who had lost loved ones on Pan Am Flight 103. Apparently not one of these men was either willing or able to enter the artist's machine for grieving.

———————————

The same week that the *New York Times Magazine* ran a piece mourning the 230 people who died when TWA Flight 800 went down, it featured an article cheerfully entitled, "His Life Is His Mind," profiling "an eminent Jungian with an overactive libido," one James Hall. After years of teaching, writing, lecturing, and philandering, late in his life Hall suffered a stroke that produced what is termed "the locked-in syndrome"—Hall's brain and his body stopped communicating with one another. The article treats us to a large photograph of Professor Hall in his office: he is suspended in a sling, his arms folded in his lap, his library of books in the background hopelessly out of reach. Hall stares into the camera, fearlessly. Having regained the use of a finger on one hand, Hall is now able to type out on a computer: "LIFE IS, IF ANYTHING, MORE INTERESTING THAN BEFORE I WAS DISABLED" (qtd. in Wedemeyer 22). He has turned his attention to the question, "What makes a person?" He believes the answers are to be found in dreams.

I know this story is supposed to be inspiring, but I just can't get it to work for me. Ah, the life of the mind, I think, so much better now that the life of the body has been nullified. I wonder what Hall's wife thinks. She says she gave up her professional career because she felt she embarrassed her more successful husband. She was aware of his infidelities, but found sustenance in her children and a charismatic church. We are informed: "Since Hall came home from the hospital in 1992 he has never been seriously sick, but Suzanne has not had a vacation. With her practical skirts and blunt-cut hair, she looks like a very weary schoolgirl" (25). She now stands by as Hall writes his book of dreams. She attends to this brain's every bodily need. She lets herself go.

During the last decade of his life, my father experienced his own version of the locked-in syndrome. As my younger brother described this time, it was as if Dad sentenced himself to solitary confinement and slowly restricted himself to whatever the aesthetic equivalent of a diet of bread and water would be, holding himself hostage for the commission of crimes of which only he was aware. He stopped listening to music; he stopped writing short stories, then poems, then any form of correspondence; he stopped speaking on the phone except when my mother was also on the line to prod him to respond. Some terrible storm had been released in his brain and he was powerless to stop it. In post-op for prostate surgery in the early 1990s, his physician prescribed Halcion, a drug which deprived him of all sense of purpose, leaving him to fall as far and as long as he could endure the terror. Having stood for so many years on the margins of society—a short-story writer, the man who stayed at home while his wife supported the family, an intellectual in the South, a quiet soul who used his writing to reach out to the world in ways he couldn't do in person—my father disappeared into the shadows.

There was no arguing with the depression that enveloped him. He fought as hard as he could against it, but the litany of his perceived failures, which played ceaselessly through his mind, was simply too great for him to bear. When his first attempt to end his life failed, those of us who were closest to him and yet stood outside the event tried to make sense of the suffering that was unfolding before our eyes. We took solace in William Styron's *Darkness Visible: A Memoir of Madness,* which recounts the author's harrowing, Halcion-driven spiral into despair. Although Styron's story found its way to us too late to have saved my father from the drug's effects, it nevertheless gave us a way to imagine where my father had been and why none of us had been able to get to him. We read about therapeutic regimes, medicinal regimes; we talked to experts, charlatans, friends, frauds; we hoped things would get better; we hoped the problem would just go away—that it was just a biochemical blip, a confluence of unfortunately timed stresses and strains, an act that had failed because, at some level, Dad had wanted it to fail.

New drugs were introduced into the system. New attitudes were improvised. And, for a time, it looked as if there was reason for cautious optimism. Dad's sense of humor returned; he had more energy; he would talk about a future where all wasn't bleak and barren. When he developed a tolerance for the new drugs, newer drugs were prescribed, then an ever-changing array of combinations and dosages. The medicinal onslaught was underway to keep him from peering back over the abyss.

In the end, nothing worked.

After his second attempt, Dad was required, as part of his state-mandated therapeutic regime, to keep a journal. The state, in effect, became his writing instructor and writing itself the instrument for representing the quality of his mental health. He would sit in circles with other unhappy people and, when it was his turn, he would point to the appropriate place on a nearby chart listing the range of possible emotions: "And how are you feeling today Warren?"

There is no question that he hated being put in this position. There are days where all he enters in his journal are a series of letters: AXB, BXC, CXD, DXE, etc. It is difficult to know how to read this. Is he playing a game? Is he giving his jailers the finger? Is this a record of his mind in the final state of its decay, the rich vocabulary, all the descriptive powers reduced to barely legible scratches? Or is it the traces of an ineffective medical intervention, a history that could not be revealed, a silence that could never be borne?

I don't know the answers to these questions.

When we still thought he would be coming back home after his stroke and had begun to think about how to retrofit the house for a wheelchair, we started cleaning out the closets to make room for the demolition work we envisioned was going to be necessary. Squirreled away in the back of Dad's closet, we found a Magnetic Poetry kit, a gift no doubt meant to rekindle the glowing embers of creativity.

It had never been used.

Weeks later, when I get back home, I break apart all the word blocks and play at making poems on the fridge. It's an homage, of sorts. As I finger the words—stuck back-to-back, jumbled together, suggestive but incoherent—I wonder if this is what it was like for him at the end. I feel the kit's restrictiveness as I try to build an image. I can't find the words I need, in the form I need. The vocabulary has been selected for immediate impact. It's just perfect for that time-honored game, "great band names." You can say, "frantic sausage worship," "bloody knife," "the silent blue heaving." You can probably even say, "the wound that never heals," if you've got the time. You get the picture—it's a Freudian field day, a way to say the same thing, over and over again. What you can't do is locate yourself in the world of language, communicate an experience, complicate its emotional content. To do that, you'd need a different set of words, a bigger box, a game less interested in being naughty and provocative. But what if these are the only words you have? What if you're locked in with a world of unexpressed memories and unexplored feelings and have no vocabulary to communicate what it is that you are experiencing?

The only text to appear twice on St. John's four-year curriculum of Great Books is the *Phaedrus*. First-year students read it during the series of seminars devoted to the Platonic dialogues and then, when they are seniors, it is assigned again as the final reading of the year. In the dialogue, Socrates describes the ideal approach to composition: "every discourse, like a living creature, should be so put together that it has its own body and lacks neither head nor feet, middle nor extremities, all composed in such a way that they suit both each other and the whole" (53). He prescribes the ideal mode of response, rebuking Phaedrus for "being more concerned with the identity of the speaker or the locale from which the account comes" than with "the truth" of the story Socrates has told about the invention of writing in Egypt. And, finally, and most famously, Socrates insists that writing is inferior to speech: "Writing, you know, Phaedrus, has this strange quality about it, which makes it really like painting: the painter's products stand before us quite as though they were alive; but if you question them, they maintain a solemn silence. So, too, with written words: you might think they spoke as though they made sense, but if you ask them anything about what they are saying, if you wish an explanation, they go on telling you the same thing, over and over forever" (69).

There's an obvious and intended irony to having these be some of the last words awaiting students at the end of four years spent reading the Great Books. Ironic readings of Plato abound, of course, and there is a whole subculture of the academy populated by those who delight in using secret decoder rings to decipher the meaning beneath all his paradoxes. A written document that denounces written documents? A college devoted to the discussion of the Great Books that concludes with a denunciation of reading and writing? The snake swallowing its tail. A riddle wrapped inside an enigma. We end where we began.

What could it all mean?

This is what I think it means. When Socrates asks Phaedrus about the speech the boy is carrying curled up in his cloak, he sets in motion a discussion that brings Lysias's discourse on love to life. Trapped in the realm of Phaedrus's private appreciation, the speech may well have had an existence of "solemn silence," whispering "the same thing, over and over forever." The silence was broken, however, when Socrates and Phaedrus read Lysias's text together and this communal reading made the text say something different, something that Lysias certainly never intended. Phaedrus, of course, has not exactly enjoyed having Lysias's argument dissected by his teacher's ruthless powers of examination. But, by the time Socrates has delivered the fiftieth deathblow to Lysias's speech and is declaring that their discussion has demonstrated the inferiority of writing, Phaedrus is in no position to point out that their discussion was entirely dependent upon the fact that Lysias's speech had been written down. Like a good student, Phaedrus knows when to shut up and let the teacher have his way.

The meaning of Lysias's speech is further altered by the fact that it has been strategically deployed by Socrates' student, Plato, as part of the drama of the dialogue. By staging the dialogue in this way, it is possible that Plato meant to suggest that Socrates was quite wrong about writing and to show that, as far as the dialogue's author is concerned, writing doesn't embalm the living word in silence or rob the mind of its powers to remember. So understood, the dialogue demonstrates that the danger of the written word is not, as Socrates claims, that it says the same thing, over and over forever, but that it allows a speaker's words to be wrenched from their original moorings and dropped in other contexts where they can be compelled to issue forth unexpected meanings. The danger of the written word is, thus, its promise; the fact that it can't be finally and completely controlled means that it forever retains the power to evoke new possibilities.

Socrates can't comprehend the promise of this technological advance; he can only see the threat it poses to his position as the ultimate arbiter of meaning. He knows that, face-to-face, he has the power to humiliate anyone who tries to come between him and his earnest search for truth; and he knows as well that he can shame most anyone he meets into silence. But he seems to sense that the written word can leave his blistering critiques behind and find more receptive audiences beyond the reach of his voice. Perhaps by condemning writing, Socrates was expressing his fear that, at some point, he would lose control of his words and that without him there to control and protect them they would stop saying what he wanted them to say over and over again and start saying something else.

Perhaps Socrates was afraid of dying after all.

On the seventh day of my father's stay in the hospital, his doctor predicted a full recovery from the stroke. I got on a plane and flew back to my family, with plans to return when he was ready to come home.

The following day, the monitor next to my father's bed, which my sister had dubbed "the TV of life," stopped scribbling his vital signs. His agony came to an end.

At the funeral, there was no casket.

At night, after I've read her bedtime stories and turned out the light, my four-year-old daughter grows philosophical. She asks about heaven, God, angels, magic, making time go backwards. "What do dead people dream about?" she asks. "We are the dreams of the dead," I tell her, "We are everything they ever hoped for." When she is older, I will tell her that we are also everything they ever feared. "Will Mommy be holding your hand when you die?" Nothing has prepared me for this question. I don't know what to say, so I say, "I hope so, honey." "You know what, Dad?" I don't respond. She wants me to know that my father is happy now. She says, "Poppy's in my heart and he's dancing."

If someone were to study the memorial service with an eye toward gaining insight into what those present believed, the researcher might begin with the various texts those involved had selected to be read, the lyrics to the hymns, the overarching liturgy. This person might zero in on the Apostle's Creed with its litany of beliefs recited in unison by the congregation; the iconography of the building; the celebration of communion; the funeral wreaths; the organization of the standings, sittings, and kneelings. The entire event could be textualized and read, a belief system abstracted.

There is a genuine pleasure in such exercises, I think. It's almost a game: how much can I learn about a people without talking to them? Indeed, at the highest levels of this game, it even becomes possible to argue that talking to the people involved in any cultural enterprise is actually unnecessary or that it distorts the pure, unmediated analysis of the knowing outside observer. According to this line of reasoning, the cultural machinery is so powerful, its dramas so thoroughly scripted, its master narratives so compelling that those involved in any public ritual have no option but to mouth the words and ideas that have been provided to them beforehand. So, to this way of thinking, what matters in this case is not what goes through the minds of those in attendance at the service, but what the service makes those in attendance do and say publicly. We stand, we sit, we appear to pray: whether we actually believe in the hermeneutic system deployed at this moment to make sense of our mortality matters not at all. What matters is that we participate in a ritualized performance that makes it appear that we believe.

For my part, I find little solace in the images of resurrection and redemption. Pascal's wager always seemed sinister to me: to choose to believe in the afterlife because no harm is done if it turns out not to exist has always seemed to me like an argument fashioned at the spiritual equivalent of a used-car dealership. So, throughout the service, I mentally amend nearly every sentence I hear and speak: I caret in the word "not" to negate beliefs I am meant to affirm; I substitute terms, rewrite sentences, move text from here to there. In other words, like all readers, I push back, I distort, I accommodate my own ways of thinking. I make a place for myself.

———————————

Back at the office, I spend my days writing memos and reports, raising money, giving talks, meeting with parents, teachers, and students, grading papers, anticipating the next crisis, trying forever to be one step ahead of the avalanche of demands. It is a world that has no natural appeal; its call, rather, is a cultural one and the joys and pleasures it affords come from losing oneself in the work of finding solutions to an ever-evolving, ever-increasing set of problems. Some of these problems, it turns out, are amenable to the application of carefully reasoned arguments that marshal evidence in an orderly fashion. Most of the problems, though, call for a different way of thinking altogether, one that sees possibility where others only see disaster, one that tries to work every angle so as to provide multidimensional responses to the multidimensional conundrums the world ceaselessly provides. While the assessments, evaluations, proposals, reports, commentaries, and critiques I produce help to keep the bureacracy of higher education going, there is another kind of writing I turn to in order to sustain the ongoing search for meaning in a world no one controls. This writing asks the reader to make imaginative connections between disparate elements; it tracks one path among many possible ones across the glistening water. This writing is the lifeblood of the humanities in action.

When I am back in the classroom, I work at getting the students to use their writing not just as a tool for making arguments, but also as a lens for exploring complexity and a vehicle for arriving at nuanced understandings of a lived reality that is inescapably characterized by ambiguities, shades of meaning, contradictions, and gaps. That's a long way to try to take undergraduates in one course in one semester, but this is what I believe the function of a secular public education should be: to provide training in the arts of solving the problems of this world, training that recognizes that people, who never leave behind their embodied histories and their cherished beliefs, can't be revised the way papers can.

Anne Fadiman's *The Spirit Catches You and You Fall Down* provides one example of what it looks like when such arts are put to use. At one point in her remarkable account of a Hmong child's fatal encounter with first-world medical practices, Fadiman pauses to describe life in the Ban Vinai refugee camp in Thailand during the 1980s. A study completed at Ban Vinai had determined that the Hmong were the least likely among all the refugees from Laos, Vietnam, and Cambodia to visit the camp's medical center, apparently because they preferred the "indigenous healing arts: shamanism, dermal treatments, herbalism" (34). The Hmong refugees didn't trust the doctors and the doctors, for their part, knew almost nothing about the Hmong, what they believed, or what brought them down from their mountain homes in Laos, across the Mekong River, to this holding station between two worlds.

In 1985, the International Rescue Committee, the relief agency in charge of Ban Vinai, asked a young ethnographer named Dwight Conquergood to design an environmental health program that would improve the effectiveness of the support services delivered at the camp. The first problem that Conquergood had to tackle was an outbreak of rabies among the dogs in the camp. The medical staff's first response had been to launch a "mass dog-vaccination campaign," but this had been a complete failure, because not one refugee responded and no dogs received inoculations. Conquergood, who had an abiding interest in shamanism and performance art and who, unlike the other volunteers, actually lived in the camp with the refugees, came up with a solution that was unimaginable to the rest of the medical staff and the camp volunteers, even though they, too, were committed to providing the best health care they could to these displaced peoples. Conquergood suggested a "Rabies Parade," featuring three important characters from Hmong folktales dressed in costumes. The parade snaked through the camp; the characters explained the etiology of rabies through a bullhorn; there was music and the banging of a drum and the next morning "the vaccination stations were so besieged by dogs—dogs carried in their owners' arms, dogs dragged on rope leashes, dogs rolled in on two-wheeled pushcarts—that the health workers could hardly inoculate them fast enough" (36–37).

If the goal is healing, what is the solution? In this case, the answer is found in art and performance, in learning how to speak in ways that others can hear, in finding a way to move and be in more than one world at once. This isn't the only answer and it isn't always the answer, but learning how to look for such answers and finding out how to implement the evanescent solutions the search itself suggests is the primary function of the humanities as I conceive them. The practice of the humanities, so defined, is not about admiration or greatness or appreciation or depth of knowledge or scholarly achievement; it's about the movement between worlds, arms out, balancing; it's about making the connections that count.

CHAPTER 1: THE DARK NIGHT OF THE SOUL

1. The boys' larger plans were laid out in Harris's diary, in which he fantasized about going to an island after the massacre or, "if there isn't such a place," he wrote, "then we will hijack a hell of a lot of bombs and crash a plane into NYC with us inside [f]iring away as we go down." Eric Harris, personal diary. For a discussion of inaccuracies in the initial characterization of the boys' interests and beliefs, see Cullen, "Inside."

2. Michael Moore's *Bowling for Columbine* rebuts these familiar explanations for the massacre in Littleton and makes the compelling argument that it is a culture of fear, particularly fear of the racialized other, that is the source of America's violent ways.

3. Harris, personal diary. "V" is short for "Vodka," Harris's code name for Dylan Klebold. For more on the contents of Harris's diary, see Cullen, "Kill Mankind," and Prendergast.

4. Harris, who was in the final semester of his senior year, had been rejected from a number of colleges in the weeks prior to carrying out the attack on Columbine. And, just before the attack, he had been rejected by the Marine Corps, apparently because he was taking the antidepressant Luvox. Although both Harris and Klebold were considered by their peers to be "brilliant, particularly in math and computers," it was Klebold who seemed to have had everything going for him: unlike Harris, he had had a date for the senior prom and he had just returned from a trip with his parents to visit the University of Arizona, where he had been admitted for the following fall (Pooley 28). Whatever their shared experiences moving through the school system and the juvenile penal system had been, it was clear to both that their paths would begin to diverge radically after graduation.

5. Kate Battan, lead investigator of the Columbine shootings, is quoted as having said, as she completed her report: "Everybody wants a quick answer. They

want an easy answer so that they can sleep at night and know this is not going to happen tomorrow at their school. And there is no such thing in this case. There's not an easy answer. I've been working on this nonstop daily [for six months] since April 20th and I can't tell you why it happened" (qtd. in Cullen, "Inside").

6. Amis does, in fact, share much in common with his successful character: he thrives on publicity; he made a name for himself early on as a modern Lothario, and his insistence during contract negotiations for *The Information* on receiving the largest advance ever given in Britain for a literary novel earned him the enmity of much of the literary community (Lyall C13).

7. Descartes was trained by the Jesuits, the religious order founded by Ignatius Loyola who became a committed Christian after a transformative experience reading *The Life of Christ.* Part of the training Descartes received involved going on a series of retreats where initiates meditated on passages from Scripture in the hope that this practice would help them to achieve a deeper understanding of the text and a more loving response to the world. That Descartes returned to the meditational form later in life is evidence of its lasting pedagogical value.

CHAPTER 2: THE NERVOUS SYSTEM

1. According to William Shatner's Web site, the "program was ultimately responsible for saving three hundred lives" during the six years it was on the air.

2. A survey of the signal events in composition's ongoing debate about the place of "the personal" in academic writing would begin with Jane Tompkins's "Pedagogy of the Distressed" and the discussions it produced; Donald McQuade's 1991 chair's address, "Living in—and on—the Margins"; David Bartholomae's "Writing with Teachers" and Peter Elbow's "Being a Writer vs. Being an Academic"; the subsequent "Interchange" between Bartholomae and Elbow; and the ever growing body of responses to these exchanges. It would include, as well, Min-Zhan Lu's "Redefining the Literate Self: The Politics of Critical Affirmation" and John Schilb's "Comment on 'The Nervous System.'"

3. In "Self-Fashioning in Discourse: Foucault and the Freshman Writer," Kurt Spellmeyer draws attention to the fact that Patricia Bizzell and Bruce Herzberg's anthology, *The Rhetorical Tradition,* effectively prevents this insight from being made because the editors chose to exclude the final part of Foucault's talk, which reconnects "Foucault's own discourse to motives, memory, intention—to the people (not the texts, but people) from whom he learned the most" (90n11). It's worth noting that the same editorial decision was made by Hazard Adams and Leroy Searle in their anthology, *Critical Theory Since 1965.* In this way, we see how, at the level of textbook production, the division between the personal and the academic gets inscribed and reinscribed.

CHAPTER 3: SMART BOMB

1. Something from this genre is a regular feature of *Harper's* September issue, e.g., Prose 1999, Gannon 2001, and Gatto 2003.

2. In her letter to the editors of *Harper's,* Lisa Kijewski reports having "encountered few classes . . . whose objectives were so poorly defined and whose assignments were so amorphous and ill-explained" as the one she took from Edmundson and she recommends, in turn, that her former professor "try teaching with a modicum of passion, enthusiasm, and respect for his students" (6–8).

3. When the World Trade Center collapsed, the cameras cut away, famously, to show a spontaneous parade in the occupied territories and Palestinians dancing in the street. Most Americans found these images, ricocheted around the world, outrageous and shocking; few seemed to recall how much pleasure the media and the military got out of those smart bombs whistling through the night during the first Persian Gulf War; few seemed to remember the laughter on this side of the Atlantic that accompanied the destruction so far away.

4. After the first Gulf War concluded, estimates of the number of enemy casualties ranged from 1,500 to 100,000, while estimates of the number of civilian casualties that resulted from the subsequent economic sanctions ranged from 10,000 to 500,000. According to Andrew Leyden, "accurate figures simply [are] impossible to determine due to the political implications of both high and low estimates" (197). The Department of Veterans Affairs has reported that, as of May 2002, more than one quarter (149,094) of the 504,047 eligible veterans from the first Gulf War had been approved for disability benefits (Veterans Benefits Administration). The source of the array of illnesses that are collected under the name Gulf War Syndrome remains in dispute, but possible causes for this syndrome include exposure to any combination of the following: chemical and biological weapons, depleted uranium (which is used in armor-piercing weaponry), pollution from oil-well fires, experimental vaccines, anti–nerve agent pretreatment pills, and stress. Robert Walpole's special report to the CIA on the use of chemical agents in the first Gulf War declared unequivocally "that Iraq did not use chemical weapons against Coalition troops" and that, after investigating "many possible releases of chemical agent from Coalition action or incidental causes," his committee could only identify one concrete instance of exposure: "inadvertent release of nerve agent from the U.S. demolition of Iraqi chemical rockets in a pit at the Khamisiyah Depot in Iraq."

5. Raphael Perl, in a report to Congress, uses this term to mark the fact that Clinton's decision to send missiles into Sudan and Afghanistan signaled a substantial shift in American foreign policy, since it was "the first time the U.S.

has unreservedly acknowledged a preemptive military strike against a terrorist organization or network." Perl goes on enumerate the possible problems with this policy shift: those who disagree with it could say that it: "(1) undermines the rule of law, violating the sovereignty of nations with whom we are not at war; (2) could increase, rather than decrease, incidents of terrorism at least in the short run; (3) leaves allies and other nations feeling left out, or endangered—damaging future prospects for international cooperation; (4) may be characterized as anti-Islamic; and (5) may radicalize some elements of populations and aid terrorist recruitment; and (6) may result in regrettable and embarrassing consequences of mistaken targeting or loss of innocent life." Obviously, this report preceded President Bush's policy of preemptive defense, which was used to support the launching of the second Iraq War in 2003.

6. Seymour Hersh reports that, following the raid on the Al Shifa plant, there was a general sense among American officials that "the target in Sudan may not have been what the CIA said it was" (35). He notes, as well, that the sixty Tomahawk missiles (costing $750,000 apiece) that were launched at suspected bin Laden camps in Afghanistan "were either poorly targeted or did not all go where they were aimed," since they destroyed, among other things, two camps controlled by the Pakistani intelligence service, which "has been far more cooperative than is publicly known in our efforts against terrorists" (38). To date, the government has not provided access to the soil sample it maintains established that the Al Shifa plant was producing chemical weapons and it has vetoed Sudan's efforts to get the United Nations to investigate the bombing and its consequences; it has, however, unfrozen the bank accounts of Saleh Idris, the Saudi millionaire who had purchased the plant just months before it was destroyed. To learn more about the Clinton administration's internal debate over the wisdom of choosing this target, see Risen.

7. That Kaczynski's psychological profile is available online for all to see would appear to confirm Kaczynski's declaration in his manifesto that technology "AS A WHOLE continually narrows our sphere of freedom" (qtd. in Douglas and Olshaker 235; par. 128; emphasis in original).

8. Robert Graysmith, who refers to Kaczynski as "The Professor," places greater emphasis on Kaczynski's formative experiences at Berkeley during the height of the Free Speech Movement, where signs of the government's abuse of power were everywhere in evidence, and on Kaczynski's love for Joseph Conrad's *The Secret Agent* and the works of Thoreau (see especially 1–14).

9. All citations from "The Unabomber Manifesto" are taken from appendix 3 of Douglas and Olshaker and include the paragraph number to assist those using other sources.

10. As fate would have it, I encountered my first computer virus while working on this meditation: the virus crashed my hard drive, neutralized my CD-ROM drive, paralyzed my machine, and cost me a day's work. Around the same time, a colleague got hit by a "tentacle virus," which erased the contents of his entire hard drive. Obviously, the Internet places in the hands of a talented, disgruntled user the power to cause considerable technological damage. It was only the Unabomber's commitment to a position of purity that prevented him from trying to harness the powers of technology to destroy technology (see Douglas and Olshaker 232–38; par. 121–32).

11. In addition to believing that his manifesto could foment an antitechnological revolution, the Unabomber also hoped that the private writing he did in his cabin would, in the event of his capture, "prevent the facts of his psychology from being misrepresented" (S. Johnson 12; pt. 1).

12. Gelernter's own theory is that Kaczynski was initially attracted to him not because of his book, *Mirror Worlds,* but because of an article that appeared in the *New York Times* early in 1992. This article was meant to be a book review, but "somehow . . . wound up in the Sunday business section instead," where the piece was "rejiggered and came out focused on [Gelernter's work with a colleague on] 'parallel programming' research" (*Drawing Life* 87).

13. In *Drawing Life,* where Gelernter gives full voice to his own critique of modernity, he pauses for a moment to imagine what the Unabomber's response must have been when he realized he'd chosen the "wrong" target: "With the exaggerated self-regard of the hardened criminal, not to mention the mathematician—and our culprit is also, it so happens, a former Berkeley professor and, almost *too* perfect, a Harvard grad!—he no doubt saw himself as the main topic of conversation and (consequently) ridicule in every *Bierstube* and Sushi bar from Bremerhaven to Yatsuhiro. . . . Not to mention every living room of Middle America. ('I jes' finished *Mirror Worlds* and lan' sakes, Mabel, that there genius bombed the only computer scientist in the whole dang country who hates computers! Don't that jes' have Harvard written all over it!' [Laughter])" (28). When Gelernter mans the ramparts of this embattled world, decrying the fact that intellectuals have deprived us all of our common decency and of our natural-born right to be judgmental, he and the Unabomber seem more fellow travelers than mortal enemies.

14. The Unabomber incorrectly renders the advertising agency's name "Burston-Marsteller" throughout his correspondence, repeating an error that was overlooked by *Earth First!*'s copy editors; the repetition of this error later served as one of the key pieces of evidence linking Kaczynski to the Mosser bombing. See *United States v. Theodore Kaczynski.* In point of fact, the Marsteller agency put together the most famous environmental commercial to date: the spot, launched

on Earth Day in 1971, depicted a Native American surveying a polluted landscape, a tear silently tracking down his cheek. Only later did it come out that glycerin was used to create the tear and that the actor, Iron Eyes Cody, was not a Native American at all, but a second-generation Italian American from Louisiana (Waldman 15A). Kaczynski was certainly unaware of these details and there is no reason to believe that he would have taken an interest in assessing the finer gradations of culpability they suggest.

15. Upon learning of the Unabomber's offer, Bob Guccioni announced right away that *Penthouse* would publish the manifesto. In subsequent correspondence, though, the Unabomber made it clear that he couldn't strike exactly the same bargain with a *second-tier* journal: "To increase our chances of getting our stuff published in some 'respectable' periodical, we have to offer less in exchange for publication in *Penthouse*" (qtd. in Douglas and Olshaker 77). So, if the *Times* and the *Post* failed him, the Unabomber would let *Penthouse* have the manifesto; he would, however, reserve the right to strike one additional human target.

16. Mello argues that the suicide attempt was "the only rational option" available to Kaczynski at this point in the trial, since he had been betrayed by his own lawyers and the judge had refused to grant him his constitutional right to represent himself (89–90). No one knows if Kaczynski had thoughts of his father who, years earlier, had ended his life with a self-inflicted gunshot wound to the head.

17. Since amazon.com does not provide a ranked list of its most-reviewed books, there's no way of knowing definitively if *The Bell Curve* is the most reviewed "academic" book on this site. On the day I checked, I could find no other academic title that had more reviews than *The Bell Curve*: Allan Bloom's *The Closing of the American Mind* had a total of 71 reviews; Cornel West's *Race Matters* had 41; W. E. B. DuBois's *The Souls of Black Folk* had 20. Just as a point of reference, on the other side of the aisle, J. K. Rowling's *Harry Potter and the Sorcerer's Stone* had 4,450 reviews.

18. All quotes are taken from reviews of *The Bell Curve* that were posted at http://www.amazon.com/ on June 10, 2004. This data set does not allow for the generation of *any* scientifically valid statements: nothing is known about the review writers, their motivations for writing, or the authenticity either of their identities or of their responses.

CHAPTER 4: FALLING BODIES

1. I first became aware of the connection readers were making between September 11 and DeLillo when a colleague brought the cover of *Underworld* to

my attention shortly after the attacks. It wasn't long before it was obvious to me that this was hardly an isolated event, as the cover came up in numerous subsequent discussions with others in my department. Segal herself mentions the cover in recounting her decision not to teach the book in the spring semester of 2002. Additional examples proliferated on the Web. See, for example: Passaro; Wilder; Bennett; Cotts. Passaro records telling DeLillo that "his name was on many people's lips" following the attacks, and getting this simple response: "Well, I wish it weren't." Of course, while the Web allows one to track evanescent reading practices of this kind, it does not preserve these events in perpetuity since there is, as yet, no means for regularly archiving the Web's contents. The record of these connections, thus, is sure to disappear without a trace.

2. Of course, DeLillo never much cared for the towers but, in the moment, this fact was as easy to overlook as the meaning behind Kertész's ominous juxtaposition of the institutions of commerce and salvation. In *Underworld,* DeLillo is less interested in the Twin Towers than he is in the Watts Towers, which are constructed out of cement and garbage. In *Mao II,* DeLillo's meditation on the relationship between art and terror, the Twin Towers are seen to have a menacing presence: here we learn, for instance, that Brita, the photographer who specializes in portraits of writers, has a darkroom in lower Manhattan with a view that is described as follows: "Out the south windows the Trade towers stood cut against the night, intensely massed and near. This is the word 'loomed' in all its prolonged and impending force" (87). For his response to the attacks, see DeLillo, "In the Ruins."

3. For more on the "witches' brew," see Davis. For studies of pregnant women, see O'Crowley; firefighters and policemen, see United States Department of Health and Human Services and Grady and Revkin; ironworkers, see United States Department of Health and Human Services; garbage haulers, see Johns Hopkins Bloomberg School of Public Health; search-and-rescue animals, see Jones.

4. For more on the time line, see Dwyer, "Fatal Confusion."

5. Indeed, it appeared in the *Sun,* a supermarket tabloid put out by American Publishers, the newspaper company based in Florida that is now better known as the site of the first anthrax attack that took place following September 11.

6. For more on the death of Father Mychal, see *St. Mychal* and Senior. The miracle is reported in "Sainthood for 9/11 Priest"; the letter is quoted in McShane.

7. For more on FEMA and the body bags, see Reilly; Dwyer and Altman. For more on determining the number of people who died in the attacks, see Lipton; Hirschkorn.

8. For those unfamiliar with New York City and its history, the name of this landfill is bound to seem unfortunate or "just not right," as one anonymous contributor to an e-bulletin board devoted to September 11 put it. The name, however, wasn't given to the landfill *after* the attacks, but rather dates back to the sixteenth century, when the Dutch were settling the area—"kills" being Dutch for "small stream." The landfill itself had been opened in 1947 as a temporary solution to the city's trash problems: when it was finally closed in 2001, New York City moved into the trash exporting business, sending more than thirteen thousand tons of residential garbage out of state everyday, at a cost of more than $650 million a year. Prior to September 11, plans were well underway for transforming the landfill "from a blight to a treasured ecological and recreational resource." As of this writing, three teams are preparing master plans for turning the surface overtop the collected remains of fifty years of the city's garbage into a nature reserve, with "golf courses, bicycling and pedestrian paths, equestrian and athletic fields, and an environmental education center" (New York Department of City Planning). There is to be, as well, a significant memorial to the heroes and victims of September 11. See Gallagher and "NYC Seeks New Ways to Dump Trash."

9. For more on the origins of the September 11 Victim Compensation Fund, see Belkin.

10. The more conventional take on Rodin's choice of subject is to describe it as "brilliant," as Ruth Butler, one of Rodin's biographers, does on the grounds that it took the bronze doors, which traditionally told "biblical stories at the entrances of religious buildings," and used them to tell "Dante's more earthly narrative of the Christian search for salvation" at the entrance to a secular museum (Butler 148).

11. For more on the amazing story of Gerald Cantor's love for Rodin, see Varnedoe et al. 7–26.

12. *The Guys* was rushed on to the stage and made into a film in less than a year. In an interview with Sam Leith of the *Daily Telegraph*, Nelson describes requests by interested major studios that she have "the fire fighter and the writer fall in love" (qtd. in Leith).

13. For *Bodies*, see University of California, Santa Cruz. For more on *Tina C*, see Monahan; *Tina C's Twin Towers Tribute*.

14. The original quote reads: "[J]'ai compati à la douleur des familles et du peuple américain. J'attends aussi en retour comme tous les Africains d'ailleurs le même élan de solidarité avec l'Afrique par rapport au paludisme, au sida, à la faim, à la soif, etc. . . ." (Ouedraogo 11).

15. The original quote reads: "Mon seul probleme, ma seule crainte, était de savoir comment une peinture abstraite, en noir et blanc, apparaîtrait dans ce qui pourrait être un musée de la Renaissance"(Iñárritu 17).

16. See Godard. A subsequent review by Deborah Young, which began by stating that reports of the film's anti-American bias were "greatly exaggerated," was all but ignored.

17. Langewiesche's account of how he gained access to the site comes from his interview with Sage Stossel, "Inside the Ruins." The omission of these details from Langewiesche's book, *American Ground,* has led to charges that Langewiesche is biased toward the Department of Design and Construction and against the New York City Fire Department.

18. For Shearer's rebuttal and links to articles on the protests of the firefighters, see the *WTC Living History Project.*

19. See "Lesson 11," *Newsday Multi-Media English Language Arts Program.*

CHAPTER 5: THE ARTS OF COMPLICITY

1. While awaiting sentencing for his first adventure at Princeton, Hogue moved to Boston, enrolled in the Harvard Extension School, landed a job at the Harvard Mineralogical and Geological Museum, and promptly set about relieving the museum of more than $50,000 in gems and minerals. How he managed simultaneously to serve time in Hopewell Township, New Jersey, for his first crime, continue his studies at Harvard, and hold down a job at the museum in Boston remains an unsolved mystery (see "Bogus Princeton Student"). For more on Hogue, see Samuels's profile in the *New Yorker,* "The Runner," and *Con Man,* the documentary by Jesse Moss. Moss was fifteen and a student at Palo Alto High School when he first came into contact with the then twenty-three-year-old Hogue, who had just joined the senior class at the high school as Jay Mitchell Huntsman and represented himself at that time as a sixteen-year-old self-taught orphan from Nevada.

2. See Cary Nelson, *Will Teach for Food* (especially Michael Bérubé's chapter, "The Blessed of the Earth"). See also GESO.

3. In a related story, when it was discovered that Lou Grammar, a C student at Cuesta Community College, had forged documents that made it possible for him to transfer to Yale, officials there scrambled to explain how such a student could have been in good standing at their university. As the story of Grammar's accomplishments at Yale spread, Donald Green, Yale's undergraduate studies director, wrote to the *New York Times* and recommended that reporters ask Mr. Grammar to produce transcripts that substantiated his claims about his scholastic performance. So much depends, it seems, on whether the fraudulent transfer student had a B or a C average.

4. See, for example, Elbow, "Pedagogy of the Bamboozled"; North; Berlin; McCormick. For examples of those committed to getting Freire's project to work

with students in the United States, see Berthoff; Shor; Kutz and Roskelly; Bizzell; Ronald and Roskelly.

5. There is not room here to pursue the influence of Martin Buber's work on Freire's thoughts about the transformative powers of language. However, if one thinks of Buber's description of the shift from an objective, "I-It," relation to the world to the communal, responsive, interactive "I-Thou" relation as both a revelation and as the ground for a spiritual revolution, the magnitude of the change Freire worked for becomes clear: conscientization is meant to lead not only to new economic and social relations, but to new spiritual relations as well.

CHAPTER 6: EDUCATING CHARLIE

1. Letter from Charles Van Doren to Scott Buchanan, Oct. 30, 1959. bMS Am 1992 (460). By permission of the Houghton Library, Harvard University. The personal correspondence in this chapter may be found either at the Maryland Archives in Annapolis, Maryland (MDA), where it is filed under St. John's College, MSA T1406; or at the Houghton Library, Harvard University, Cambridge, Massachusetts, where it is filed with the collected papers of Scott Buchanan, bMS AM 1992.

2. For a full resume of Van Doren's educational experiences, see Stone and Yohn, 115–17.

3. See United States Cong. Stempel's testimony all occurred on Oct. 6.

4. Redford has responded to criticism of this kind with the assertion that he was "very careful not to stray too far from the truth, especially where somebody's reputation was concerned" (qtd. in Bernstein), only to be accused, in turn, of trying "to harness the power of history, to provoke the thrill that an audience feels when it thinks it's witnessing reality, and when it suspends the knowledge that the words and faces and scenes on screen are the creations of invisible hands" (Frankel).

5. Attanasio offered that other explanation for the film's poor showing at the box office, the one that is always ready to hand: "What we attempted to do was criticize the culture, and that's never going to be popular" (qtd. in "An Enigma").

6. Mark Van Doren met Buchanan in 1927 when Buchanan, who was organizing lectures for Cooper Union's People's Institute in New York City, asked him to present a series of talks on the great comic writers of the world. Van Doren was amazed that someone who earned his degree at Harvard, having completed his dissertation in philosophy on the idea of "possibility" under Alfred North Whitehead, would throw himself so completely into educating "people in New York whose minds had had no formal training comparable with his." Buchanan's strength, Van Doren continued, "lies in his faith that every living person has an

intellect: the human intellect. The people who came to the Library were possibly as important, he could believe then, as Whitehead himself" (qtd. in Charles Nelson, *Scott Buchanan,* 43–44).

7. Mark Van Doren to Scott Buchanan, Sept. 11, 1937, bMS Am 1992 (463). By permission of the Houghton Library, Harvard University.

8. Scott Buchanan to Mark Van Doren, Oct. 30, 1942, bMS Am 1992 (794). By permission of the Houghton Library, Harvard University.

9. Fadiman, who enthusiastically reviewed Adler's *How to Read a Book* in 1940 for the *New Yorker,* eventually went on to join the editorial board for *Encyclopedia Britannica* and published, in 1960, *The Lifetime Reading Plan,* which seeks to make "life companions" of the great works of Western civilization. (Revised and updated many times, *The Lifetime Reading Plan* remains in print to this day.) His daughter Anne has published *Ex Libris: Confessions of a Common Reader,* which includes an account of her family's love affair with reading, language, and big words, and her own reaction to Redford's film: "When I saw the movie *Quiz Show,* I squirmed in my seat because the literary-hothouse atmosphere of the Van Doren ménage was all too familiar" (12).

10. Scott Buchanan to Mortimer Adler, Aug. 21, 1938, MDA.

11. Mortimer Adler to Scott Buchanan, Sept. 16, 1938, MDA.

12. The attractiveness of such a move did not increase or change over time. When Buchanan and Barr resigned from St. John's at the end of 1946, Mark Van Doren turned down the board's invitation to be considered as a candidate for the college presidency (Smith 96). The elder Van Doren also declined Buchanan and Barr's invitation to join their effort to establish a new colony for the study of the Great Books in Massachusetts, on the grounds that he "did not care to dislocate [his] life" (*Autobiography* 296).

13. Scott Buchanan to Mark Van Doren, Oct. 30, 1942, bMS Am 1992 (794). By permission of the Houghton Library, Harvard University.

14. For more on Buchanan and Barr's resignation, see Miller 107–17.

15. This quotation and those following are from Van Doren Statement 3, Nov. 2, 1959, bMS Am 1992 (460); see especially pages 4–8. By permission of the Houghton Library, Harvard University.

16. To get a sense of the relative size of Van Doren's winnings and of his contract with NBC, consider that his starting salary as an assistant professor in the English department at Columbia University in 1955 was $4,000 per year.

17. The rest of the mail was of an entirely different cast: "From The Bronx to Basutoland, fans have deluged [Van Doren] with 2,000 letters, including 20 outright proposals of marriage, numerous veiled ones, solicitations from investment houses and wildcatters, requests for handouts that add up to more money than he has won" ("Wizard" 49).

18. Charles Van Doren to Scott Buchanan, Jan. 27, 1960, bMS Am 1992 (460). By permission of the Houghton Library, Harvard University.

19. It's worth observing, in passing, that when Mortimer Adler came up with the *Syntopicon*, his catalogue of the 102 Great Ideas discussed in the Great Books, his list included neither "woman" nor "equality." As should be evident by this point in the discussion, the Great Conversation, as conceived by its creators, was largely carried out among men about works by men for a society that was conceived of as consisting primarily of men. Hutchins, for example, described the work of his Center for the Study of Democratic Institutions in the following terms: "The Center consists of twenty-five men who meet every day in a Spanish style building known to the members as El Parthenon. The men, one of whom is a woman, are writers, philosophers, scientists, social scientists, and lawyers, with two bishops and two ex-college presidents thrown in" (qtd. in "History of the Center"). It is in the interests of not covering over this glaring limitation in this pedagogical approach that I have self-consciously retained the universal use of "he," "mankind," and "men" throughout. For those who wish to claim that the meaning of these terms has changed over time and that, in the past, they were meant to serve as universals that included women, see Anne Fadiman's account of her conversations with Clifton Fadiman about this very issue, in which the elder Fadiman is quoted as saying: "I viewed the world of literature—indeed, the entire world of artistic creation—as a world of males, and so did most writers. Any writer of fifty years ago who denies that is lying. Any male writer I mean" (*Spirit* 62).

20. Buchanan uses this phrase in his letter to Mark Van Doren proposing a set of television programs on the Great Books that he envisioned marketing to NBC or Mutual of Omaha. Scott Buchanan to Mark Van Doren, Oct. 30, 1942, bMS Am 1992 (794). By permission of the Houghton Library, Harvard University.

21. Wofford, fresh back from the war, met Buchanan as he was trying to decide whether to use the GI Bill to take him to St. John's or the University of Chicago. He ultimately settled on the University of Chicago and has ever since, he says, "been trying to make up for the books, the foreign languages and the mathematics I missed at St. John's" (Charles Nelson, *Scott Buchanan*, 75). Over the last two years of Buchanan's life, Buchanan granted Wofford a number of interviews, which were posthumously published under the title *Embers of the World*. Wofford, one of the early architects of the Peace Corps, went on to serve as the president of Bryn Mawr College, was subsequently elected to the U.S. Senate, and is currently Professor of Practice at the University of Maryland.

22. Scott Buchanan to Harris Wofford, Dec. 13, 1959, bMS Am 1992 (810). By permission of the Houghton Library, Harvard University.

23. This and the previous quote: Scott Buchanan to Mark Van Doren, Nov. 10, 1959, bMS Am 1992 (794). By permission of the Houghton Library, Harvard University. The Center for the Study of Democratic Institutions was established with seed money from the Ford Foundation's Fund for the Republic, which was created in the wake of the McCarthy era to combat the abuse of civil liberties in America. Hutchins, who helped administer this fund after stepping down as the chancellor of the University of Chicago, persuaded the board to set up a permanent center in Santa Barbara for studying the maintenance of civil liberties in a democracy. Buchanan was the first senior fellow brought to the center in 1959 (for more, see "History of the Center"). Hutchins served as the director of this center until the end of his life in 1977.

24. All quotes in this paragraph: ibid. In the end, the only crime that was committed in the quiz-show deceptions occurred when those involved lied under oath to the grand jury. All who were charged for this crime either had the charges against them dismissed or received suspended sentences. See "Quiz Show Scandals."

25. In the following account of the evolving relationship between the University of Chicago and the *Encyclopedia Britannica*, I have drawn heavily on Hyman and Kogan.

26. Declining sales forced the William Benton Foundation to sell the *Encyclopedia Britannica* in 1995, with the proceeds, rumored to be around $500 million, going directly to the University of Chicago (See Feder, "Deal is Set."). This contribution to the university's endowment, coupled with the $125 million that the *Encyclopedia Britannica* contributed to the university in royalties over the years (see Landler), makes Benton's lunch with Wood an example of truly high dining.

27. Scott Buchanan to Mortimer Adler, Aug. 14, 1946, bMS Am 1992 (528). By permission of the Houghton Library, Harvard University.

28. Scott Buchanan to Robert Maynard Hutchins, Dec. 5, 1946. bMS Am 1992 (642). By permission of the Houghton Library, Harvard University.

29. In an addendum to "The Book-of-the-Millennium Club," Dwight Macdonald's scathing review of *Great Books of the Western World*, Macdonald credits his earlier review with having adversely affected sales in the early 1950s. Macdonald's criticisms of what he saw as a monument to middlebrow culture, he tells his readers, were no match, though, for "Mr. Hardin and his banner-bearing colleagues" who had been hired to sell the series door-to-door (261).

30. For Van Doren's remarks in their entirety, see his "The Biggest Challenge of All." The account of the audience response comes from Chajet.

CHAPTER 7: SPEAKING WITH THE DEAD

1. Adler has insisted that this critical self-assessment was actually made by Hutchins himself (129).

2. Scott Buchanan to Robert Maynard Hutchins, Feb. 12, 1937, bMS Am 1992 (642). By permission of the Houghton Library, Harvard University. The personal correspondence in this chapter may be found at the Houghton Library, Harvard University, Cambridge, MA, where it is filed with the collected papers of Scott Buchanan, bMS AM1992.

3. Scott Buchanan, "The Classics and the Liberal Arts Number 1," n.d., bMS Am 1992 (642). By permission of the Houghton Library, Harvard University.

4. Images of *Dark Elegy,* along with a statement by Lowenstein, may be found at <http://www.geocities.com/CapitolHill/5260/suzy.html>.

Ackroyd, Peter. *T. S. Eliot: A Life.* New York: Simon, 1984.

Adams, Hazard, and Leroy Searle, eds. *Critical Theory since 1965.* Tallahassee: Florida State UP, 1986.

Adler, Mortimer. *Philosopher at Large: An Intellectual Autobiography.* New York: Macmillan, 1977.

"After Complaints, Rockefeller Center Drapes Sept. 11 Statue." *New York Times,* Sept. 19, 2002: B3.

Althusser, Louis. "Ideology and Ideological State Apparatuses (Notes Towards an Investigation)." *Lenin and Philosophy and Other Essays.* Trans. Ben Brewster. London: New Left, 1971. 121–73.

Amis, Martin. *Experience: A Memoir.* New York: Hyperion, 2000.

———. *The Information.* New York: Harmony, 1995.

Anzaldúa, Gloria. *Borderlands/La Frontera: The New Mestiza.* San Francisco: Spinsters/Aunt Lute, 1987.

Ashmore, Harry S. *Unseasonable Truths: The Life of Robert Maynard Hutchins.* Boston: Little, 1989.

"The Atta Document in Full." *Observer,* Sept. 30, 2001: 17.

Barbier, Nicole. "The Plasters of Meudon." *Beaux Arts Magazine* 47 (June 1987): 62–67.

Barron, James. "Warnings from a Student Turned Killer." *New York Times,* May 1, 1999: A12.

Barry, Dan. "At Morgue, Ceaselessly Sifting 9/11 Traces." *New York Times,* July 14, 2002, sec. 1: 1.

Barry, Dan, and William K. Rashbaum. "Born of Hell, Lost after Inferno; Rodin Work from Trade Center Survived, and Vanished." *New York Times,* May 20, 2002: B1.

Bartholomae, David. "Interchange: A Response to Peter Elbow." *College Composition and Communication* 46.1 (1995): 84–87.

————. "Inventing the University." *When A Writer Can't Write.* Ed. Mike Rose. New York: Guilford, 1985. 134–64.

————. "Writing with Teachers: A Conversation with Peter Elbow." *College Composition and Communication* 46.1 (1995): 62–71.

Belkin, Lisa. "Just Money." *New York Times,* Dec. 8, 2002, sec. 6: 92.

Bennett, Samuel. "September 11th." *Adolescent Love Poetry.* Sept. 2001. Feb. 5, 2003 <http://adolescentlovepoetry.com/911/sept11.htm>.

Berlin, James. "Not a Conclusion: A Conversation." *Into the Field: Sites of Composition Studies.* Ed. Anne Ruggles Gere. New York: MLA, 1993. 193–206.

Bernstein, Richard. "For $64,000, What Is 'Fiction?'" *New York Times,* Sept. 4, 1994: B1.

Berthoff, Ann E. *Reclaiming the Imagination.* Upper Montclair, NJ: Boynton/ Cook, 1984.

Bérubé, Michael. "The Blessed of the Earth." Cary Nelson, *Will Teach* 154–82.

Bizzell, Patricia. *Academic Discourse and Critical Consciousness.* Pittsburgh: U of Pittsburgh P, 1992.

Bizzell, Patricia, and Bruce Herzberg. *The Rhetorical Tradition.* Boston: Bedford St. Martin's, 1990.

Bloom, Allan. *The Closing of the American Mind.* New York: Simon, 1988.

"Bogus Princeton Student Held in New Crime." *New York Times,* May 16, 1993: A25.

Bourdieu, Pierre. *Distinction: A Social Critique of the Judgement of Taste.* Trans. Richard Nice. Cambridge, MA: Harvard UP, 1984.

Bowling for Columbine. Dir. Michael Moore. United Artists, 2002.

Brinley, Maryann. "What's in the Dust?" *UMDNJ HealthState* 20.1 (2002): 28–29. Feb. 1, 2003 <http://www.eohsi.rutgers.edu/pdf/HSdust.pdf>.

Buber, Martin. *I and Thou.* New York: Scribner's, 1955.

Buchanan, Scott. Personal correspondence. Maryland Archives, Annapolis, MD (MDA). Filed under St. John's College, MSA T1406.

————. Personal correspondence. Houghton Library, Harvard University. Cambridge, MA. Filed under bMS Am 1992.

Butler, Ruth. *The Shape of Genius.* New Haven: Yale UP, 1983.

Chajet, Clive. Letter. "On Charles Van Doren." *Columbia College Today Online,* Nov. 1999. Feb. 16, 2003 <http://www.college.columbia.edu/cct/nov99/ nov99_letterseditor.html>.

Chase, Alston. "Harvard and the Making of the Unabomber." *Atlantic Monthly,* June 2000: 41–65.

Chen, David. "Worst-Hit Firm Faults Fairness of Sept. 11th Aid." *New York Times,* Sept. 17, 2002: A1.

Con Man. Dir. and prod. Jesse Moss. HBO, 2002.

Cosentino, Geraldine. "The World Trade Center Collapse: A Disaster for Art." *OIA OnlineNewsletter,* Spring 2002. Feb. 1, 2003 <http://www.oiaonline.org/newsletter.htm>.

Cotts, Brian. "911." *30* 30.VIN.17, Sept. 11, 2001. Feb. 5, 2003 <http://briancotts.tripod.com/cottsweb/thirty/thirtyvin17.html>.

Cronkite, Walter. "What Is There to Hide?" *Newsweek,* Feb. 25, 1991: 43.

Cullen, Dave. "Inside the Columbine High Investigation." *Salon.com,* Sept. 23, 1999. Feb. 22, 2003 <http://www.salon.com/news/feature/1999/09/23/columbine>.

———. "Kill Mankind. No One Should Survive." *Salon.com,* Sept. 23, 1999. Feb. 19, 2003 <http://www.salon.com/news/feature/1999/09/23/journal>.

Davis, Maia. "Dust from WTC Contained 'Witches' Brew' of Pollutants." *Record,* Feb. 16, 2002. Feb. 7, 2003 <http://www.eohsi.rutgers.edu/pdf/recordarticle.pdf>.

DeLillo, Don. "In the Ruins of the Future." *Harper's Magazine,* Dec. 2001: 33–40.

———. *Mao II.* New York: Penguin, 1991.

———. *Underworld.* New York: Scribner, 1997.

Denby, David. *Great Books: My Adventures with Homer, Rousseau, Woolf, and Other Indestructible Writers of the Western World.* New York: Simon, 1996.

Descartes, René. *Discourse on Method and Meditations on First Philosophy.* Trans. Donald A. Cress. 4th ed. Indianapolis: Hackett, 1998.

Devlin, Bernie, Stephen E. Fienberg, Daniel Phillip Resnick, and Kathryn Roeder, eds. *Intelligence, Genes, and Success: Scientists Respond to* The Bell Curve. New York: Springer, 1997.

Douglas, John, and Mark Olshaker. *Unabomber: On the Trail of America's Most Wanted Serial Killer.* New York: Simon, 1996.

DuBois, W. E. B. *The Souls of Black Folk.* New York: Blue Heron, 1953.

Dwyer, Jim. "Fatal Confusion: Inside the Tower." July 7, 2002. Audio portion of interactive article. *New York Times on the Web,* Nov. 9, 2002 <http://www.nytimes.com>.

———. "Investigating 9/11: An Unimaginable Calamity, Still Largely Unexamined." *New York Times,* Sept. 11, 2002: A19.

Dwyer, Jim, and Lawrence K. Altman. "After the Attacks: The Morgue: Loads of Body Bags Hint at Magnitude of Grisly Task." *New York Times,* Sept. 13, 2001: A10.

Dwyer, Jim, Eric Lipton, Kevin Flynn, James Glanz, Ford Fessenden, Alain Delaqueriere, and Tom Torok. "102 Minutes: Last Words at the Trade Center: Fighting to Live as the Towers Died." *New York Times,* May 26, 2002: A1.

Edmundson, Mark. "On the Uses of the Liberal Arts." *Harper's Magazine,* Sept. 1997: 39–49.

Educating Rita. Dir. Lewis Gilbert. Columbia/Tristar, 1983.

"Effort to Identify Remains of 9/11 Victims Ends." Associated Press wire article, Feb. 23, 2005.

Elbow, Peter. "Being a Writer vs. Being an Academic." *College Composition and Communication* 46.1 (1995): 72–83.

———. "Interchange: A Response to David Bartholomae." *College Composition and Communication* 46.1 (1995): 87–92.

———. "Pedagogy of the Bamboozled." *Embracing Contraries.* New York: Oxford UP, 1986. 85–98.

11'09"01 Press Kit. Studio/Canal Press, 2002. Dec. 10, 2002 <http:// www.bacfilms.com/site/september11/index.php3>.

Eliot, T. S. "The Metaphysical Poets." Rpt. in *Selected Prose of T. S. Eliot.* Ed. Frank Kermode. New York: Farrar, 1975. 59–67.

———. "Tradition and the Individual Talent." Rpt. in *Contemporary Literary Criticism.* Ed. Robert Con Davis and Ronald Schleifer. 2nd ed. New York: Longman, 1989. 25–31.

Emerson, Steven, and Brian Duffy. *The Fall of Pan Am 103: Inside the Lockerbie Investigation.* New York: Putnam's, 1990.

"An Enigma of 'Quiz Show': No Crowds." *New York Times,* Feb. 12, 1995: H19.

Fadiman, Anne. *Ex Libris: Confessions of a Common Reader.* New York: Farrar, 2000.

———. *The Spirit Catches You and You Fall Down.* New York: Farrar, 1998.

Farrell, John Aloysius. "The Patriot Gulf Missile 'Didn't Work': Defense Secretary Cohen Speaks Out." *Boston Globe,* Jan. 13, 2001: A1.

Feder, Barnaby. "Deal Is Set for Encyclopedia Britannica." *New York Times,* Dec. 19, 1995: D2.

Ferri, Daniel. "Education by the Numbers." *Harper's Magazine,* July 1998: 19–23.

Finnegan, William. "Defending the Unabomber." *New Yorker,* Mar. 16, 1998: 52–63.

Fischer, Claude, et al. *Inequality by Design: Cracking the Bell Curve Myth.* Princeton, NJ: Princeton UP, 1996.

Fisk, Robert. "Free to Report What We're Told." *Independent,* Feb. 4, 1991: 19.

Foucault, Michel. "The Order of Discourse." *Untying the Text.* Trans. Ian McLeod. Ed. Robert Young. New York: Routledge, 1981. 48–78.

———. *The Use of Pleasure.* Trans. Robert Hurley. New York: Vintage, 1985.

Frankel, Max. "This Is Your Life." *New York Times Magazine,* Oct. 9, 1994: 32.

Fraser, Steven, ed. *The Bell Curve Wars: Race, Intelligence, and the Future of America.* New York: Basic, 1995.

Freeman, Barbara Claire. "Pedagogy and Psychoanalysis: A True Story." *Common Knowledge* 4.1 (1995): 7–15.

Freire, Paulo. *Pedagogy of the Oppressed.* Trans. Myra Bergman Ramos. New York: Continuum, 1989.

Gallagher, Mariellen. "Better Waste Management May Reduce NYC Deficit, Columbia Earth Institute Says." *Columbia News,* Feb. 27, 2002. Dec. 10, 2002 <http://www.columbia.edu/cu/news/02/02/waste_mgm_study.html>.

Gannon, Frank. "English 99: Literacy among the Ruins." *Harper's Magazine,* Sept. 2001: 45–48.

Garrett, Laurie. "Air of Infirmity: City Struggles to Contend with Widespread WTC Cough." *Newsday,* Sept. 30, 2002: A6.

———. "Under the Plume: September 11 Produced a New Kind of Pollution, and No One Knows What to Do about It." *American Prospect* 13.19 (Oct. 2002): 22–24.

Gatto, John. "Against School: How Public Education Cripples Our Kids, and Why." *Harper's Magazine,* Sept. 2003: 33–38.

Gelernter, David. *Drawing Life: Surviving the Unabomber.* Boston: Free Press, 1997.

———. *Mirror Worlds, or the Day Software Puts the Universe in a Shoebox . . . : How It Will Happen and What It Will Mean.* New York: Oxford UP, 1991.

Germano, William. "The Way We Read Now." *Chronicle of Higher Education,* Oct. 5, 2001: B9.

GESO (Graduate Employees and Students Organization). "Casual in Blue: Yale and the Academic Labor Market." Spring 1999. Apr. 8, 2005 <http://yaleunions.org/geso/reports/Casual_in_Blue.PDF>.

Gingrich, Newt. *Lessons Learned the Hard Way: A Personal Report.* New York: Harper, 1998.

Giroux, Henry A., and Susan Searle. "*The Bell Curve* Debate and the Crisis of Public Intellectuals." Kincheloe, Steinberg, and Gresson 51–70.

Godard, Francois. "Canal Plus 9/11 Pic Courts Controversy: Anti-U.S. Elements Permeate Project." *Variety,* Aug. 20, 2002. Apr. 8, 2005 <http://www.variety.com/index.asp?layout=upsell_article&articleID=VR1117871633&cs=1>.

Goldberg, Natalie. *Writing Down the Bones.* Boston: Shambala, 1986.

Goldstein, Bill. "Let Us Now Praise Books Well Sold but Seldom Read." *New York Times,* July 15, 2000: B11.

Grady, Denise, and Andrew Revkin. "Lung Ailments May Force 500 Firefighters Off Job." *New York Times,* Sept. 10, 2002: A1.

Graysmith, Robert. *Unabomber: A Desire to Kill.* Washington DC: Regency, 1997.

Green, Donald P. "Did Yale Imposter Really Earn B Grades?" *New York Times,* Apr. 24, 1995: A27.

Gross, Jane. "Out of the House, but Still Focused on Family." *New York Times,* Apr. 29, 1999: B2.

"Ground Fires Still Burning." *NewScientist.com*, Dec. 3, 2001. Jan. 5, 2003 <http://www.newscientist.com/news/news.jsp?id=ns99991634>.

Hagan, Joe. "Gould's Wife Takes on *Atlantic* Scribe." *New York Observer*, Oct. 21, 2002: 17.

Harris, Eric. Personal diary (excerpts). *Westword.com*, Dec.12, 2002 <http://www.westword.com/special_reports/columbine/files/index_html>.

Harrison, Kathryn. *The Kiss*. New York: Bard, 1996.

Hasson, Judi. "The Republican Brain Trust." *USA Today*, Dec. 9, 1994: 8A.

Hawkes, Nigel. "Racism Versus Science." *Times*, Oct. 19, 1994: 16.

Herbert, Bob. "In America: Throwing a Curve." *New York Times*, Oct. 26, 1994: A27.

Herrnstein, Richard J., and Charles Murray. *The Bell Curve: Intelligence and Class Structure in American Life*. New York: Touchstone, 1996.

Hersh, Seymour. "Annals of National Security: The Missiles of August." *New Yorker*, Oct. 12, 1998: 34–41.

Hirschkorn, Phil. "WTC List May Name Some Who Are Still Alive." *CNN.com*, Sept. 14, 2002. Jan. 5, 2002 <http://www.cnn.com/2002/US/09/14/wtc.missing>.

"History of the Center." *Center for the Study of Democratic Institutions Collection*. Davidson Library, University of California, Santa Barbara. Feb. 16, 2003.

Hong, Joy. "A Matter of Interpretation." Student paper. "Literature and Society: An Introduction to Cultural Studies." Prof. Richard Miller, Rutgers University, Apr. 1995.

hooks, bell. *Teaching to Transgress*. New York: Routledge, 1994.

Hotz, Robert Lee. "Probing the DNA of Death: Experts Examine 14,994 Remains to Try to Identify the 9/11 Dead." *Los Angeles Times*, Oct. 9, 2002: 1.

Hughes, Marvalene. "A Post–September 11th Mandate for Education." *New York Times on the Web*, Jan. 15, 2002. Feb. 8, 2003 <http://www.nytimes.com/2002/01/15/college/HUGH.html>.

Hutchins, Robert Maynard. *The Great Conversation*. Great Books of the Western World 1. Chicago: Encyclopedia Britannica, 1952.

———. *The Higher Learning in America*. New Haven: Yale UP, 1936.

Hyman, Sidney. *The Lives of William Benton*. Chicago: U of Chicago P, 1969.

"Identification of Bodies a Slow Task." *Death Care Business Advisor* 6.7 (2001).

Iñárritu, Alejandro González. *11'09"01 Press Kit*. Studio/Canal, 2002. Feb. 8, 2003 <http://www.bacfilms.com/site/september11/index.php3#>.

Jacoby, Russell, and Naomi Glauberman, eds. *The Bell Curve Debate: History, Documents, Opinions*. New York: Times, 1995.

Johns Hopkins Bloomberg School of Public Health. "Health Assessment Finds World Trade Center Cleanup Workers Suffering from Acute Respiratory

Problems." Press release, Aug. 23, 2002 <http://www.jhsph.edu/PublicHealth News/Press_Releases/PR_2002/WTC_health.html>.

Johnson, David. "World Trade Center History: Magnificent Buildings Graced Skyline." *FactMonster.* Feb. 5, 2003 <http://www.factmonster.com/spot/wtcl.html>.

Johnson, Jim. "Cleaning up a Horror: Crews Work to Remove Mountains of Debris after Terrorist Attack." *Waste News,* Sept. 17, 2001: 1.

Johnson, Sally C. "Forensic Evaluation of Theodore Kaczynski." No. CR-S-96–259-GEB. The United States District Court for the Eastern District of California, Sept. 11, 1998. Jan. 3, 2003 <http://www.unabombertrial.com/documents/psych_report1.html>.

Jones, Rebecca. "With Cold, Wet Nose: Odie Named Top Dog for His Work at WTC." *Rocky Mountain News,* Sept. 23, 2002: 4d.

Kakutani, Michiko. "The Order and Chaos of Clearing Ground Zero." *New York Times,* Oct. 22, 2002: E1.

Karr, Mary. *The Liars' Club.* New York: Viking, 1995.

Kaysen, Susanna. *Girl, Interrupted.* New York: Vintage, 1994.

Kennedy, Helen, Robert Ingrassia, and Corky Siemaszko. "Defiant McVeigh Is Put to Death: Bomber Remains Silent, Unrepentant to Very End." *Daily News,* June 12, 2001: 2.

Kennedy, Randall. "The Phony War." Fraser 179–86.

Keyes, Daniel. *Flowers for Algernon.* New York: Harcourt, 1959.

Kijewski, Lisa J. "Letter." *Harper's Magazine,* Dec. 1997: 6–8.

Kincheloe, Joe L., and Shirley R. Steinberg. "Who Said It Can't Happen Here?" Kincheloe, Steinberg, and Gresson 3–50.

Kincheloe, Joe L., Shirley R. Steinberg, and Aaron D. Gresson III, eds. *Measured Lies: The Bell Curve Examined.* New York: St. Martin's, 1996.

Kogan, Herman. *The Great EB: The Story of the Encyclopedia Britannica.* Chicago: U of Chicago P, 1958.

Krakauer, Jon. *Into the Wild.* New York: Villard, 1996.

Kutz, Eleanor, and Hephzibah Roskelly. *An Unquiet Pedagogy: Transforming Practice in the English Classroom.* Portsmouth, NH: Boynton/Cook, 1991.

Landler, Mark. "Slow-to-Adapt Encyclopedia Britannica Is for Sale." *New York Times,* May 16, 1995: D1, D22.

Langewiesche, William. *American Ground: Unbuilding the World Trade Center.* New York: North Point, 2002.

Leith, Sam. "The Fire Captain and Me." *Daily Telegraph,* Aug. 12, 2002. Feb. 5, 2003 <http://www.telegraph.co.uk/arts/main.jhtml?xml=/arts/2002/08/12/btnelson12.xml>.

Lelyveld, Joseph. "All Suicide Bombers Are Not Alike." *New York Times Magazine*, Oct. 28, 2001: 49.

Le Normand-Romain, Antoinette. *Rodin: The Gates of Hell*. Paris: Musee Rodin, 1999.

"Lesson 11: Writing an Editorial." *Newsday Multi-Media English Language Arts Program*, 2002. Feb. 8, 2003 <http://www.newsday.com/other/education/ny-news_111902.story>.

Lewis, Neil A. "Bush Weighing Brief Opposing College on Race." *New York Times*, Jan. 15, 2003: A1.

Leyden, Andrew. *Gulf War Debriefing Book: An After Action Report*. Grants Pass, OR: Hellgate, 1997.

Lioy, Paul. "Characterization of the Dust/Smoke Aerosol that Settled East of the World Trade Center (WTC) in Lower Manhattan After the Collapse of the WTC, September 11, 2001." Working paper, n.d. Feb. 6, 2003 <http://www.eohsi.rutgers.edu/wtc/images/PJLweb_files/v3_document.htm>.

Lioy, Paul, and Michael Gochfeld. "Lessons Learned on Environmental, Occupational, and Residential Exposures from the Attack on the WTC." Working paper, n.d. Feb. 8, 2003 <http://www.eohsi.rutgers.edu/wtc/Lessons%20Learned%20Manuscript.pdf>.

Lipton, Eric. "Giuliani Says City Was Prepared for 9/11." *New York Times*, Sept. 29, 2002: A45.

Lu, Min-Zhan. "Redefining the Literate Self: The Politics of Critical Affirmation." *College Composition and Communication* 51.2 (1999): 172–94.

Lugg, Catherine A. "Attacking Affirmative Action: Social Darwinism as Public Policy." Kincheloe, Steinberg, and Gresson 367–78.

Lyall, Sarah. "Martin Amis's Big Deal Leaves Literati Fuming." *New York Times*, Jan. 31, 1995: C13.

Macdonald, Dwight. "The Book-of-the-Millennium Club." *New Yorker*, Nov. 29, 1952. Rpt. *Against the American Grain: Essays on the Effects of Mass Culture*. Ed. Dwight Macdonald. New York: Press, 1983.

McBride, James. *The Color of Water: A Black Man's Tribute to His White Mother*. New York: Riverhead, 1996.

McCormick, Kathleen, "Always Already Theorists: Literary Theory and Theorizing in the Undergraduate Curriculum." *Pedagogy Is Politics: Literary Theory and Critical Teaching*. Ed. Maria-Regina Ketcht. Urbana: U of Illinois P, 1992. 111–31.

McCourt, Frank. *Angela's Ashes: A Memoir*. New York: Scribner, 1996.

McQuade, Donald. "Living In—and On—the Margins." *College Composition and Communication* 43.1 (1992): 11–22.

McShane, Larry. "Canonization Urged for NYPD Chaplain, 9/11 Victim." *Boston Globe,* Dec. 25, 2002: A3.

Mello, Michael. *The United States of America Versus Theodore John Kaczynski: Ethics, Power, and the Invention of the Unabomber.* New York: Context, 1999.

Milbank, Dana. "Whatever Happened to the Class of 1994? *New York Times Magazine,* Jan. 17, 1999: 36–40.

Miller, Richard E. *As If Learning Mattered: Reforming Higher Education.* Ithaca: Cornell UP, 1998.

Modern Language Association. "MLA Special Ballot." MLA, June 1996.

———. "Professional Notes and Comment," *PMLA* 111.3 (1996): 542.

Monahan, Mark. "Edinburgh Reports: What's All the Fuss About?" *Daily Telegraph,* Aug. 19, 2002. Dec. 10, 2002 <http://www.telegraph.co.uk/arts/main.jhtml?xml=/arts/2002/08/19/btwin19.xml>.

Morrison, Toni. *The Bluest Eye.* New York: Penguin, 1994.

Moses, Paul. "Bad Air Days From 9/11 Hit Brooklyn Hard." *Newsday,* Nov. 14, 2002: A36.

"A Nation Challenged: Notes Found After the Hijackings." *New York Times,* Sept. 29, 2001: B3.

Nelson, Cary. "Between Crisis and Opportunity. The Future of the Academic Workplace." Nelson, *Will Teach* 3–31.

———. "Lessons from the Job Wars: What Is to Be Done?" *Academe: Bulletin of the American Association of University Professors,* Nov.–Dec. (1995): 18–25.

———, ed. *Will Teach for Food: Academic Labor in Crisis.* Minneapolis: U of Minnesota P, 1997.

Nelson, Charles, ed. *Scott Buchanan: A Centennial Appreciation of His Life and Work.* Annapolis: St. John's College P, 1995.

New York Department of City Planning. "Department of City Planning Announces the Winner of the Internal Competition for a Conceptual Design and Master Plan for the Future of Fresh Kills." Press release #022–01, Dec. 18, 2001. Dec. 10, 2002 <http://www.ci.nyc.ny.us/html/dcp/html/about/pr121801.html>.

North, Stephen M. "Rhetoric, Responsibility, and the 'Language of the Left.'" *Composition & Resistance.* Ed. C. Mark Hurlbert and Michael Blitz. Portsmouth, NH: Boynton/Cook, 1991. 127–36.

"NYC Seeks New Ways to Dump Trash." *wnbc.com,* Feb. 20, 2002. Dec. 10, 2002 <http://www.wnbc.com/news/1244442/detail.html>.

O'Crowley, Peggy. "N.J. Scientists Study Birth Defects for Link to 9/11 Stress and Dust." *Home News Tribune,* Sept. 11, 2002: 1.

Oklahoma City National Memorial. Feb. 7, 2003 <http://www.oklahomacitynationalmemorial.org>.

O'Shaughnessy, Patrice. "More than Half of Victims ID'd." *New York Daily News,* Sept. 11, 2002: 8.

Ouedraogo, Idrissa. *11'09"01 Press Kit.* Studio/Canal, 2002. Dec. 10, 2002 <http://www.bacfilms.com/site/september11/index.php3>.

Passaro, Vince. "DeLillo and the Towers." *Mr. Beller's Neighborhood,* Oct. 10, 2001. Feb. 5, 2003 <http://www.mrbellersneighborhood.com/story.php?storyid =403>.

Perl, Raphael. *Terrorism: U.S. Response to Bombings in Kenya and Tanzania: A New Policy Direction?* Congressional Research Service Report for Congress, 98–733F. Sept. 1, 1998. Jan. 3, 2003 <http://usinfo.state.gov/topical/pol/terror/crs98091 .htm>.

Plato. *Phaedrus.* Ed. R. Hackforth. Cambridge: Cambridge UP, 1972.

———. *The Republic.* Trans. Allan Bloom. New York: Basic, 1968.

Pooley, Eric. "Portrait of a Deadly Bond." *Time,* May 10, 1999: 26–32.

Postol, Theodore. "Letter to John Conyers Jr." *The Federation of American Scientists,* Sept. 8, 1992. Feb. 19, 2003 <http://www.fas.org/spp/starwars/docops/pl920908.htm>.

Prendergast, Alan. "I'm Full of Hate and I Love It." *Denver Westword,* Dec. 6, 2001. Feb. 25, 2003 <http://www.westword.com/issues/2001–12–06/news.html/1/index.html>.

Prose, Francine. "I Know Why the Caged Bird Cannot Read: How American High School Students Learn to Loathe Literature." *Harper's Magazine,* Sept. 1999: 75–84.

Quiz Show. Dir. Robert Redford. Hollywood Pictures, 1994.

"The Quiz Show Scandals." *The American Experience.* PBS, 2000. Transcript. <http://www.pbs.org/wgbh/amex/quizshow/filmmore/transcript/index.html>.

Rakoff, David. "The Way We Live Now: Questions for Eric Fischl: Post-9/11 Modernism." *New York Times,* Oct. 27, 2002, sec. 6: 15.

Reilly, William M. "NY Digging for Dead, Survivors." *United Press International,* Sept. 12, 2001. Jan. 3, 2003 <http://www.lexisnexis.com/>.

Revkin, Andrew. "After Attacks, Studies of Dust and Its Effects." *New York Times,* Oct. 16, 2001: F1.

Rich, Adrienne. "When We Dead Awaken: Writing as Re-Vision." *On Lies, Secrets, and Silence: Selected Prose 1966–1978.* New York: Norton, 1979. 33–50.

Ricks, Delthia. "Assessing the Scope of WTC Ailments: Experts Study How Lungs May Worsen." *Newsday,* Oct. 1, 2002: A39.

Riding, Alan. "An American Tragedy Viewed through 11 Foreign Prisms." *New York Times,* Sept. 9, 2002: E1.

Risen, James. "Question of Evidence: A Special Report: To Bomb Sudan Plant, or Not: A Year Later, Debates Rankle." *New York Times,* Oct. 27, 1999: A1.

Rodriguez, Richard. "The Achievement of Desire." *Ways of Reading*. Ed. David Bartholomae and Anthony Petrosky. 3d ed. New York: Bedford Books, 1993. 481–504.

Ronald, Kate, and Hephzibah Roskelly. *Reason to Believe: Romanticism, Pragmatism, and the Possibility of Teaching*. Albany: State U of New York P, 1998.

Rose, Mike. *Lives on the Boundary: The Struggles and Achievements of America's Underprepared*. New York: Free Press, 1989.

———. *Possible Lives: The Promise of Public Education in America*. Boston: Houghton, 1995.

Ryan, Michael. *Secret Life: An Autobiography*. New York: Vintage, 1996.

The Saint John's Story. Videocassette. St. John's College, 1954.

"Sainthood for 9/11 Priest." *Sun*, Jan. 21, 2003.

Samuels, David. "The Runner." *New Yorker*, Sept. 3, 2001: 72–85.

Schilb, John. "Comment on 'The Nervous System.'" *College English* 59.2 (1997): 220–21.

Schneider, Andrew. "NYC under an Asbestos Cloud." *Seattle Post-Intelligencer*, Jan. 14, 2002. Feb. 8, 2003 <http://seattlepi.nwsource.com/national/54382 _asbestos14.shtml>.

Scott, James. *Domination and the Arts of Resistance: Hidden Transcripts*. New Haven: Yale UP, 1990.

Segal, Carolyn Foster. "The Solace of Literature." *Chronicle of Higher Education*, Oct. 5, 2001: B7.

Senior, Jennifer. "The Fireman's Friar." *New York Magazine*, Nov. 12, 2001. Feb. 8, 2003 <http://www.newyorkmetro.com/nymetro/news/sept11/features/5372/>.

"The September 11th Victims' Fund: De Factos of the Matter." *Economist*, Sept. 21, 2002: 35.

Shatner, William. *The Official Shatner Web Site*. Feb. 1, 2002 <http://www.william shatner.com/>.

Shor, Ira, ed. *Freire for the Classroom: A Sourcebook for Liberatory Teaching*. Portsmouth, NH: Boynton/Cook, 1987.

Simpson, David. *The Academic Postmodern and the Rule of Literature: A Report on Half-Knowledge*. Chicago: U of Chicago P, 1995.

Smith, J. Winfree. *A Search for the Liberal College: The Beginning of the St. John's Program*. Annapolis: St. John's College P, 1983.

Sommers, Nancy. "Between the Drafts." *College Composition and Communication* 43.1 (1993): 23–31.

Spellmeyer, Kurt. "Self-Fashioning in Discourse: Foucault and the Freshman Writer." *Common Ground: Dialogue, Understanding, and the Teaching of Composition*. Englewood Cliffs: Prentice, 1993. 67–92.

Stone, Joseph, and Tim Yohn. *Prime Time and Misdemeanors: Investigating the 1950s TV Quiz Scandal.* New Brunswick, NJ: Rutgers UP, 1992.

Stossel, Sage. "Inside the Ruins." *Atlantic Online,* June 17, 2002. Feb. 8, 2003 <http://www.theatlantic.com/unbound/interviews/int2002–06–17.htm>.

St. Mychal. Feb. 8, 2003 <http://www.saintmychal.com/main.html>.

Styron, William. *Darkness Visible: A Memoir of Madness.* New York: Random House, 1990.

Thomas, Jo. "McVeigh Defense Suggests Real Bomber Was Killed in Blast." *New York Times,* May 23, 1997: A1.

———. "McVeigh Speaks at Last, Fleetingly and Obscurely." *New York Times,* Aug. 15, 1997: A14.

———. "2 Sides Agree to Exhume One Victim in Bomb Case." *New York Times,* Feb. 28, 1996: A10.

Thomson, Alex. *Smokescreen: The Media, the Censors, the Gulf.* Tunbridge Wells, Eng.: Laburnham and Spellmount, 1992.

Tilove, Jonathan. "In the Shadow of *The Bell Curve.*" *Plain Dealer,* Feb. 5, 1995: 1C.

Tina C's Twin Towers Tribute. Dec. 10, 2003 <http://www.tinac.net/twintowers .html>.

Tompkins, Jane. "Pedagogy of the Distressed." *College English* 52.6 (1990): 653–60.

United States Cong. House Committee on Interstate and Foreign Commerce. *Investigation of Television Quiz Shows.* 86th Cong., 1st sess. Oct. 6–10, 12, 1959.

United States Department of Health and Human Services. "HHS Awards $10.5 Million for Training, Research to Address Health Concerns Related to World Trade Center Attacks." Press release, May 8, 2002. Jan. 5, 2003 <http:// www.hhs.gov/news/press/2002pres/20020508.html>.

United States v. Theodore Kaczynski. No. CR-S-96–259 GEB, 1998 WL22017 (E.D. Cal. Trans. Jan. 22, 1998). Jan. 20, 2003 <http://www.unabombertrial.com/ transcripts/012298kz.html>.

University of California, Santa Cruz. "UC Santa Cruz Student Work Chosen for International Arts Festival." Press release, July 19, 2002. Feb. 8, 2003 <http:// www.ucsc.edu/news_events/press_releases/text.asp?pid=177>.

Van Doren, Charles. "The Biggest Challenge of All." *Columbia College Today Online,* Sept. 1999. Feb. 16, 2003 <http://www.college.columbia.edu/cct/sep99/ 30a_fr.html>.

———. *The Joy of Reading: 210 Favorite Books, Plays, Poems, Essays, etc.: What's in Them, Why Read Them?* New York: Harmony, 1985.

Van Doren, Dorothy. *The Professor and I.* New York: Appleton-Century-Crofts, 1959.

Van Doren, Mark. *The Autobiography of Mark Van Doren.* New York: Greenwood, 1968.

Varnedoe, Kirk, Rachael Blackburn, Aida Audeh, Antoinette Le Normand-Romain, Mary L. Levkoff, Daniel Rosenfeld, and Jacques Vilain. *Rodin: A Magnificent Obsession.* London: Merrell, 2001.

Veterans Benefits Association. *May 2002 Gulf War Veterans Information Briefing for: National Gulf War Resource Center.* Office of Performance Analysis and Integrity, Data and Information Systems, Sept. 10, 2002. Feb. 4, 2003 <http://www.ngwrc.org/pdf/GWVISreportSeptember2002.pdf>.

Waldman, Amy. "Iron Eyes Cody, 94, an Actor and Tearful Anti-Littering Icon." *New York Times,* Jan. 5, 1999: A15.

Walker, Alan, and Pat Shipman. *The Wisdom of the Bones: In Search of Human Origins.* New York: Knopf, 1996.

Walpole, Robert. *Chemical Warfare Agent Issues During the Persian Gulf War.* Persian Gulf War Illnesses Task Force. Office of the Director of Central Intelligence, Apr. l, 2002. Feb. 25, 2005 <http://www.odci.gov/cia/publications/gulfwar/cwagents/cwpaper1.htm#key1>.

Watkins, Evan. *Work Time: English Departments and the Circulation of Cultural Value.* Palo Alto: Stanford UP, 1989.

Weber, Bruce. "Inside the Meritocracy Machine." *New York Times Magazine,* Apr. 28, 1996: 44–68.

Wedemeyer, Dee. "His Life Is His Mind." *New York Times Magazine,* Aug. 18, 1996: 22–25.

Weeks, Linton. "Publisher Yanks Unabomber Book." *Washington Post,* Nov. 6, 1999: C2.

Weigle, Richard D. *Recollections of a St. John's President, 1949–1980.* Annapolis: St. John's College P, 1988.

Welch, Nancy. "Resisting the Faith: Conversion, Resistance, and the Training of Teachers." *College English* 55.4 (1993): 387–401.

West, Cornel. "Nihilism in Black America." *Race Matters.* New York: Vintage Books, 1993. 15–32.

Wilder, Matthew. "Before and After—The Movie." *CityPages.com* 23:1110, Mar. 13, 2002. Feb. 5, 2005 <http://www.citypages.com/databank/23/1110/article10232.asp>.

"The Wizard of Quiz." *Time,* Feb. 11, 1957: 44–50.

WTC Living History Project. Dec. 10, 2002 <http://www.wtclivinghistory.org/wtclivinghistory.htm>.

Wyatt, Edward. "Designers Draw Praise for Trade Center Ideas." *New York Times,* Nov. 22, 2002: B1.

Young, Deborah. "11'09"01." *Variety,* Sept. 5, 2002. <http://www.variety.com>.

versus culture in, 175–76; public role of, 150–52, 164–69; public versus hidden transcripts in, 166–69; purpose of, ix–x, 27, 197–98; social justice and, 26; taste and, 34–35; testing in, 52; as violation, 185; violence and contemporary, 1–3, 26. *See also* classroom; graduate students; Great Books program; reading; students; teaching; writing
Elbow, Peter, 30
11'09"01 (film), 107–9
Eliot, Charles W., 160
Eliot, T. S., 176–81
Embers of the World (Wofford), 210n21
Emerson, Ralph Waldo, 88, 120
Encyclopedia Britannica, 157–64, 211n26
Engels, Friedrich, 69
Enright, Dan, 144–45, 164
Environmental Health Perspectives, 95, 98
Epstein, Charles, 64
Euclid, 183–84
Ex Libris: Confessions of a Common Reader (Fadiman), 209n9
expertise: academy and, 117; ideology and, 124
Exxon Corporation, 65–66

Fadiman, Anne, 197, 209n9, 210n19
Fadiman, Clifton, 148, 209n9, 210n19
false consciousness: Freirean pedagogy and, 121–25; in higher education, 117–18; public versus hidden transcripts and, 127–29; teaching as exposure of, 131
FBI (Federal Bureau of Investigation), 61, 99, 100
Feinberg, Kenneth, 101–2
FEMA (Federal Emergency Management Agency), 94, 98
Fencing with Words (Varnum), 139
Ferri, Daniel, 52
Finnegan, William, 68
Fischl, Eric, 107
Fisk, Robert, 56
Flannigan, Steven, 189
"Flowers for Algernon" (Keyes), 164–65
Ford Foundation, 211n23
forensics, 98–101

Foucault, Michel, 31–34, 48, 116
Freedman, Albert, 144–45, 150
freedom: Descartes', 16–19; in *Into the Wild*, 15. *See also* liberation
Freeman, Barbara Claire, 116
Freire, Paulo, 5, 119–25, 128, 130–31, 208n5

The Gates of Hell (Rodin), 103–6
Geertz, Clifford, 126–27
Gelernter, David, 64–65
gender: grief and, 190; language and, 210n19
George Mason University, 86
Germano, William, 87–88
Ghiberti, Lorenzo, 104
Gilbert, Lewis, 165
Gingrich, Newt, 79, 80–81
Giroux, Henry, 74
Giuliani, Rudy, 98, 103
Goldberg, Natalie, 111–12
Goya, Francisco de, 107
graduate students: teaching seminar for, 43–45, 171–72, 174–75, 179; unionization by, 115
Gramm, Phil, 80
Gramsci, Antonio, 127
Great Books of the Western World, 160–63, 211n29
Great Books program: Chicago background of, 158–64, 182; cultural role of, 148; doubts about, 145–46, 149–50, 158; founding of St. John's College's, 146, 183; goal of, 153–56, 162; nature of, 142–43, 147; promotion of, 153–56; staffing problems for, 148–49; uniqueness of, 142–43, 146
Great Conversation, 154, 155, 161–63, 179, 182
The Great Conversation, 162–63
Greenfield, Jeff, 145
Grutter v. Bollinger (2003), 81
The Guys (play and film), 107

Halcion, 191
Hall, James, 190–91
Harris, Eric, 1, 3, 4–5, 25, 26, 199n4
Harrison, Kathryn, 20

See also autobiography; memoirs; personal approach

September 11, 2001 attacks. See World Trade Center attacks (2001)

Shearer, Rhonda Roland, 112

Simpson, David, 187–88

Six Centuries of Great Poetry, 180

Skinner, John, 94

smart bombs, 54–56

social connection: absence of, 15; in Karr's *The Liars' Club*, 24; Plato's *Phaedrus* on, 194; through book discussions, 4; Unabomber's lack of, 57; writing to create, 25. *See also* dialogue; Great Conversation

Socrates, 168, 183–84, 193–94

Sommers, Nancy, 30, 32

Spearman, Charles, 70

Spellmeyer, Kurt, 31–32

The Spirit Catches You and You Fall Down (Fadiman), 197

Spivak, Gayatri, 185

St. John's College, 142–50, 153–56, 183–85, 193

The St. John's Story (film), 153–56

Steinberg, Shirley, 74

Steinhaeuser, Robert, 2

Stempel, Herb, 144–45

students: authenticity of, 126–27, 130–31; as benefactors/victims, 166; compliance of, 121–27, 132–33, 135, 137–38; first encounters with actual, 172; Freirean pedagogy and, 119–25; place of, in higher education, 114–18; preparation of, for life in bureaucracy, 140–41; self-analysis of education achievement, 174–75; as subordinates, 129–30. *See also* graduate students

Styron, William, 191

Suhr, Danny, 96

suicide, 28, 184–85, 186, 192

Syntopicon, 160, 210n19

Tanaina Plantlore, 14

taste, 34–35, 148

teaching: coming out in, 43–44; conditions of, 52–53, 169, 173; democratic, 82–83; as domination, 130–31; Freire and, 119–25; graduate students and, 43–45, 171–76, 179; impossibility of, 176; liberation as goal of, 120–25, 130–31, 138–39, 169, 172; motivation for, 171–73; personal versus academic in, 48; and preparation of students for life, 140–41; roles for, 137. *See also* classroom; education

Teaching to Transgress (hooks), 119

technology: as cause of social cataclysm, 4; smart bombs, 54–56; smart classrooms, 51–52; Unabomber on, 59–60, 62–67, 69

testing, government-mandated, 52

text-world relationship, 13–14, 33

theory, 5, 187–88

The Thinker (Rodin), 104, 106

Thomson, Alex, 54

Thoreau, Henry David, 12, 13, 120

The Three Shades (Rodin), 104, 106

Tic Tac Dough (television show), 164

Time (magazine), 66, 147, 151, 152

Tina C's Twin Towers Tribute, 107

Tinberg, Howard, 139

Tinkering Toward Utopia (Tyack and Cuban), 139

Tolstoy, Leo, 12

Tompkins, Jane, 30, 119

toxins, from World Trade Center collapse, 94–96, 98

"Tradition and the Individual Talent" (Eliot), 176–77, 182

transcripts, public versus hidden, 127–32, 166–69

truth and falsity: Descartes on, 17–18; Great Books program and, 143–44; in Karr's *The Liars' Club*, 23–24; in *Into the Wild*, 15

"Tumbling Woman" (Fischl), 107

Turkana Boy, 109–11

TWA Flight 800, 189, 190

Twenty-One (television show), 143–45, 147, 150–51

Tyack, David, 139

Unabomber. *See* Kaczynski, Theodore

Underworld (DeLillo), 88–94

unions, graduate student, 115